Aristophanes
Plays: Two

Wasps, Clouds, Birds, Festival Time, Frogs

Aristophanes was a conjurer, mixing magic and fantasy with political reality to create a crucible wherein the issues of the day were distilled into finely honed comic masterpieces. Slapstick and bawdy, satire and fantasy were his tools but the plays of his which remain give us vivid images of the social, moral and political issues of his day. *Wasps* shows the conflict of old and new, corruption and justice, age and youth, father and son. *Clouds*, a funny lighthearted play is very loosely centred around the philosopher Sokrates and sets up a debate between loud-mouthed ignorance and intellectual hokum. *Birds* is an escape into a kind of utopia, a fantasy place which threatens to become a tyranny. *Festival Time* centres around the women's secret festival or Thesmophoria where Euripides is to be condemned for his supposed misogyny, and *Frogs* is a battle between the Aristophanic Aeschylus and Aristophanic Euripides when Dionysos goes to Hades to save the drama festivals.

Aristophanes was born in Athens about the middle of the fifth century BC. His first play was performed in 427 but produced, perhaps because of his youth, under the name of Kallistratos. The first surviving play is *Acharnians*, one of the nine that represent all we have of what has come to be known as Old Comedy. All of these nine were written against the backdrop of the Peloponnesian War in which Sparta finally defeated Athens in 404BC. Two last plays from the fourth century show a change in mood and emphasis to a more social drama and are therefore published separately along with two plays of Menander. Aristophanes probably died in 385BC.

ARISTOPHANES

Plays: Two

Wasps

Clouds

Birds

Festival Time (Thesmophoriazousai)

Frogs
translated by Kenneth McLeish

*introduced by J. Michael Walton
and Kenneth McLeish*

series editor: J. Michael Walton

B L O O M S B U R Y
LONDON · NEW DELHI · NEW YORK · SYDNEY

Bloomsbury Methuen Drama

An imprint of Bloomsbury Publishing Plc

50 Bedford Square	1385 Broadway
London	New York
WC1B 3DP	NY 10018
UK	USA

www.bloomsbury.com

Bloomsbury is a registered trade mark of Bloomsbury Publishing Plc

This edition first published in Great Britain in 1990 by Methuen Drama

Visit www.bloomsbury.com to find out more about our authors and their books
You will find extracts, author interviews, author events and you can sign up for
newsletters to be the first to hear about our latest releases and special offers.

British Library Cataloguing-in-Publication Data
A catalogue record for this book is available from the British Library.

ISBN: PB: 978-0-4136-6910-0
ePDF: 978-1-4725-0397-8
ePUB: 978-1-4725-0396-1

Library of Congress Cataloging-in-Publication Data
A catalog record for this book is available from the Library of Congress.

CONTENTS

EDITOR'S INTRODUCTION

'Every person of stature or standing
You put in plays, comes out ragged and tatty –'

So runs Aeschylus' accusation against Euripides in
Aristophanes' *Frogs* (lines 1063-4) when, as a character
within the play, he complains that Euripides has led the
theatre down the slippery slope of naturalism. At first
sight this might seem a peculiar charge, even allowing for
the fact that Aristophanes' stage caricatures tend to
stretch their real-life originals to the point of distortion.

Naturalism, the attempt to produce on stage life as it is
really lived, was a short-lived, if hydra-like, dramatic movement associated with the latter years of the nineteenth
century. Inspired initially by the French novel and quickly
picked up throughout Europe and America, the search for
'truth for truth's sake' on stage was as quickly dropped
when it proved incapable of addressing the basic paradox
that realistic theatre embodies. As a reaction to the con-
trived worlds of romanticism and melodrama, the concerned playwright might set out to address topics which
would examine the realities of living in the new scientific
age. In practice stage performance proved, both in content
and in form, inevitably reliant upon the dramatic artifice
which has always been the theatre's most powerful means
of expression.

In the light of the performance conditions of the fifth
century BC, any mention of naturalism demands an expla-
nation. Aristophanes' world is patently a stage world where
gods and monsters, animals and fictional characters may
share adventures and experiences with actual people – or
rather, with their stage personae, the real-life versions of
whom were, as like as not, sitting in the audience. What
could be more theatrical or less realistic than a city in mid-
air or a trip to Hades? What could be more blatantly artifi-
cial than this drama of masks, music, dance and slapstick?
How could such a blend of comic and fantastical elements
prove anything other than a consolation for the cheerless

realities of daily living, the Greek equivalent of the romantic evasions which 19th-century naturalism had set out to overtake?

Nevertheless, the development of drama in Athens, as the fifth century progressed, is relentlessly in the direction of a kind of realism. In tragedy the super-heroes of Aeschylus are superseded, first by the real heroes of Sophocles, then by the 'ragged and tatty' anti-heroes of Euripides. The comedian Aristophanes, younger than any of these tragic playwrights, moves firmly away from the world of mythology in the direction of a complex mix of real life and stage life, fantastical but far from escapist. Aristophanes is a conjuror, an enchanter, a weaver of magic carpets. But fly as he may above the troubles besetting his war-torn Athens, with its internal disputes as damaging as the ever-threatening Spartans outside, Aristophanes refuses to allow his audience to forget for too long who they are and what their own responsibilities may be. In the guise of high fantasy, all the issues of the day are present, social, moral and political.

That Aristophanes was aware of the move towards realism in tragedy as the fifth century BC progressed is firmly spelled out in *Frogs*, where Euripides' treatment of sordid themes and unheroic characters spawns the sort of criticisms which later greeted the social dramas of Ibsen. Aristophanes, it must be admitted, was an equal contributor to this move towards a drama of real issues and living people. The solutions to problems may take dramatic flight but the problems are earth-bound enough, rooted in a community harried by war and a decaying social fabric. However oblique his route to stage truth, Aristophanes approaches the serious issues of his day with the zeal of a reformer and the harshness of a moralist.

In play after play the central character or characters are ordinary Athenians. What happens to them is extraordinary. They meet up with all manner of creatures and deities, many of them hostile to humanity. These ordinary men and women – and this was the first appearance of

'ordinary' men and women on the European stage – tackle
the problems of life in Athens in the last twenty years of
the Peloponnesian War. If the blood and the grief are left
to Euripides and a 'realistic' tragic world, the day-to-day
problems of simply being alive, from constipation to paying
the bills, are the flesh on Aristophanes' fantastical skeletons. It is the blending of those aspects of romance and
melodrama with the savage tang of actual experience that
gives his plays their serious aftertaste.

Much of this is achieved by juxtaposing the real and the
unreal with dramatic devices such as 'turning a joke'. In
Birds, produced in 414BC, Peithetairos and his companion
Euelpides have left Athens, fed up with living in the city.
They seek out the advice of the mythical King Tereus who
was transformed into a hoopoe. When they find him
Peithetairos suggests that what the birds should do is build
their own city in mid-air in order to assert their former
power over humankind and over the gods:

> 'Who do you lord it over now? Grasshoppers, flies.
> Then, it'll be the whole human race. Lock, stock
> And barrel. Not to mention starving out the gods.
> It worked with the Melians.' (lines 186-8)

In 416BC, a little over a year before the performance of
Birds, the Athenians had attacked the island of Melos for
wishing to remain neutral in the war. When the Melians
finally surrendered, the entire male population was put to
death, the women and children sold into slavery. It was an
atrocity that appalled many Athenians, particularly after
the Melian ambassadors had come to Athens and presented their case to the Assembly with dignity and logic, as
the historian Thucydides recorded.

Within the first two hundred lines of *Birds*, a play which
initially seems to be a paean to idealism, comes the first
mention of the new city, a Utopia which will release its citizens from all the problems besetting Athens. But at the
very moment when Aristophanes might seem to be leaving
the world of the war behind and offering a retreat into
escapism, however briefly, to an audience who in 414 would

sorely have welcomed an escape, he introduces that reference to Melos, a bleeding wound on the Athenian conscience. The effect is to warn the audience that this is a serious comedy, a play of ideas whose heart may be in the heavens but whose feet are still in the trenches.

The didactic function of theatre is the one aspect of the playwright's art on which Aeschylus and Euripides, the two dead but not forgotten dramatists, are agreed in their confrontation in Hades in *Frogs*, first performed at the Lenaia of 405BC as the Peloponnesian War was reaching its disastrous conclusion. 'Children have teachers to teach them, and grown-ups?/Have playwrights. To set good examples', says Aeschylus (lines 1054-5). Euripides agrees, disputing only the teaching methods. As Aristophanes has created both characters, we may perhaps assume that he regards his own comic art as every bit as educational as that of the tragedians.

The theatre in Athenian life was always political, in the sense that it dealt with affairs of the *polis*, the city itself. The tragedies of Aeschylus, Sophocles and Euripides were stories developed from the complex world of myth. Myth has the advantage of never being fixed. This gives the playwright a flexibility constantly to renew familiar tales and find in them an immediate message. All the three tragedians wrote plays which covered similar ground but their treatment allowed for major changes of emphasis. The fictional plot was tried by Agathon, who appears as a character in *Festival Time*, but the experiment was not a success and tragedy reverted to its familiar series of plots.

The position with comedy was less clear-cut. At the end of the group of three tragedies which a playwright submitted for the Great Dionysia, there was an addendum, a satyr play. The satyrs, crude animalistic devotees of Dionysos, had licence to open up the tragic debate to a comic dimension, presenting to humankind a distorted view which nevertheless restored the balance. In a world of arbitrary fate and unconscionable calamity, the satyrs offered perspective, the chance to relax and an antidote to despair. These satyr plays were formulaic, following one aspect of, or at least a theme from, the series of plots presented in the serious group. If Aristotle is to be believed, the satyr play had a pedigree longer than Tragedy and much longer than Old Comedy.

The inclusion of a comic afterpiece to every tragic submission may well have led to Old Comedy developing late as an independent form. The loss of every text from the Old Comedy before Aristophanes may not have deprived today's stage of many masterpieces, but at least one play from one of his contemporaries would have provided a valuable point of comparison. Our assumptions about Old Comedy have to be based almost entirely upon Aristophanes. His reputation assures us of his supremacy but he achieved this supremacy, perhaps, by being different from the others, by being atypical. He was certainly controversial and doubtless made enemies. Not every play won first prize. The first version of *Clouds* – our text is a revision – was placed third, *Wasps* and *Birds* only second. But however they were judged in their own time, his plays offer a vision which is theatrically and socially unique.

The real point of speculation revolves around how much his stage portraits reflected actual prejudice. When the audience for *Clouds* saw a Sokrates flown in swinging on the stage crane as a leader of the sophistic movement, did this appear a gross, if funny, distortion? Or did it contribute to a hostile view of Sokrates which built up over the years, culminating in his being condemned to death a few years after Athens' final defeat in the Peloponnesian War?

When a primarily male set of spectators saw in *Festival Time* the Thesmophoria mocked as an occasion for women to get drunk and air their grievances, how accurate a picture did they take it to be? When Euripides is seen in a panic because the women may condemn him for portraying them in such an unflattering manner, does that mean that we are wrong today to consider him as sympathetic to the likes of Phaidra and Medea, women apparently driven to extremes by the insensitivity of men?

When a whole play, *Wasps*, is devoted to lawcourt satire; when the aim of the main character in *Clouds* is to learn how to cheat the legal system; when the prime reason for the protagonists' desire to leave Athens in *Birds* is dissatisfaction with lawyers, is this a coincidence amongst the small number of plays which have survived or a mark of the frustration felt by a majority of the population with a state system which had run out of control?

If all these questions must remain open – and the audience reaction of any age is difficult to pin down – the plays of Aristophanes do provide a number of pointers to a level of theatrical sophistication amongst the Athenians which makes their entire drama amenable to a modern perception. This can be most easily demonstrated by examples from *Frogs*, something of a special case as it is both a play about theatre and a play about the theatre.

The battle between the Aristophanic Aeschylus and the Aristophanic Euripides, each claiming superiority in some aspect of the dramatic art, is a relief to the modern reader because the terms of reference are ones that are recognisable as part of a contemporary critical approach. When Euripides complains of the Aeschylean 'silent figure', he is pointing to a visual theatrical device which a modern sensitivity to performance values will pick up from an Aeschylus text. Euripides' acknowledgement of the device gives licence to us today to recognise it as a calculated effect. When Aeschylus castigates the stage costume of Telephos and condemns the prosiness of Euripidean argument, he admits Euripides as the standard-bearer of the new realism in staging as well as in sentiment.

The traditional view that Aristophanes preferred Aeschylus to Euripides is one that *Frogs* will barely sustain, for all that Euripides has proved the most enduring satirical target elsewhere. The grounds for resurrecting Aeschylus rather than Euripides turn out to be not artistic but political. As in so many of his plays, Aristophanes starts out with one declared aim – Dionysos goes to Hades to save the drama festivals – and cunningly contrives to switch horses in midstream. The blatant message about the exiled Alkibiades shows the serious commentator using his theatre as a platform and simultaneously rejoicing in its process.

In another way *Frogs* celebrates the whole business of theatre. The protagonist is Dionysos, the god in whose honour the festivals of the Lenaia and the Great Dionysia were held. Portrayed as a buffoon, this Dionysos may be a surprise to anyone expecting a figure of respect. On the way to Hades with his servant Xanthias, the two swap disguises until Aiakos proposes beating the pair of them to discover which is truly the god. The god, naturally, will feel no pain. An actor, naturally, will, whatever part he is playing. The gag depends on the audience's dual perception, a perception exploited or extended in some way in almost every scene Aristophanes ever wrote.

How the people of any period view their theatre offers a private insight into that society. In times when the audience has been exclusive or privileged, such as the theatre of the court masque or restoration comedy, the view is partial. The huge open-air stages of the world have largely been for the benefit of audiences of any class or condition. Accordingly, they make for better mirrors of society. So it was in Athens where enlightenment was a by-product of diversion but where, by the closing years of the century, the theatre was proving itself a place for the debate of immediate as well as long-term issues. In this, Euripides and Aristophanes were linked. Kratinos was even to coin the verb *euripidaristophanizein*, 'to innovate like Euripides and Aristophanes'. Through such a medium, each of the two playwrights, in his own way, aimed to present his audience with truths as formidable and frequently unpalatable as did those revolutionary playwrights and practitioners who sought to reflect the new scientific age at the end of the nineteenth century.

It is here, in his desire to create for the audience a portrait of their daily lives, but a portrait framed in magic, that Aristophanes blended reality and fantasy and blended them as has no playwright since. That the Athenians applauded his plays and ignored his advice is a further reflection on the temper of his times: a frustration he shared with Euripides. Had he never written a scene, the conduct of the war would doubtless have proceeded exactly the same. The world of informers, charlatans and political chancers would have been neither more nor less corrupt. But the Athenians would have been diminished by missing the experience of his vision and we, today, would have forfeited our one opportunity to see beyond his plays to the Athenians as real people, living in a real and uncomfortable world.

J. Michael Walton
University of Hull, 1993

Transliteration from Greek into English presents problems of consistency. The names of the playwrights are more familiar as Aeschylus, Sophocles and Menander than as Aischulos, Sophokles and Menandros. Otherwise direct transliteration has normally been adopted while allowing for previous translations in the series.

TRANSLATOR'S INTRODUCTION

Aristophanes and the surreal

In a sense, no stage play is ever 'real'. By their very nature as created works, plays offer a select and organised view of our 'reality'. The presence of author, performer and spectators in a theatre show imposes a kind of irony between 'reality' and what is being represented. We always know, in the theatre, more than is being shown to us, and that knowledge is part of what makes the show. This is so in every kind of serious drama. I am thinking not just of Edgar's masquerades in *Lear*, say, or George's and Martha's charades in *Who's Afraid of Virginia Woolf?*, but of the content of such avowedly 'realistic' works as *A Doll's House* or films such as *Silkwood* or *All The President's Men*. The show itself is a kind of objective correlative by which we judge the show.

This is especially the case in comedy. In comedy, our feeling that we are watching a performance, our appreciation of the performer, is vital to enjoyment. One can 'lose oneself' in serious drama, surrender disbelief. But the surrender in comedy is different: a giving up of oneself to hilarity, to the hysteria (individual or mass) which is one of the main kinds of ecstasy Dionysos was said to provoke, and which comedians and comic actors deliberately encourage. Comic performers always have 'attitude'. They always take a stance to their material, approaching it laterally instead of entering into its world, as performers do in tragedy. This creates the ironic distance which makes a comedy performance 'work' – an irony quite different from that in serious plays.

In performances of the 'high', or 'literary', comedy of the last few hundred years, it can be difficult to see this process at work. The actor playing John Worthing or Elyot Chase, for example, may seem at first sight to have surrendered to 'realism' just as much as someone playing Ejlert Løvborg or Konstantin Treplev. Such an actor may seem to have little in common with such 'low' comedy performers as Jacques Tati or Steve Martin. We might think that they are not so much saying, 'Isn't this silly?' as *embodying* silliness, as one might embody jealousy or saintliness. But in both kinds of comedy, 'high' and 'low', ironic distance is the same. In 'low' comedy the performer is able to stand aside from what he or she is doing, and invite us to mock it; in 'high' comedy that function is performed by the author, whose laterality to life is what makes the comedy.

Since Aristophanes was born too early to benefit from literary criticism, and was therefore unaware that comedy could be divided into such categories as 'high' and 'low', he was able to have the best of both worlds. The ironical distance in performances of his plays comes equally from author and performer. This happens in other writers' comedies – in the scene in *l'Avare*, for example, where Argan rounds on the audience, accusing them of stealing his miser's hoard – but in Aristophanes' plays it is all-pervasive, a main feature of his style. Comedy is consistently made from the hinge between the 'real' world of the audience and the 'fantasy' world of the stage action – and above all, from the comedian's own position, as it were beside this hinge, moving it this way and that and inviting us to admire and laugh at him as he does so.

It is established that the 'great and mighty deed' (as Dikaiopolis calls it in *Acharnians*) moves each Aristophanic plot from 'reality' to 'surreality', from the world of the everyday to magic. Each play begins with the hero outlining an intolerable situation, domestic, political or both, and deciding to take some extraordinary step to resolve it. The step is taken, and the rest of the play examines its consequences. Aristophanes' plots have elements in common with fairy stories. Flying to heaven on a dung-beetle, going to join the birds or engineering a women's takeover of the affairs of state replace rubbing a magic lamp or summoning one's fairy godmother. But as soon as the magic deed is done, the bounds of possibility are exploded in exactly the same way. We accept it as natural, in fairyland, that birds and wasps should talk, that gods should be fools and gluttons, that the hero can undergo every kind of transformation. But Aristophanes goes further. Having operated the hinge to swing us from 'real' to 'surreal', he equally casually moves it the other way. His wasps, birds, gods turn from their fantasyland to tell us, the audience, home-truths about our own 'real' lives. The very unexpectedness of this gives such comments extra pungency. But they remain incongruous and 'absurd' in context – essential features of a comic show.

Despite such occasions, it is debatable whether Aristophanes ever *does* actually speak to us in his own 'real' voice. This is not, I feel, what comedy – any comedy, and his in particular – is about at all. The *parabases* of Aristophanes' plays are often held up as prime instances of the author 'dropping his mask' and speaking to us directly. The word *parabasis* itself even means 'walking forward' or 'stepping aside'. But the Chorus who perform each *parabasis* never, in fact, do step aside from their character in the show. Wasps remain wasps, birds remain birds, knights remain knights. I think that the pretence they make of dropping the mask is itself a mask, a carefully- organised pirouette in the direction not of 'reality' but of a different kind of 'attitude' and irony. They no more enter the 'real' world in the *parabasis* than they do when they perform those short passages of scurrilous personal abuse, irrelevant to the action, which punctuate the second halves of many plays.

If there is a movement from 'reality' to 'surreality' and back, it is left to the actors, and to the main actor in particular, to control it, to manipulate it for maximum hilarity and acerbity. Thus, for example, Dikaiopolis and Trygaios often seem – even claim – to speak Aristophanes' mind on social issues relevant to the time of *Acharnians* or *Peace*; Strepsiades' comments about Sokrates in *Clouds* are presented as if they are 'real' opinion. But I question whether Dikaiopolis, Trygaios or Strepsiades really do ever slip out of their roles, letting Aristophanes' 'own' voice take over. The *actor* slips momentarily in or out of character, and so creates another kind of comc irony in performance. But this is not to say that he becomes Aristophanes, however pointful or 'real' his remarks may seem. In the only place where – we are led to believe – Aristophanes' authentic utterance *is* reported, in Plato's *Symposium* (see *Clouds* introduction, page xxii), the two things he avoids doing are making specific comments *ad rem* or *ad hominem*, and making jokes. Are we to take as 'real' criticism the mockery of Euripides indulged in by Mnesilochos, Trygaios, the Chorus in *Lysistrata* or a dozen other characters? Could it not have been there simply to raise a laugh – as a modern comedian or character in comedy might get a laugh by sending up Shakespeare? And if that is the case, is it not possible that political, social and other apparently 'real' remarks should not have been there for similar effect? Perhaps, when a comedian assures us, with a very straight face indeed, 'I never joke', that is perhaps the most crucial joke of all.

As in *Aristophanes: Plays One*, I should like to end this general introduction by thanking friends who have made my work on Aristophanes even more pleasurable: William Arrowsmith, Kenneth Dover and Michael Walton. Particularly warm thanks are due to my wife Valerie McLeish, and to Frederic Raphael, to whom this volume, like the preceding one, is dedicated in thanks for a friendship which has now lasted undimmed for twenty years.

Wasps

Wasps was first produced at the Lenaia in January, 422BC, and won second prize. Aristophanes was in his mid-twenties, and *Wasps* was his seventh play. It is the fourth of his plays to survive.

In the summer before the production, the two main adversaries in the Peloponnesian War, Athenians and Spartans, had signed a one-year truce. The urgency of war, and Kleon's military and political strategies, are therefore not the background to this play. Instead, Aristophanes turns the searchlight of his satire on the law. At the time of the play, cases were heard before a jury picked from a pool of 6000 men, each of whom served for a year. The jurors were paid a pittance – Kleon had recently raised the daily amount to three obols (half a drachma) – and for this they had to make themselves available throughout the year. These factors tended to deter able-bodied men, in full employment, from volunteering, and the pool of jurymen therefore consisted of elderly citizens, for whom jury pay was a kind of dole.

The cases such jurymen tried were many and varied. But the principal target of Aristophanes' wrath is the system of *euthune*, 'calling to account'. The law stipulated that holders of public office, once their terms of service were finished, should be subjected to public scrutiny, and should be fined if irregularities were found in their accounts. *Euthune* was one of the main tasks of the Athenian democratic juries – and by the time of *Wasps* Kleon and his followers were using it as a political instrument, attacking and vilifying their opponents. Cases were not heard in front of judges, with expert barristers or attorneys. Instead, points were made by oratory, and the jurors – sometimes as many as several hundred at a time – were likely to be as much affected by rhetoric as by the merits of the case. Although the idea of a pool of jurymen, representing the whole people of Athens, is admirably democratic, the possibilities for corruption – especially in the hands of a man like Kleon, noted equally for rhetorical skill and political unscrupulousness – were legion. Kleon proclaimed himself 'watchdog of the state'; his enemies called him 'Dog'; Aristophanes, in the domestic court-scene in *Wasps*, satirises him as a real dog, the thieving cheesehound 'Snatch'.

The play's legal background lends itself to one of Aristophanes' favourite comic themes: the conflict between generations. Lawcourt matters are the excuse for a father-son struggle even more convulsive than that in *Clouds* (first produced in the previous year). Philokleon ('Kleon-lover'), the father, stands for the old generation, the good old times and the good old songs; he is also a reprobate, shameless, sly and irrepressible. Bdelykleon ('Kleon-puke'), the son, is zealous, humourless – and on the side of the angels. The battle between such characters is one of the oldest and most reliable themes in comedy.

Even by Aristophanes' standards, Philokleon is a particularly challenging role to play. The actor must be a master of the mask, the complicated wasp-costume (at least until he discards it for the second half of the play), and of slapstick (for example in the escape-scenes from the netted house at the start of the play, or his later conflict with the Bread-woman and outraged citizen). He must sing, both comic songs and tragic burlesque. He must be a master of verbal comedy (for example in the *agon* and trial scene). He has a spectacular drunk scene, and closes the play with a display of comic dancing. He is onstage for four-fifths of the play's action, and dominates the comedy. There is similar gusto in other Aristophanic leading roles at the time – indeed, the similarity of comic style between Agorakritos (*Knights*, 424), Strepsiades (*Clouds*, 423), Philokleon (*Wasps*, 422) and Trygaios (*Peace*, 421) makes one wonder if the same comedian may not have been involved in all four plays.

Another much-discussed aspect of the play is the character of the Chorus. Philokleon's gusto, the profusion of slapstick, and the arrival of a troupe of comic dancers (Karkinos and his three sons) for the dance-contest at the end, not to mention the presence of the boys with torches who usher in the Chorus at the start of the play, have suggested to some scholars that this particular group of Chorus-men were elderly, even geriatric. Unfit for energetic dance, they left it to others, confining themselves to stately group movement or a version of military drill distantly remembered from war-service sixty years before. It is an appealing notion, and nothing in the play conflicts with it. But there is nothing to justify it either, and these Chorus-men may have danced as energetically as any others. If they did, they would have provided one more element of display in what is already a spectacular piece of theatre.

Because people are wary of the detail of Athenian law-court procedures, *Wasps* is seldom performed: in Britain, its main outings this century have been the Cambridge production of 1909 for which Vaughan Williams wrote incidental music, and one at King's College, London, in 1981 – both of them amateur affairs, in ancient Greek. (There have however been two separate, highly successful, productions by the Greek National Theatre in Athens.) In fact legal detail hardly obtrudes, and is perfectly comprehensible. In performance, Philokleon's character, slapstick and the verve of the script should carry all before them.

The setting is a street or open space outside Philokleon's house (which is covered by a net). One doorway, an upper window and access to the roof are essential.

Clouds

Clouds was first produced at the Great Dionysia in late March or early April 423BC. Aristophanes was in his mid-twenties. The play won third prize, and some eight or nine years later Aristophanes revised it. This revision is the version which survives. In it, Aristophanes claims (lines 522ff) that *Clouds* was his best play to date – though this may be no more than anyone might say in similar circumstances. The revision was not performed in his lifetime.

Down the centuries, *Clouds* has attracted scholarly attention not for its comic excellence or theatrical ingenuity, but simply because one of its central characters is called Sokrates. In real life, Sokrates (in his forties at the time of the play) was a philosopher who made his reputation by use of the method of reduction: when you have considered every aspect of a question, and eliminated all irrelevancies and mistaken ideas, what is left – with luck – is truth. He subjected everything to this method, from cosmology to ethics, from the nature of memory to the existence of the soul. None of his own teaching survives; he is principally known because he features in dialogues written by his pupils and followers (notably Xenophon and Plato), and because of his trial and execution in 399BC for 'corrupting the young'. He knew Aristophanes personally, and Plato's *Symposium* shows them as fellow-guests at a post-play dinner-party given by Agathon, debating the nature of love into the small hours. There is a story that during the performance of *Clouds*, hearing some visitors to the city whispering 'Who is this Sokrates?', he stood up for everyone to see.

The Sokrates of *Clouds* is a completely different figure. He is a conman who runs an eccentric school. In the school, pupils ponder the heavens and the Earth, consider such deep questions as how many of its own feet a flea can jump, and above all learn word-play, the art of making bad seem good. None of this has anything to do with the real-life Sokrates, and the play would be just as successful if its charlatan were renamed 'Professor X'. *Clouds* contains no parody of Sokrates' real ideas or real teaching techniques. The only real activities parodied are initiation ceremonies into a mystery cult (Strepsiades must be sprinkled, and must listen to prayers and hymns, before he can be enrolled in the school), and the rhetorical debates (in this case, between Right and Wrong) which were a feature of higher education among the Athenian upper class. It is sometimes claimed that Aristophanes' satire of Sokrates was more biting than I suggest, on the analogy of his treatment of Kleon in other plays. But the contrary may equally well be the case. If his satire on Sokrates (about whom we know a great deal) is so superficial, using the man's name merely as an adventitious joke, perhaps his lampoons of Kleon or Euripides (about whom we know far less) are by no means as specific as they seem.

Clouds is really 'about' its central character, Strepsiades. He is a boorish, street-wise old man, a buffoon with pretensions to grandeur – learned perhaps from his snooty wife and upwardly-mobile son. Beset with debts incurred by his son's mania for horses, he goes to Sokrates' *phrontisterion* to learn how to outwit his creditors. (I have translated *phrontisterion* as 'Thinkery'. *Phrontisteria* still exist, all over Greece: they are 'crammers', providing intensive tuition for specific exams.) The play is about the confrontation between Strepsiades' loud-mouthed ignorance (standing for 'the old ways') and the slippery wordplay and intellectual hokum peddled at the *phrontisterion* (standing for 'the new ways'). Eventually, Strepsiades is so outraged by the teaching of the school that he burns it down and chases away the frauds. This ending uses stage sleight-of-hand to produce a 'moral' outcome which has not been logically prepared. The old rogue Strepsiades suddenly ends up on the side of the angels, scattering freaks and poseurs as farce-heroes have always done. Aristophanes is pandering to the prejudices of a large, heterogeneous audience at an international festival – a group rarely noted for 'advanced' opinions on education, philosophy, the generation-gap or anything else.

Clouds, despite the identity of its Chorus, is a sunny, happy play. It eschews politics, and indeed serious issues of any kind at all. (Even Right and Wrong are concerned less with philosophical niceties than with social etiquette.) The Cloud-chorus, for the most part, sings words which have a kind of serene inconsequentiality, stately and aloof from the slapstick of the main action. Even their advice to the judges in the *parabasis*, and their lampooning of perverts and frauds, seem more disembodied than in Aristophanes' other comedies. How they danced, their costumes and the nature of their music are, in the circumstances, matters of considerable interest, and lack of evidence is more than usually frustrating.

The play's setting is a street with two doors, those of Strepsiades' house and the *phrontisterion*. The action requires characters to climb on the roof, and also makes use of the theatre crane. There seems at one point to be a tableau, in which Sokrates' students are revealed inside the phrontisterion. On how this may have been done, see Note 15, page 380.

Birds

Birds was first produced at the Great Dionysia in March or April, 414BC, and won second prize. Aristophanes was in his early thirties.

At the time of this production, politics in Athens were dominated by the Sicilian Expedition, which had set off some six months before, with high hopes of subduing Sparta's allies in Syracuse. Its outcome was still uncertain; all that could be said was that it had not so far lived up to people's expectations – that it would be a triumph, a decisive national adventure which would, at a stroke, restore Athens to the military and political supremacy it had held 60 years before, at the end of the Persian War. *Birds* has been seen, ingeniously, as an allegory of this expedition (with the gods as Spartans, Peithetairos as Alkibiades, and so on). Such overtones may have given extra spice to the piece (which is otherwise notably free of politics), but it seems to me to be too prescriptive and heavy-handed an allegory to sustain an entire comedy, particularly one as effortless and airy as *Birds*. In the same way, the gloss other commentators put on the play – that it is a satire on the utopian speculations fashionable at the time (and which culminated, so far as modern readers are concerned, in Plato's *Republic*) – seems equally over-emphatic. On the evidence of Aristophanes' other surviving plays, he was not a man for utopias. His ideal states are not of the mind, but practical places in which the injustices and follies of the here-and-now are set right not by reason but by an earthy magic which simply restores the *status quo*, with different people in charge.

This last miracle, in fact, is precisely what happens in *Birds*. In Athens at the time of the play, one of the main concerns of what we would now, perhaps, call the 'chattering classes' was the dichotomy between *polypragmosune* and *apragmosune*. *Polypragmosune* was an unquenchable bustle of concern for your own and other people's affairs. It was said to be characteristic of the Athenian people. In its benign manifestations, it led to such things as social awareness, democracy, personal decorum, an ordered polity and paternal affection for the allies. Its malign symptoms were busy-bodying, informing, imperialism and a hyperactive inability to let any social or intellectual idea alone. *Apragmosune* was the opposite: not so much *laissez-faire* as a philosophy of 'get it right and then stop tinkering'.

It is to escape from *polypragmosune* that Peithetairos and Euelpides leave Athens. The city, for them, is polluted by other people's fervour; all they want is somewhere quiet, a place they can roll up in as in a blanket. However, as soon as Peithetairos puts his flash of inspiration into practice, and the bird-city is built, he spurns the unfussy life and adopts a refined, personal form of *polypragmosune*. He becomes a dictator: issuing orders, enforcing his will and maintaining his state by military means. He blockades the gods – a move deliberately reminiscent of the Athenians' real treatment of the island of Melos: see Editor's Introduction, pages ix–x. If *Birds* is political allegory or satire, such actions are the nub of its argument, and Aristophanes' point is doubly devastating because of the understated irony with which it is made. Peithetairos' final apotheosis, when he usurps Zeus' powers, marries Sovereignty and takes over the universe, is not only a satisfyingly orgiastic conclusion to the comic action, but a devastatingly ironical comment on human (Athenian?) ambition. The message – if this is the message, if comedies *do* have messages – is delivered with geniality and lightness, but it is hardly less effective because of that.

As a comic type, Peithetairos differs from all Aristophanes' other main characters except Lysistrata. Most Aristophanic heroes are rumbustious, life-guzzling extroverts. Peithetairos, by contrast, is almost entirely serious. In the first section of the play, he leaves most of the joke-making to Euelpides (a far less subtle character, a typical buffoon). Once the bird-state is created, he becomes a self-confident figure of authority, a kind of totem-pole round which the antics of other characters revolve. This authoritative stillness serves Aristophanes' irony: despite the outrageousness of what Peithetairos is actually doing, his demeanour makes him seem the one sane figure in a lunatic universe. It also determines the structure of the play. In form, *Birds* is a series of vignettes:

there are, for example, seventeen *alazon*-scenes ('sponger'-scenes), four times the Aristophanic average. In most of them, Peithetairos plays the 'straight-man' role, and comic dynamism comes not from him but from his interlocutors. This kind of part is rare in stage comedy, but has been a staple of radio in the last 60 years (in Britain, examples range from *ITMA* and *Much Binding in the Marsh* to *Round the Horne* and *Beyond Our Ken*). In performance, although the main actor is crucial to every single scene, his stillness gives enormous scope to the rest of the cast. *Birds* teems with characters, and the actors' constant reappearance in new roles, their sheer bustle, may have been one of its main attractions. The pace slows down only for the last *alazon*-scene of all, the arrival of the delegation from Heaven – and the effects of this *rallentando* are, first, to enhance our feeling that the whirl we have been watching has been a purposeful progression, which is now approaching resolution; and second, to give a few minutes' relaxation before the marriage-celebrations which close the play.

Though pace and comic dynamism came from the actors, equally vital energy must have been contributed by the music and dance. The Chorus of birds, at such a lavish festival as the Great Dionysia, was trained and costumed, one imagines, with an extravagance befitting the occasion. Internal evidence of spectacle is provided both by announcements of the various birds which arrive – each species, real or imaginary, introduced as if by a flunkey at a reception – and, at another level, by the extent and quality of the choruses. The songs in this play, accompanied by flute music and redolent with imitated bird-song, are among the most varied and kaleidoscopic in all Greek poetry. They give the play an ethereal, dream-like quality, and a feeling of genial grandeur which is matched (in Aristophanes' surviving work) only in *Clouds*. Like Shakespeare's *The Tempest*, *Birds* is a play whose mystery is apparent but intangible, and it is unaffected lyricism which makes it so.

Stage spectacle provided by music, dance, costumes and the coming and going of a large number of characters, is framed by extreme simplicity of setting. *Birds* needs only one doorway, and makes brief use of the theatre crane (for the entry and exit of Iris). Otherwise, a bare stage is all it needs.

Festival Time

Festival Time was first produced in 411BC, the same year as *Lysistrata*. Aristophanes was in his early thirties. There is discussion about which festival gave occasion to the play. Tradition says that *Festival Time* was performed at the Great Dionysia, *Lysistrata* at the earlier Lenaia. But there is no evidence, and either play would have fitted either festival. (For more on this, see Introduction to *Aristophanes Plays: One*, pages xiii–xiv and xxviii.)

The Greek title of *Festival Time* is *Thesmophoriazousai* ('Women at the Thesmophoria'). The Thesmophoria was a festival in honour of 'The Twain': Demeter, goddess of harvest, and her daughter Persephone, queen of the Underworld and bringer of spring. It was celebrated throughout Greece; in Athens it was a three-day festival at the end of autumn. Attendance was restricted to free women, married or widowed: slaves and virgins were barred. Like all ceremonies in honour of Demeter and Persephone, the Thesmophoria involved mystery rituals, known only to devotees. The participants set up camp on the festival site, and – so far as is known – spent their time fasting, sacrificing and feasting. The event seems to have been regarded with awe by the participating women – and with tolerance or scurrility by men. To make farce of it, as Aristophanes does, may have given his (largely male) audience a *frisson*, and caused ripples of outrage among women, in a way we can hardly recapture today. A possible analogy is the way modern British (male) initiates, and women, might react to a farce set among Freemasons.

In fact, *Festival Time* is concerned neither with the Thesmophoria itself nor with gender politics. It is a straightforward farce, whose slapstick invention is rivalled in Aristophanes' surviving work only by the beating-scene in *Frogs* and the last third of *Women in Power*. Euripides, well-known (at least in comedy) as a misogynist and slanderer of women, is to be condemned by women at their secret festival; to speak for him, he smuggles his buffoon relative Mnesilochos ('Remember the trap') into the festival, disguised as a matron. Mnesilochos is unmasked, and Euripides tries to save him by using rescue-scenes out of his own tragedies. The plot is simple and of infinite potential, a farcical donnée of purest gold. Aristophanes' invention continues unflagging: in later times, only Feydeau ever created such an unstoppable escalation of logical, absurd disaster. Scholars cherish the play because it is the sole source for several snippets of real Euripides. Aristophanes-lovers consider it one of the funniest of all his plays, its dazzle undimmed by age.

At this stage in Aristophanes' career – at least to judge by the surviving plays – he was structuring his plays in ways which undercut the hierarchy of protagonist and other actors apparent in his earlier work. In *Birds* he experimented with 'company' articulation of the action, giving comic impetus not to the leading actor but to the actors playing lawyers, diplomats, priests, gods and other interlopers. In *Lysistrata* he changed the function of the *alazon*-scenes, and made new structural, dynamic use of the divided Chorus. *Festival Time* centres not on a single actor, but on what we would nowadays think of as a double-act. Mnesilochos is the 'protagonist' in the sense that he is onstage for most of the action, and speaks more lines than anyone else. His character – a boastful, not too bright old rogue willing to try anything – is important. But something else also fuels the comedy: his relationship with Euripides. They seem, as a couple, to come from a world outside the narrow action of the play. It is as if they know secrets which the audience do not, as if we are eavesdropping on private remarks and jokes. In this double-act, neither partner is exclusively 'straight man' or 'comic': the initiative shifts between them in every scene.

This feeling that the partners in a double-act have a relationship outside the immediate action is common today, adding greatly to the appeal of such comedy. In *Festival Time* it parallels another sense of familiarity in the play: that between us, the audience, and Euripidean drama. We are encouraged to think that we know these plays – not only their general tone and style, but also specific details. This, too, has modern parallels. Mnesilochos as Andromeda or Helen of Troy plays off Euripides as Perseus or Menelaus much as the partners in a modern double-act might give 'their' Juliet and Romeo or Cleopatra and Anthony. A great part of our pleasure, in both ancient and modern plays, is the feeling that we are revisiting theatre classics with a pair of irreverent and unceremonious guides. In *Festival Time*, we also laugh at the women guards and policeman who fail to see through the masquerade: complicity with the comedians, always a crucial part of the success in comedy, is encouraged and reinforced at every step. Books have been written about Euripides' or Sophocles' use of irony; Aristophanes' irony, in this and other plays, is a neglected but no less energetic resource.

Festival Time needs one doorway, that of Agathon's house. Possibly the scenery showing the house-front was wheeled away to show Agathon inside, or he was wheeled out on the *ekkuklema*: the situation is similar, and the problems are the same, as with the Dikaiopolis-Euripides scene in *Acharnians*. The main action takes place in an open space in the women's encampment in the Festival area – again analogous to the setting of other plays, this time Euripides' *Hecuba* and *Women of Troy*. Use may have been made of an upper level, or at least of a raised structure on to which Mnesilochos climbs for sanctuary, out of reach. At one point Euripides flies in and out on the theatre crane, disguised as Perseus riding the winged horse **Pegasos**.

Frogs

Frogs was first performed at the Lenaia in January 405BC, and won first prize. Aristophanes was in his early forties.

In January 405BC, the people of Athens seem to have been in a particularly volatile, not to say jumpy mood. Some four months before, the Athenian fleet had won its greatest victory so far in the Peloponnesian War, at Arginousai – and after the celebrations, the people had rounded on the successful generals, tried them for abandoning injured sailors among the wreckage, and executed six of them. This extraordinary piece of national hysteria seems to have been the result of lack of firm leadership, and to have been regretted as soon as it happened, adding a kind of sullen shame to the war-exhaustion which already gripped the people, and which Arginousai itself had only momentarily relieved. If Aristophanes caught a political mood in *Frogs*, it was one of uneasiness – and, perhaps like many people in the city, he focused it on the figure of Alkibiades, possibly the only person of stature left alive in Athenian politics, but now banished and in disgrace. When Dionysos in the play tries to decide which playwright to take back to Athens by asking Aeschylus and Euripides what should be done about Alkibiades, he may well be touching on one of the most hotly-debated 'real' issues of the moment.

In the world of the theatre, there was also cause for gloom. In 406, a few months before *Frogs*, Euripides (aged about 80) had died, and soon after the play went into rehearsal, Sophocles had also died (aged about 90) – two of the last links with the great theatrical past and with the 'fifty years' of Athenian political and cultural supremacy under Perikles. Remaining poets, according to Dionysos, were floor-sweepings. But for all its overt purpose, his journey to the Underworld was not merely to bring back a good old poet, but symbolically to restore the good old days. Yearning for the past underlies the play, helping to create the autumnal feeling which touches even its most outrageous satire. Its heart is not bubbly frog-songs or slapstick literary criticism, but a Chorus of Initiates evoking the hymns and processions of the Eleusinian Mysteries (rituals in which devotees were supposed to be granted the power to pass freely between the Upper World and the Underworld), and then turning to the audience and making a direct comparison between the good old days and present-day corruption and uncertainty.

The standoff between old and new is reflected in the poetic contest itself. For centuries, *Frogs* has been mined for literary-critical detail, as if the opinions Aristophanes puts into his characters' mouths are somehow rigorous, scholarly and a fair representation of 'enlightened opinion' of the time. (As well trust the attitudes to Shakespeare and Shaw in the 1970s musical update of *Frogs* by Burt Shevelove and Stephen Sondheim. Comedians out to entertain a large audience use rigorous attitudes and techniques, but they are not those of literary criticism.) In fact the contest is between representatives of the Old Spirit and the New Spirit. Aristophanes sends them both up equally, and when it comes to a choice, makes Dionysos select Aeschylus not because of what he has heard, but simply because he feels like it. Throughout Aristophanes' career, he allied himself with the conservative, broad-brush nostalgia characteristic of comedy audiences: save in a very few instances (people who went to see Lenny Bruce in his heyday, for example, or who go to see Ben Elton in his), audiences are rarely as radical, or as alert, as some commentators on Aristophanes would like us to believe.

Formally, *Frogs* is the most innovative of all Aristophanes' surviving plays using 'Old Comedy' styles and structures. The only traditional element left undeveloped is the *parabasis*, and even that is turned into a sermon, far more serious-seeming and specific than we (at our distance from the circumstances of the first performance) might think appropriate. The *alazon*-scenes are not clustered in the second half of the play, but appear from the start, and are wholly integrated into the action: the Corpse-scene is particularly felicitous. Indeed, at times it is almost as if Dionysos and Xanthias are themselves *alazones*, 'droppers-in' on other people's lives who get their slapstick comeuppance. The *agon* ('contest' or 'debate') is extended and developed until it takes over the whole second half of the play, and requires additional structuring – an escalation of slapstick – to hold our attention. And the acting-company hierarchy of Aristophanes' early plays, which he had begun subverting as early as *Birds* a decade before, has now almost disappeared. Comic and dramatic initiative are shared equally between all three main actors. In the first half Dionysos and Xanthias perform in the 'double-act' style familiar from *Festival Time* (see Introduction, page xxviii), and also have particularly effective 'triple-act' scenes (in which all three actors are equal) with Herakles and Aiakos. In the second half, the initiative shifts between Dionysos, Aeschylus and Euripides in a way quite different from the *agones* in *Acharnians* or *Wasps* (where the main character takes a major part in the debate), or in *Clouds*, where the debate is a formal, fighting-cock affair in which the main character plays no part at all. The Chorus stands well apart from the main action, in a way foreshadowing its more perfunctory roles in Aristophanes' last two surviving comedies, *Women in Power* (*Ekklesiazousai*) and *Wealth*.

The staging of *Frogs* requires two entrances: Herakles' house and the gate of the Underworld. Otherwise an open space is sufficient. Dionysos rows across it in Charon's boat, accompanied by the Chorus of Frogs. It would be neat to imagine that this space, in the Greek theatre, was the *orchestra* or central circle, but there is no evidence. As to the Frogs themselves, scholars suggest three alternative ways in which they may have been staged in the ancient theatre. (1) The Frogs were played and danced by boys, who sang their own song and later joined the main Chorus; (2) The Frogs were played by acrobats and dancers, and their song was provided by Chorus-men offstage; (3) The Frogs were unseen throughout, and their song was provided by the offstage Chorus.

Note: line-numbers alongside the texts relate to the Greek original rather than to this translation. Superior numbers in the texts refer to Notes at the end of the book.

WASPS

Characters

SOSIAS
XANTHIAS
BDELYKLEON
PHILOKLEON
BOY
CITIZEN
BREAD-WOMAN

silent parts:

BOY DANCERS
CHAIREPHON
DARDANIS (dancing girl)
DOGS (SNITCH and SNATCH)
DONKEY
DRUNKS
KARKINOS (dancer)
KITCHEN UTENSILS
PUPPIES
SLAVES (CRUSHER, GNASHER, GRINDER)
WITNESS

CHORUS OF AGED JURYMEN (the 'Wasps')

Athens. Open space outside PHILOKLEON's *house. The house is covered by a net. Night.* BDELYKLEON *is asleep on the flat roof.* XANTHIAS *is asleep beside the door. Enter* SOSIAS.

SOSIAS.
  Oi, Xanthias. Pea-brain. What're you doing?

XANTHIAS.
  Night duty. And I'm in training. Go away.

SOSIAS.
  You'll be in agony if Sir arrives.
  Have you forgotten the Thing we're supposed to guard?

XANTHIAS.
  I *was* trying to forget. Shake off dull care...

SOSIAS.
  Don't let me stop you. I know just what you mean.
  I'm having to prop my eyelids open too.

XANTHIAS.
  What else are you doing? Sleep-walking? Too much
    beer?

SOSIAS.
  Fat chance. I'm fighting Mr Sandman.

XANTHIAS.
  Ha!
  I'm fighting a desertful of Sandmen,   10
  Camels and all. Except that *isn't* all:
  I'm having nightmares.

SOSIAS.
  Funny. So am I.
  You start with yours.

XANTHIAS.
  It's shopping day. We're in the market place.
  A huge great eagle swoops out of nowhere, grabs
  Something round and shiny, soars away –
  Then turns into Kleonymos and drops it.

SOSIAS.
  A shield-shedder!

XANTHIAS.
Pardon?

SOSIAS.
It's like that tongue-twister
20   You say to prove you've not been drinking.
Cool Cat Kleonymos Sheds Several Shields.

XANTHIAS.
Tongue-twister, nothing. It's an omen, a dream
like that.

SOSIAS.
Of course it's not. An omen. What, exactly?

XANTHIAS.
Who knows? It's just not normal. Shedding
shields...
What about yours, then?

SOSIAS.
Ha! A big one, mine.
I dreamt about...the hull of the ship of state.

XANTHIAS.
The whole hull, huh? Up anchor, then. Get
30   launched.

SOSIAS.
I'd only just dozed off. The dream began.
I was in the Assembly. A flock of sheep,
With walking sticks and cloaks. Listening. In rows.
And who was doing the talking? A great fanged
whale
With a voice like a furious ferret.

XANTHIAS.
Bleah!

SOSIAS.
What?

XANTHIAS.
Stop.
It stinks. It stinks of Kle – er, HIM.

SOSIAS.
There's more.
This whale took a scale and a short sharp knife
And started carving up a carcass.

XANTHIAS.
No!   40
It *was* him! Carving up the state. Wake up!

SOSIAS.
I saw Theoros, sitting on the ground,
Like a crow at a sacrifice, watching, waiting...
In fact he *was* a crow. You could tell by the caws.
You know Theoros: anything for the caws.

XANTHIAS.
The caws? Oh, the cause. Of course!

SOSIAS.
It's no joke. Theoros – crow?

XANTHIAS.
That's an omen, and a good one.

SOSIAS.
How?

XANTHIAS.
Man – well, Theoros – turns into crow, right?
What happens next? That's obvious: he croaks.   50

SOSIAS.
You're good, you know. I spent two drachs just now
At Madam Sosostris'. *She* didn't think of that.

XANTHIAS.
It's time to tell the audience the plot.
A word or two to get them going. Ahem.
Don't panic. There's nothing heavy here. We're clean.
No slapstick, either. We *could* have offered sex,

Free popcorn, hunky attendants peddling nuts.
60 We *could* have had a pie-fight: others do.
We *could* have stuck one on Euripides,
Made giblets of Kleon. We don't, we won't –
Though *why* we avoid such good material...
Never mind. This is what you'd call a fable,
A theatrical legend. 'The hottest show in town';
'Fight to get seats' – you know the kind of thing.
That's Sir up there. Our master. On the roof,
Asleep. 'Watch Dad', he said. 'Don't let him out.
70 He's got to stay inside, in quarantine.'
What's wrong with the old fool? It's quite unique.
You'll never guess. What, want to try? All right.
You, sir. Yes, you, sir.

SOSIAS.
Nymphomania,
He says.

XANTHIAS.
He always does. Takes one to know one. Next!

SOSIAS.
He was right about the 'mania'. What's that?
Dipso...? There's someone there saying dipso.

XANTHIAS.
Nah.
80 Too classy. What he's got's not dipso. Next!

SOSIAS.
Dog-lover? What d'you mean? What's wrong with
that?

XANTHIAS.
Not dog-lover, dummy, *dog*-lover. Filthy minds.

SOSIAS.
How could you? He *told* you: it's not that kind of
show.

XANTHIAS.
You're wasting your time. You'll never get it.

Shut up and listen, if you want to know.
I'll straight unfold his lordship's tragic case.
He's a trialophile¹, and there's no known cure.
Ever since that law of Kleon's, paying jurymen,
He's been hooked on passing sentence. Moans and
    groans
If a day goes past without a verdict. Lies awake   90
All night, can't get a grain of sleep –
Or dozes off, clutching his voting-stone so tight
That he wakes up with his thumb and fingers sticky,
As if he'd been...no, no, we said we wouldn't.²
You know those graffiti –
'Show cats in transit';
'*We've* seen the Parthenon' – ?
Well, *his* says 'Jurymen do it with voting urns.'
We had a cock once, crowed at bedtime. Sir   100
Starts raving and cursing, saying it was late,
It was taking bribes to keep him out of court –
Some state official, accounts up for audit –
Starts yelling 'Shoes!' as soon as supper's done,
Rushes off to court, camps out all night,
Head of the queue, clinging to the noticeboard
Like a geriatric barnacle. And once he's in,
He's strict! Maximum damages, rigour of the law –
It gives him a buzz like a beehive. His voting-stones:
He's so afraid of running out, he keeps   110
A beach. You won't talk him out of it.
He's an addict. He's got it bad –
And that's where *we* come in. He's locked inside,
No exit. We see to that. It's the son I'm sorry for.
Him on the roof. He's at his wits' end. What else
Can he do? He tried being nice to him,
Tried asking him politely to take off his cloak
And stay at home. The verdict? No. He tried
All the usual cures for madness: purges, baths:
No joy. He tried dervishes, whirling dervishes –
And the old man twirled into court to hear the next
    case
Complete with long white skirt and tambourine.   120

We shipped him to Aegina, the Healing Shrine –
And next morning he was back in court as usual.
Since then we've not let him out at all.
He tried trickling down the drain;
We stuffed the hole with rags.
He hung a ladder out the window
And started hopping down,
130   Shouting 'Who's a pretty boy, then?'
That's why we slung that net;
That's why we're here, on guard.
There. I think I've told you everything. Oh no.
The old man's name. You won't believe it:
Philokleon: he's a Kleon freak as well.
His son's called Bdelykleon: Kleon-puke.
So, it's a mouthful. It's still a good idea.

BDELYKLEON (*from the roof*).
Xanthias! Sosias!

XANTHIAS.
Oops.

SOSIAS.
What now?

XANTHIAS.
His Nibs.

BDELYKLEON.
Quick, one of you, run round the back. Dad's out.
He's in the kitchen, looking for mouseholes.
140   Watch the waste-pipe, in case he runs out there.
Xanthias, lean on the door.

XANTHIAS.
A pleasure, Boss.

BEDLYKLEON.
What's that in the chimney? Funny noises. Hey!
Who's there?

PHILOKLEON (*from inside the chimney*).
Not 'who', son, 'what'.

He sticks his head out.

A puff of smoke.

BDELYKLEON.
You're joking.

PHILOKLEON.
I'm smoking – and that's no joke.

BDELYKLEON.
Get back inside. Faugh! Soot! Get down!
The chimney cover...there. This log of wood...
That'll hold him. Any other bright ideas?
Ye gods, I'm not enjoying this. O-ee,　　　　　　150
All mortal misery makes mock of me.

XANTHIAS.
He's pushing the door now.

BDELYKLEON.
Lean, then. Harder.
I'm coming down. Catch hold of the latch!
He won't get far if you brace that bar.

PHILOKLEON (*inside*).
What are you doing? Bastards! Let me out!

He sticks his head out of a window.

It's Drakontides on trial today. D'you want
Him acquitted?

BDELYKLEON.
What's that to you?

PHILOKLEON.
My horoscope.
I heard it in Delphi, on that day trip:
'Let anyone off, you'll wither away and die.'　　　160

BDELYKLEON.
Horoscopes now! What next?

PHILOKLEON.
Please let me out. I *must*.

BDELYKLEON.
Oh, no you mustn't.

PHILOKLEON.
I'll chew the net away.

BEDELYKLEON.
What with?

PHILOKLEON.
Right then. You wait. I'll see to you.
A sword. A summons. Don't go away. Stay there.

He withdraws his head. Pause.

BDELYKLEON.
Now what are you doing?

PHILOKLEON *sticks his head out again.*

PHILOKLEON.
Nothing. If you must know,
I'm getting Neddy ready. It's market day.
170   I'm loading him with stuff to sell.

BDELYKLEON.
Can't I do that?

PHILOKLEON.
I'll see to it myself.

He withdraws his head.

BDELYKLEON.
Big deal.

PHILOKLEON (*inside*).
Right. Open up.

SOSIAS.
It's a trick. Don't do it, sir.
He's trying to con you.

BDELYKLEON.
He can try all he likes.

I know what he's up to. *I'll* fetch the donkey out.
He won't get past.

He goes inside, and reappears holding reins,
trying to coax a (still invisible) donkey out
of the house.

Come on, Neddy. What's wrong with you?
Stop groaning. Don't you want to go to market?
You do seem to be carrying a lot of weight.   190

The donkey comes out. It is loaded with garden
produce, which hangs down like a curtain to the
ground³.

SOSIAS.
    It's like Odysseus in the story.
    There's someone underneath.

BDELYKLEON.
    Where? Show me. Oi,
    Who's there?

PHILOKLEON.
    No One.

BDELYKLEON.
    No One who?

PHILOKLEON.
    At All. No one at all⁴.

BDELYKLEON.
    Never mind No One. No Win. Pull him out.
    The dirty old devil: look where he's stuffed himself.
    This is Neddy, you fool, not a voting urn.

PHILOKLEON.
    Get off. D'you want a fight?   190

BDELYKLEON.
    What's to fight about?

PHILOKLEON.
    Donkey-doos.

BDELYKLEON.
You slithery, slippery, sly old man.

PHILOKLEON.
What d'you mean, slithery? I'm tasty, me.
Delicious. Have a bite.

BDELYKLEON.
Oh, get inside.
Take Neddy with you.

PHILOKLEON (*as he is pushed inside*).
Jurymen! Kleon! Rape!

BDELYKLEON.
Howl all you like. This door stays shut.

(*to* XANTHIAS *and* SOSIAS)

200   Block it with stones. Wedge in that plank.
Now help me roll this millstone. There.

SOSIAS.
Ow!
Something's showering me with dirt.

XANTHIAS.
Mouse in the eaves.

SOSIAS.
Mouse? Juryman. Up there.
He's prising up the tiles.

BDELYKLEON.
He thinks he's a pigeon now.
Pass me that net. Shoo! Shoo! Get back inside.

210   It's like being curator in a monkey-house⁵.

SOSIAS.
Look, sir, he's in. He's quiet. He won't get out.
We've time for forty winks. Well, twenty. *Please.*

BDELYKLEON.
You're joking. Five minutes, they'll all be here:
The rest of them, his fellow-jurymen,
Calling to fetch him.

SOSIAS.
    It's hardly dawn.

BDELYKLEON.
    Exactly. They're late already.

    (*to the audience*)

    They come in the middle of the night,
    By lamplight, singing the good old songs,
    Humming and chuntering,
    Mumbling and muttering,
    Humping him, bumping him, right out of bed.   220

XANTHIAS.
    No problem. We'll scare them away with stones.

BDELYKLEON.
    You can't do that.
    These aren't just any old grandads.
    They're sparks in the chimney,
    Leaping and roaring.
    They're wasps in a wasps' nest.
    They've stings in their backsides[6].
    They zoom, they buzz, they bite.

SOSIAS.
    Don't you worry, sir. I've got my stones.
    No sit-on-the-jury wasps can frighten me.

    Exit BDELYKLEON. XANTHIAS *and* SOSIAS *settle
    down to sleep. Enter* CHORUS, *led by* BOYS *with
    lamps.*

CHORUS.
    Quick, men, march. Pick up your feet.   230
    Reeve, don't drag. You'll be left behind.
    Once you beat us all; now even Finer's faster.
    Judge, dear friend, where are you?
    Proctor? Sherriff? Here they come now.
    Those were the days! Remember them?
    Thrace? Fifty years ago?
    You and me, night exercise,

Snaffling that salad bowl for firewood?
I can taste that porridge still.

240   Hurry now. It's Laches' trial today.
Treason. 'Be there. Crack of dawn,'
Lord Protector Kleon told us.
'Three days' rations: frowns, bile, fury.
He's loaded, and where did it come from? You!
It was you he betrayed; you punish him.'
Don't hang back. It's nearly morning.
Light your way. Mind out for stones.

BOY.

Daddy, daddy, mind the mud.

CHORUS.

Use a stick: prick up the wick.

BOY.

250   This is just as good. Look, see!

CHORUS.

Don't use *that* to prick the wick!
Stupid boy! Oil's rationed. You
Don't pay through the nose for it. I do.

BOY.

Hey! That hurt. Just one more slap
And we drop these lamps and head for home.
You can paddle in the puddles,
Like the silly old coots you are.

CHORUS LEADER.

I've cooted bigger than you, my lad.
Cheeky devil. Yarg! What's that?

260   What am I treading in? Why won't it *rain*?
Four more days. They promised. Look:
Fuzz, here on the wick. Sure sign.
Good thing too. The crops are parched.
Showers, north wind: that's all they need.

Funny. This is the house. We're here.
No Philokleon. Not *late*?

He's usually first in line,
Leading the singing. He loves the good old songs.
That's it! Gather round, men. Ready?   270
Sing him out of bed. Serenade him,
Tickle his ears, entice him out.

CHORUS.
What's keeping you? Come out. Return our calls.
It's time to go.
Have you stubbed your toe?
Bruised ankles? Poisoned kneecaps? Swollen balls?
That's tough,
That's rough,
No joke for a man your age.
We need your fire, your rage.
When they mumble and moan,
When they grumble and groan,
You butt 'em,
You nut 'em,
You're hard as stone.   280
That bastard yesterday got off. What for?
Pleading glances,
Extenuating circumstances,
Distinguished Undercover Work in Time of War.
That's rough,
That's tough:
No wonder our old friend frets.
Come on, man, no regrets.
There's a pigeon to pluck today.
Make him run out of luck today.
Filthy traitor!
Athens-hater! –
Let's make him pay!

No response from the house.

CHORUS (*to the* BOY).
Get a move on, get a move on.   290

BOY.
Will you give me

All I ask for?
Go on. Please, Dad.

CHORUS.
　Ask away, son.
　What d'you fancy?
　Bag of marbles?

BOY.
　Bag of figs, Dad.
　Fat and juicy.

CHORUS.
　Little bastard!
　Always scrounging.

BOY.
　Right, that does it.
　No more lamp-light.

CHORUS.
300　Half a drach a day I earn. That's poor.
　Sticks for the fire, porridge-oats. No more.
　And figs! He asks for figs!

BOY.
　Dad, I'm frightened. If the court's closed,
　Nothing doing
　Till tomorrow,

　Where's your money?
　Where's our breakfast?
　Empty bellies.
　Dad, I'm starving.

CHORUS.
　Do stop moaning.
310　What can I do?
　Larder's empty.
　Not a penny –

BOY.
　I'm your son, Dad.

CHORUS.
  You're a millstone.

BOY (*sobbing*).
  Gods, we're doomed. No hope. It's heaven's curse.
  What earthly use is an empty purse?
  Woe! Wail and howl.

  Lamentation. PHILOKLEON *pokes his head out of*
  an upstairs window.

PHILOKLEON.
  Woe! I weep for you,
  Dear friends, I howl for you,
  I hear you, here.
  How can I weep, how wail my woe?
  I'm tragically trapped.
  They're watching me, them there.
  I've a jury to serve on,   320
  I've verdicts to vote on,
  I yearn for the urn!

  Zeus! O Zeus, look down,
  Thunder-lord, hear, help.
  Let me slip away like mist,
  Like dust, like smoke.
  Send lightning, lord.
  Roast me, toast me,
  Crunch me to crumbs, to ashes
  Blown on the balmy breeze –   330
  Or turn me to stone, to voting stone.

CHORUS.
  Who did it, who?
  Who dungeoned you
  And threw away the key?

PHILOKLEON.
  My son. Up there.
  Asleep. Take care.
  Don't wake him. Rescue me.

CHORUS.
But what have you done
To annoy your son?

PHILOKLEON.
He says I'm a pest,
I'm obsessed,
I'm besotted.
340   I tell him, 'Get knotted'.
He says I can choose:
There'll be dancing girls, booze –

CHORUS.
What a swine! What a smarty!
To bribe you with party!
The treacherous rat,
Making offers like that!

There's only one way out: escape.
Get down before he notices.

PHILOKLEON.
But how? I'm going mad in here.
I need that urn. I need it, now.

CHORUS.
350   Find a chink, a crack. Squeeze through –

PHILOKLEON.
What d'you take me for, cream cheese?
Not even a flea could squeeze through these.

CHORUS.
D'you remember that time in Naxos,
When you stuck those kebab-sticks in the wall
And used them like a ladder?

PHILOKLEON.
I was young then, I had my health and strength –
And I wasn't guarded. Not like now.
360   It's a fortress here. There are grim, gruff guards
(Well, two of them) to watch my every move,

As if I was pussy prowling round the larder.
They've got kebab-sticks, mate, not me.

CHORUS.
You've got a date.
It's getting late.
Find some way out. Some trick.

PHILOKLEON.
What if I chew
The net right through?
Tough on the teeth, but quick.

CHORUS.
You're right.
Get chomping. Bite!   370

PHILOKLEON.
I'll soon be out.
But please don't shout,
Don't wake my son.
It'll soon be done.

CHORUS.
Don't fret about sonny.
If he tries to be funny
We'll make him sweat.
Just bite that net.

Tie a rope round your middle.
Swing down, like a spider on a thread.   380

PHILOKLEON.
Like a fish on a line, you mean.
Suppose he sees me, and reels me in?

CHORUS.
Just lower yourself down. We'll see to him.
He won't be reeling, he'll be squealing.

PHILOKLEON.
All right. Here goes. But remember:
If anything...nasty...happens, gather me,

Weep for me, lay me to rest – under Witness Box
Three.

CHORUS.
Nothing nasty's going to happen.
Say your prayers; get lowering.

PHILOKLEON.
Lord of lawsuits, judge and juryman supreme,
390 You love to hear defendants howl and scream.
I'm on the ropes (well, rope); send help divine,
I'll never fart again inside your shrine.

He starts lowering himself.

BDELYKLEON.
Sst! Wake up.

XANTHIAS.
What is it?

BDELYKLEON.
I thought I heard something. Is it Dad?
Is he wangling his way out again?

XANTHIAS.
Not wangling, dangling.

BDELYKLEON.
Push him back, you fool!
Fetch the yard-brush, give him a helping hand.

PHILOKLEON.
400 Help! Who's got a case this year?
Ladies and gentlemen, the mercy of the court.
Help me! D'you want to see me hauled inside?

*Pandemonium. PHILOKLEON is halfway up, halfway
down. BDELYKLEON is tugging from above, XANTHIAS
is poking from below. The CHORUS mill about,
taking off their cloaks to reveal wasps' costumes
underneath.*

CHORUS.
Now he's done it. This means trouble.

Bring your stings, men. At the double.
Beat him, bite him,
Fix him, fight him,
Sting that pacifist, that traitor,
Spartan-lover, city-hater.   410
Stir your anger, feed your fury.
Teach him not to touch the jury.

BDELYKLEON.
Quiet! Please! Shut up and listen.

CHORUS.
Louder, men!

BDELYKLEON.
He's here and here he stays.

CHORUS.
Tyrant! Dictator!
You stand here in Athens,
Cradle of democracy, land of the free,
And say he's here to stay?

SOSIAS.
Look out, sir. They do have stings.   420

BDELYKLEON.
Sharpened up in court.

CHORUS.
Sharpened up for *you*. That's right, men:
HUP. All together now, look FIERCE.
You're wasps, remember. He poked your nest.
Stings OUT. By the right, quick JAB.

XANTHIAS.
I'm not fighting this lot. I daren't.
Look at those skewers.

CHORUS.
Let him go, or you'll be sorry.
You'll wish you'd a shell, not skin.

PHILOKLEON.
This way! Stick the bastard, quick!   430

Buzz him, prong him, poke him.
Sting his fingers. Prick his bum.

BDELYKLEON.
Crusher, Grinder, Gnasher, help!

Three SLAVES *come out.*

Grab the old man. Don't let him go.
Get on with it. Whips, chains, say NOW.
Don't mind *them:* they're nothing but fuss and buzz.

CHORUS.
And stingers. D'you get me, stingers. Down!

PHILOKLEON.
The shame of it! D'you see this now?
An Athenian juryman, a soldier for democracy,
By his own slaves, HANDLED. Who taught you
      pain?
440   Who gave you knuckle sandwiches? You *owe* me!

CHORUS.
Ladies and gentlemen, there's a lesson here.
The Pains of Old Age. He lavished himself
On these young men. Cloaks, tunics, shoes –
Oh those winter chilblain-chasers! –
And how do they thank him? How do they repay
      him?
They HANDLE him.

PHILOKLEON.
Pig, let go.
D'you remember when you stole that bunch of
      grapes?
450   How I tied you to the olive tree, skinned you alive,
Made you the talk of the household. All that, for
      this!
Put me down. You too. Before my son comes back.

CHORUS.
Do it now, or else. You'll be sorry. Soon.
You can see by our faces the sort of men we are:

Street-fighters for justice, pepper nostrils, mustard
eyes.

BDELYKLEON, XANTHIAS *and* SOSIAS *rush out*
with brooms, sticks and blazing torches.

BDELYKLEON.
Beat them, bash them, bang them.

XANTHIAS.
Smoke them, choke them, char them.

SOSIAS.
Shoo! Get back. Don't make me –

XANTHIAS.
Push, sir! Now! Attack!
They're falling back.   460

BDELYKLEON.
I knew they wouldn't last it.
Just thank your stars they're past it.

CHORUS.
Don't be cheeky.
That was sneaky,
Creeping up behind to grab us,
Slinking round the side to nab us.
Why such treachery, such treason?
Tell the truth. Explain. Give reason.   470

BDELYKLEON.
No more fighting? No more shouting?
Negotiations? Patience? Calm?

CHORUS.
Negotiations? Calm? With you?
Traitor, Spartan-lover,
Long-haired, namby-pamby freak!

BDELYKLEON.
I think I'll let father go.
I don't need broadsides like this every day.

CHORUS.

480   Broadside? That? You've heard nothing yet.
    If it's a meal of mouth you want,
    Just wait till we get you in court.
    'Conspiracy', 'Public enemy' –
    They'll eat you for dinner and spit out your bones.

BDELYKLEON.

    Oh, go away. I've had enough of this.

CHORUS.

    'Broadside'. 'I've had enough of this.'
    Who *do* you think you are? His Mighty Majesty?
    This is class war, comrade – and you're the enemy.

BDELYKLEON.

    It's always the same with you.
    The minute things don't go the way you want,
    It's 'Class war', 'His Majesty.'
    We're a republic...comrade.
490   Class war's been obsolete for fifty years,
    And suddenly it's as common as toasted cheese.
    If you try to buy trout instead of kippers,
    It's 'Working-class fish not good enough?'
    If you ask for extra salt or vinegar,
    It's 'Watch it. We know your kind round here.
    This is Athens. Everybody equal.
    If you want free handouts,
    Shove off somewhere else.'

XANTHIAS.

    The same thing happened to me, yesterday.
500   It was lunchtime, bloody hot,
    So I asked her Lusciousness
    To do it doggy-fashion, for coolness –
    And she says, 'Lie down and like it,
    Like all the rest of us.''

BDELYKLEON.

    They love it when you talk like that:
    Look at them. What's their lifestyle?

Crack-of-dawny,
Hungry-yawny,
Raggle-taggle
Hubble-bubble
Bibble-babble –
I try to rescue Dad from that,
To make him a proper gent, to give him dignity
(You know, like Morychos) – and what do I get?
'Tyrant! Traitor! Freak!'

PHILOKLEON.
Well, so you are. I like my lifestyle.
Who needs your nibbles and fancies and dainties –   510
Money to burn?
I'll stick to plain old nourishing lawsuits –
Done to a turn.

BDELYKLEON.
I told you: addicted, obsessed.
If you shut up a minute, and listen,
I'll show you you're wrong.

PHILOKLEON.
Being a juryman's wrong?

BDELYKLEON.
What's wrong is sucking up
To men who treat you like an idiot,
A slave.

PHILOKLEON.
Excuse me: slave? I hold the reins.

BDELYKLEON.
Oh yes! Democracy's chariot, the good Greek law!
You're a carthorse who thinks he's a driver, Dad.   520

PHILOKLEON.
Rubbish. And I can prove it. Let *them* decide.

BDELYKLEON.
Fine. Let him go.

PHILOKLEON.

First give me a naked blade.

He strikes an attitude, as if to stab himself.

If I fail this test, bare blade bite breast.

BDELYKLEON.

Very good. And if you give up halfway?

PHILOKLEON.

I'll forfeit my pay.

CHORUS.

Gloves off, scrum down, on guard.
Shower him with arguments, good and hard.

BDELYKLEON (*to* SOSIAS).

Fetch an umbrella, there's a good fella.
530   I think it just might rain.

CHORUS.

Be as quick as a ferret,
As sharp as a knife.
There's honour, there's merit
In a juryman's life.
Speak up for us all:
Don't stall.

BDELYKLEON.

What a face, what a frown! I'll write all this down.

PHILOKLEON.

I'm really quite nervous. No gain without pain.

CHORUS.

540   He's got to be told,
It's no sin to be old.
We're not dregs,
Empty boxes on legs.

Speak up for us now, make a powerful effect:
We're old but we matter; they owe us respect.

PHILOKLEON.
    Right. 'We're old but we matter.' How true.
    That's the point. We're respected. We count.
    We're just pensioners, ordinary – BUT
    The whole world bends the knee to us, scrapes   550
    To us, pampers us, treats us like kings.
    I get up in the morning; I stroll
    Down to court – and they're waiting, they're there:
    Great hulking defendants, men in their prime,
    Queuing up to be nice to me – me! –
    Shaking hands (fingers sticky with bribes),
    Sickly grins, voices oozing respect.
    'Honoured sir, please have pity. I grant
    I was tempted – but *you* know the score:
    You've got style, you're a man of the world' –
    Total strangers! Unless they remember
    From last time who voted 'Not guilty'.

BDELYKLEON.
    Fine. Crawlers. I'm writing that down.

PHILOKLEON.
    Right. I promise; I swagger inside –   560
    And forget every word that I said.
    It's a floor-show. They're racking their brains
    For the best way to tug at our heartstrings.
    Plead poverty, pile up their debts
    Till they bounce off the sky? Tell us jokes,
    Funny stories from Aesop? They think
    We'll be kind if we're splitting our sides.
    They're mistaken. They bring in their kids,
    Their 'princesses', their 'darling boys' –
    And I sit stony-faced while they huddle and bleat,
    While their Daddy goes down on his knees   570
    And beseeches me, 'Pass my accounts,
    And my lambkin will leap for your lordship –
    Unless you like piggy-wigs better...'
    I know what he's saying. I slacken my rage.
    That's our power for you, that's our respect:
    Take a rich man and fart in his face.

BDELYKLEON.
> I'm writing. '...and fart in his face.'
> Nothing better? There has to be more.

PHILOKLEON.
> Right. At coming-of-age time, we make
> All the candidates show their credentials.
> Remember Oiagros last year?
> Starred in Aeschylus; summonsed; up;
> 580 Gave us his *Niobe*; lovely; got off.
> A musician's acquitted; he plays
> Us his thanks, our old favourites. A man
> Makes a will, leaves his goods and his cash
> To his daughter. Will challenged in court.
> Stuff the documents – who gets the money?
> Whoever speaks nicest to *us*.
> You can challenge a magistrate, launch
> An appeal – but you can't challenge us.
> We decide and it happens. That's power.

BDELYKLEON.
> Very good, that. But stuffing that poor
> Daughter's documents? Not very nice.

PHILOKLEON.
> 590 Right. Another thing. Matters of state.
> Arbitration. Our pigeon. Our job.
> Politicians make eyes at us, men
> Like Euathlos, Kleonymos – men! –
> Shed a tear, shed a shield,
> Say they'll never betray us, they'll fight
> For the people, for Athens. Unless
> We're available, nothing gets done.
> Even Kleon, His Hugeness, respects us,
> Bites others but leaves us alone,
> Cradles us, dandles us, brushes the flies
> From our faces – as you never do.
> Lord Theoros, a toff of toffs, a V.I.P.,
> 600 Kneels and sponges our boots.

This is power, and you lock me inside,
You insist I'm a slave. I'm a king!

BDELYKLEON.
Is there anything else? Is there more?
You're a bum, Dad, and talking won't change you.

PHILOKLEON.
Right. Best thing of all: I come home
With my pay, they all fall on my neck.
'Daddy, darling!' (my daughter) 'Sit down.
Your poor feet must be aching. That purse
Looks so heavy. I'll put it down here.'*
Then the Missus comes bustling in. 'Look,   610
Darling: biscuits, fresh-baked, just for you.'
Well, I'm partial to that. I adore it.
Just because I'm retired, I don't see
Why I have to sit waiting for you
And your butler to ladle out lunch.
All that grumbling and muttering. Look:
I've emergency rations: a sandwich,
A donkey of wine. Cheers! Up yours!
Ha! You can see what he thinks about you.
I'm a lord, I'm a king,   620
I'm as good as a god.
When I thunder and growl
People shudder and shake.
When my lightning-flares flash
Every nob, every toff
Who's got something to hide
Sits there wetting himself.
You're afraid of me, too,
You don't know what to do.
But I'm not scared of you.   630

He dances.

CHORUS.
What wit! What class! What style!
Who'll outsmart you? You've won by a mile.

PHILOKLEON.
Who patronised Da-da? Who thought I was ga-ga?
I thought you'd change your mind.

CHORUS.
You left nothing unstated,
Left nothing to chance.
We're impressed, we're elated,
Our hearts want to dance.
640 We're in paradise.
It's nice.

PHILOKLEON.
He's shuffling, he's stumbling, he's moping, he's
mumbling.

BDELYKLEON.
I'm working up wordplay. You'll find what kind.

CHORUS.
You'd better be quick,
And you'd better be slick.
We don't play by the rules,
We're not fools.
We're a prejudiced, difficult jury.
Convince us, or flinch from our fury.

BDELYKLEON.
650 'COMIC WRITER CURES ALL CITY'S ILLS' –
It's a challenge. I'll do what I can.

(*praying*)

Father, lord –

PHILOKLEON.
Don't you 'Father, lord' me.
You're to prove I'm a slave. If you don't
Then you're done for. Unpleasant but true.

BDELYKLEON.
Right, Dad, listen. Don't make such a face.
You can start with some finger-work: add

Up the cash Athens rakes in each year.
There's imperial revenue, mines,
Markets, harbour-tax, fees, rents and fines.
What's the total? A million? Now add   660
Up what *you* get, your jurymen's pay.
At three obols a day, every day,
It's a couple of thousand – at most.

PHILOKLEON.
It's a fraction! It's peanuts!

BDELYKLEON.
Exactly.

PHILOKLEON.
So who gets the rest?

BDELYKLEON.
Dad, you said it yourself. You admire
Them, you trust them. 'We'll never betray
You, we'll fight for you (credulous scum)' –
Doesn't that get your vote every time?
They grow fat on the profits they make
From the empire. Protection. 'Pay up   670
Or expect stormy weather.' *They* say.
You're too busy with scrag-ends and scraps.
When our allies catch sight of you,
Gulping and guzzling on air, empty air,
It's no wonder they hurry right past
And deposit their bribes with those bigmouths:
Wine, pickle, cheese, sesame seeds,
Honey, cushions, cups, necklaces, crowns.
It's *your* empire: you sweated and fought
To amass it, and what do you get?
Not even free garlic to flavour your soup.

PHILOKLEON.
Yes, I bought some today.   680
But that's business. You say I'm a *slave*.

BDELYKLEON.
Yes, of course you're a slave. Look who lords it

With toadies and stooges: it's them.
Look who drools for three obols a day –
Obols *you* went to war for, *you* marched,
Toiled and rowed for. Three obols – you're slaves!
You're being used! It gets right up my nose
When some baby-faced barrister swans
Up and stands there, like this – no, like this –
And announces, 'Tomorrow. Dawn Call.

690   If you're late, kiss your obols goodbye.'
No one threatens *his* fee. No one dares.
They're all in it together. They share
Every bribe fifty-fifty; they slice
Up the action like men with a saw –
Mine-mine, mine-mine, mine-mine –
And you're blind. Obols dazzle your eyes.

PHILOKLEON.

No, you're joking. That's not what they do.
He's convincing, though. What if it's true?

BDELYKLEON.

If those crooks hadn't tied you in knots,
You'd be rich, every citizen, rich.

700   You've an empire, north, east, west and south,
And it brings you three obols, loose change.
Even that they begrudge you, they pay
You by drip-feed. It suits them. They want
You to fawn on the bosses who feed you –
And then, when you're trained, they can set
You to savage their enemies, go for the throat.
If they chose, there'd be goodies for all.
It's no problem. How many big towns
In the empire? A thousand. Give each
Twenty families in Athens to feed,
And hey presto! Your problems are solved.
No more queuing for handouts; you're rich,

710   You can feast on the fat of the land –
And what else do old soldiers deserve?

PHILOKLEON.
I've come over all flabby. My sword!
It's too heavy to brandish. I'm limp.

BDELYKLEON.
When they panic, they promise the Moon.
Public subsidy, corn by the ton.
Do you get it? Do pigs get to fly?
Half a cupful of barley a day.
It's because of all this
That I locked you inside.
They won't make *you* look daft.   720
Pompous frauds! I'll look after you,
Pamper you, treat you –
Far more than three obols a day.

CHORUS.
Never prejudge the issue, they say.
Hear both sides of the argument first.
Well, I've heard, and I've judged, and you've won.
No more anger. I lay down my arms.
As for you, dear old friend,
Accept his case.
It's no disgrace.   730
I wish my son
Promised me such fun.
Your lucky day,
Is here to stay.
So go with the flow.
Don't answer no.

BDELYKLEON.
Leave everything to me.
I'll supply all his needs:
Nice new clothes, nice soft food,
A blanket
To warm him up here,
A woman
To warm him down *here* –   740

What's the matter? He's gone very quiet.
No complaints? I don't like this at all.

CHORUS.
It makes him sad
To think how bad
He was before,
What a daft old bore.
Now you've had your say,
He'll do things your way.
He'll accept,
He'll show respect.

PHILOKLEON (*a huge tragic cry*).
Ee-oh, mo-ee, mo-eeee!

BDELYKLEON.
What's up now, Dad?

PHILOKLEON.
750   What good are your blankets, your goodies,
Your women, to me? All I want
Is the old days, the happy, golden days
When I stood in the voting-queue – last.
How I savoured that, waiting till last!

Hot foot now, soul! Where *is* my soul?
Dark shades, engulf – oh gods,
No more judging...not even of Kleon!

BDELYKLEON.
760   Do listen, Dad. For heaven's sake give in.

PHILOKLEON.
Oh, I give in. Whatever you say. Just don't –

BDELYKLEON.
Don't what?

PHILOKLEON.
Don't say my judging days are done.
I *need* to judge, I've *got* to judge –

BDELYKLEON.
Of course you do.
But not down *there:* it's miles away.
We'll give you a court at home. A family court.

PHILOKLEON.
Judge here? You're crazy. Who? What?

BDELYKLEON.
Everything.
That naughty girl who never shuts the door⁹ –
You can confiscate her assets every time.
It's no different from any other court.   770
Suppose it's a sunny day? Judge in the garden.
If it's snowing, judge by the fire, inside.
If it's raining, don't go out at all. Lie in bed
Till lunchtime; no one will take your name.

PHILOKLEON.
Keep talking.

BDELYKLEON.
And if someone goes on and on and on
You won't have to sit with your stomach rumbling,
Growling at the defendant.

PHILOKLEON.
Judge *and* eat?
Think with my mouth full? I can't do that.   780

BDELYKLEON.
Of course you can. You've heard
Of 'chewing things over', 'digesting the facts' –

PHILOKLEON.
I like this more and more. There's just
One problem left. My fee.

BDELYKLEON.
I pay that.

PHILOKLEON.
Great.

Saves all that fiddling about with change.
I remember once...you know that practical joker
Lysistratos? He and I were paid together once:
A drachma between us. We went to get change
790 In the fish market; he gave me three mullet-scales;
I thought they were obols and stowed them in my
    mouth.
God, they were foul! I spat them out and grabbed
    him.

BDELYKLEON.
What did *he* say?

PHILOKLEON.
'I thought you were hungry.
Human dustbin. You're always munching change.'

BDELYKLEON.
Well, now you see: there'll be no more of that.

PHILOKLEON.
I'm not complaining. Let's get on with it.

BDELYKLEON.
I'll fetch what you need out here. Don't go away.

He goes inside.

PHILOKLEON.
See how everything comes true?
790 ERECT YOUR OWN DOMESTIC COURT.
JUDGE CASES IN THE COMFORT OF YOUR
    GARDEN.
FUN FOR ALL THE FAMILY.
THIS SIDE UP. SATISFACTION GUARANTEED.

BDELYKLEON *comes back, with* SLAVES *carrying
furniture and props for the court.*

BDELYKLEON.
Here you are. I think that's everything.
A potty, in case you're taken short.
I'll hang it here.

PHILOKLEON.
  Very thoughtful.
  You understand my weakness:
  When an old man has to go, he has to go.   810

BDELYKLEON.
  A fire, and a plate of beans
  In case you get peckish.

PHILOKLEON.
  Brilliant!
  Now even if I'm dying of flu, I'll still feel full
  Of beans. They're bringing a cock. What for?

BDELYKLEON.
  In case of boring speeches. You doze off;
  He crows; hey presto.

PHILOKLEON.
  I like the sound of that.
  So far so good. There's one thing missing.

BDELYKLEON.
  What?

PHILOKLEON.
  A statue of Justice.

  BDELYKLEON *improvises.*

BDELYKLEON.
  Here. Complete with scales.   820

PHILOKLEON.
  She was here all the time. I never saw.

BDELYKLEON.
  She looks like Kleonymos to me.

PHILOKLEON.
  Exactly.
  One step out of line, she'll come down on you
  Like...a ton of shields.

BDELYKLEON.
It's time for the first case.
Sit down.

PHILOKLEON.
I am. Get on with it.

BDELYKLEON (*aside to himself*).
All right, who's first?
What master criminals do we have inside?
I know: this morning Thratta burnt the soup.

PHILOKLEON.
Hold on! Don't start! We need a podium.
830   You were going to start without a podium.
A podium's essential. We all know that.

BDELYKLEON.
You're right. We haven't got a podium.

PHILOKLEON.
I know the very thing.

He rushes round the back of the house.

BDELYKLEON.
He's gone to get one.
A podium! Fancy me forgetting that.

XANTHIAS *comes out, furious.*

XANTHIAS.
Where are you? I'll teach you. Bloody dog!

BDELYKLEON.
What's the matter?

XANTHIAS.
Snatch[10] is the matter.

BDELYKLEON.
Snatch?

XANTHIAS.
The dog.

Creeps into the kitchen, chomps a cheese and *whoof!*
He's off.

BDELYKLEON.
  That's it! Case Number One. Stay here.
  You'll have to prosecute.   840

XANTHIAS.
  Not me, sir. Snitch.
  The other dog. He's asked to take the case.

BDELYKLEON.
  All right, call both of them.

XANTHIAS.
  Call Snitch and Snatch.

  He goes inside. PHILOKLEON *reappears from
  behind the house, with a piece of wicker fence.*

BDELYKLEON.
  What's that?

PHILOKLEON.
  A podium.

BDELYKLEON.
  It's the pigsty wall.

PHILOKLEON.
  Who's quibbling? Get on with it. I'm feeling...fine.

BDELYKLEON.
  I'll fetch the case-notes and the files.

PHILOKLEON.
  All this delay! I'm fine! I'm dying to fine!   850

BDELYKLEON.
  There.

PHILOKLEON.
  Start, then.

BDELYKLEON.
  The court's in session. Case Number One.

PHILOKLEON.
No, damn it. I forgot the urns.

BDELYKLEON.
What urns?

PHILOKLEON.
The voting-urns.

BDELYKLEON.
Use these. Not flower-pots: urns.

PHILOKLEON.
Perfect. I'm ready. No I'm not. No clock.
No water-clock.

BDELYKLEON (*brandishing the potty*).
What about this? When it's full, case ends.

PHILOKLEON.
No expense spared. No expense at all.

BDELYKLEON.
860   A stick of incense, quick. A light. A wreath.
As soon as the prayers are said, the trial begins.

CHORUS.
Excuse me: prayers?
We'll see to those.
You're friends again:
No more yelling and cussing,
No fighting and fussing:
Domestic bliss.

BDELYKLEON.
Let the prayers begin.

CHORUS.
Apollo, lord,
870   On this young man, his father,
His garden festival, his friends
(That means us),
Send blessings.

BDELYKLEON.
Work a miracle, lord. Take my Daddy.
He's pernickety, fussy and faddy,
He's embedded, encrusted in folly.
Make him kindly and gentle and jolly.
Make him mild   880
As a sweet-natured child,
No more stinging and hitting –
Acquitting.

CHORUS.
Our turn again.
Apollo, lord,
On this young man, so thoughtful,
So devoted to his elders
(That means us),   890
Send blessings.

BDELYKLEON.
Gentlemen of the jury, take your places.
No further admittance. Let the case begin.

  SNATCH *and* SNITCH, *two dogs, are brought in by*
  SOSIAS *and* XANTHIAS.

PHILOKLEON.
Which one's on trial?

BDELYKLEON.
This one.

PHILOKLEON.
He's for it, then.

BDELYKLEON.
The clerk will proceed to read the charge. Ahem.
Accused: Snatch, of The Kennel, Our House: here.
Accuser: Snitch, a mongrel, same address.
Charge: that the defendant Snatch did gourmandise
One entire Sicilian cheese, and furthermore
Denied a share to the accuser, Snitch.
Fixed penalty if guilty: wooden bone.

PHILOKLEON.
  He'll die like a dog, if it's up to me.

BDELYKLEON.
  The defendant, Snatch.

PHILOKLEON.
  He's obviously guilty.
900 Did you see that smarmy grin?
  Where's the other one, the accuser, Snitch?

SNITCH.
  Wow wow.

XANTHIAS.
  He says he's here.

PHILOKLEON.
  He's as bad as the other one.
  Good for nothing but barking, licking plates.

BDELYKLEON.
  Silence in court.

  (*to* SNITCH)

  Step forward. Address the court.

PHILOKLEON.
  Just a minute. I'll help myself to beans.

  XANTHIAS *puts* SNITCH *on the 'stand'*. SNITCH
  whines and snarls, and XANTHIAS *interprets*.

XANTHIAS.
  Your honour, the facts of this case
  Are exactly as stated: a crime against me,
  Against all cheesehounds everywhere. He snatched
  And ran. In a dank, dark den he chomped that
910 cheese.

PHILOKLEON.
  You can say that again. He belched just now.
  What a stink of cheese! The court was not amused.

XANTHIAS.
On being reminded, 'Share and share alike',
He refused. Ignored the golden rule:
At this address, we feed the watchdog first.

PHILOKLEON.
At this address, we've all been deprived of cheese.
This fanatic, this hothead – ow! These beans!

BDELYKLEON.
Look, Dad, you can't condemn him out of hand.
You've got to hear *his* side.

PHILOKLEON.
Who cares about his side?   920
The case is clear.

He gestures at SNITCH, *who is howling to* XANTHIAS.

Howls for itself.

XANTHIAS.
The quality of mercy...oh, forget it.
He's guilty as hell: a monophagist,
A snatcher-and-grabber, an asset-snaffler,
A rind-eradicator –

PHILOKLEON.
I'm drowning here.

XANTHIAS.
We demand exemplary punishment.
We invoke the principle 'One den, one thief'.
We remind the court of our own position here:
Snitch gets the cheese, or Snitch don't bark.   930

He helps SNITCH *down from the 'stand'.*

PHILOKLEON.
Ooh, ooh,
That swine, that criminal. If this is true...
That bastard. Don't you think so, cock? He blinked.
He does. Just a minute. Clerk! I need the potty.

BDELYKLEON.
  Fetch it yourself. I've witnesses to call.

  PHILOKLEON *takes down the potty and uses it.*

  In the case of People Versus Snatch,
  Be upstanding: pestle, grater, barbecue,
  Pot, saucer, dish – and anyone else
  With fish to fry, I mean a case to try.

  Enter KITCHEN UTENSILS.

940 Get on with it. Sit down. Put down that potty.

PHILOKLEON.
  I'll keep it, thanks. He may be needing it.

BDELYKLEON.
  You never stop. You never smile. You sink
  Your teeth in a juicy case, you won't let go.
  Step forward, prisoner. Address the court.

  SNATCH, *assisted by* SOSIAS, *takes the 'stand',
  but is too terrified to speak.*

  Come on.
  There's nothing to be afraid of.

PHILOKLEON.
  What can he say?
  He's guilty.

BDELYKLEON.
  No. It often happens. *He*
  Makes his usual speech, in his usual way,
  And they're frozen solid. Mesmerised.
  Prisoner, stand down. I'll make your speech myself.
950 Ahem. Unaccustomed as we are to making pleas
  For slandered dogs, we'll try. He's good at his job –
  Wolf-scaring.

PHILOKLEON.
  He's a liar and a thief.
  There aren't any wolves round here.

BDELYKLEON.
I told you he was good.

PHILOKLEON.
He's good at eating cheese.

BDELYKLEON.
What d'you expect?
He's a dog: he barks, he wags his tail.
We don't give degrees to dogs round here.

PHILOKLEON.
You should.
Degrees in cheese-eating. He'd be first in line.   960

BDELYKLEON.
At least let's hear the witnesses.
Step forward, grater. That's it. Now, speak up.
You keep an eye on all the cheese round here?
You count it all in, count it all out? Ah, right.
This afternoon – was any left ungrated? No?
You see, she says no.

PHILOKLEON.
She's lying in her teeth.

BDELYKLEON.
We ask the court's indulgence. Look at him:
He's a dog of good character, industrious:
Always scratching and sniffing for buried bones –
Always on active service, while his opponent...lolls.   970
Lolls and demands his share. Lolls and demands and
      bites.

PHILOKLEON.
Aaa-haah. What's wrong with me? I'm weakening.
I don't feel well. I think I'm going to...listen.

BDELYKLEON.
Don't fight it, father. Pity the prisoner,
Don't ruin him. Where are his poor wee pups?

Enter PUPPIES.

That's right. Surround him. Lick him, whimper.
Aaah.
Look up at him with big round eyes. Kiss him –

PHILOKLEON.
All right, all right. You've made your point.

BDELYKLEON.
'You've made your point'. Does that mean 'yes' or
980   'no'?
We've still no verdict, Dad. You have to say.

PHILOKLEON (*to the* PUPPIES).
Get off! Get down! It's these confounded beans.
I'd have managed, I wouldn't have lost control
If I hadn't been knotted inside with beans.

BEDELYKLEON.
Guilty or not guilty?

PHILOKLEON.
I'm making up my mind.

BDELYKLEON.
Be merciful. It's easy, look. You take
The voting-stone, like this...you stand up straight,
You walk to the *second* urn, you shut your eyes,
You drop it in. Not guilty.

PHILOKLEON.
I won't. I can't.
It's first urn or nothing. Guilty.

BDELYKLEON.
Come on then.
990   I'll hold your hand.

He steers PHILOKLEON *to the second urn.*

PHILOKLEON.
Is this the urn? The first urn?

BDELYKLEON.
Yes.

PHILOKLEON.
There. Done.

BDELYKLEON.
You said it. Done. It's time to count the votes.

PHILOKLEON.
What's the verdict?

BDELYKLEON.
Just a minute. Here we are.
In the case of People Versus Snatch: Not Guilty.
Dad, what's up? Good grief! Fetch water, quick!
Sit up, Dad. Speak to me.

PHILOKLEON.
'Not Guilty'?

BDELYKLEON.
Yes.

PHILOKLEON.
I'm finished.

BDELYKLEON.
Of course you aren't. It's quite all right.

PHILOKLEON.
How can I face myself? 'Not guilty'. Why?
What's to become of me now? Oh gods, I'm sorry,   1000
I didn't mean to, it wasn't like me at all.

BDELYKLEON.
Don't panic. You'll be all right. I'll see to you.
I'll look after you, I'll take you everywhere:
To dinners, to parties, to theatre shows.
No more politics. Your life will be such *fun!*
Come on. Let me take you in.

PHILOKLEON.
If you say so, son.

They go inside, accompanied by XANTHIAS,
SOSIAS, SNATCH, SNITCH, *the* PUPPIES *and*
the KITCHEN UTENSILS.

CHORUS.
    Off you go. Good luck.
1010 Now, ladies and gentlemen,"
    Countless millions:
    A little interlude,
    Words to the wise.
    You *are* wise, aren't you?

    Please excuse me for being so frank,
    But our author deserves far more praise.
    He's been putting on plays here for years,
    First of all incognito, a ghost,
    A ventriloquist making his points,
1020 Telling jokes, through another man's lips,
    Then quite openly, racing to fame
    In a comedy chariot all of his own.
    And despite all the prizes, the praise,
    He was modest and shy, never preened
    In the wrestling-schools, looking for trade,
    Never stooped to write slander or lies
    For a boyfriend, discarded, who said
    'If you lampoon my lover, I'll pay.'
    From the start, from his very first play,
    He left ordinary mortals alone,
    All his targets were monsters, and huge.
1030 He was braver than Herakles, swam
    Through the stink and the leather-lunged threats
    Of the Tannery, bearded the Beast
    In its lair, with its eyes popping fire
    And its tangle of toadies, its voice
    Like a camel's, its seal-stink, its balls –
    Oh those unwashed, incredible balls!
    He was fearless, he grappled and fought,
    He resisted all bribes, he was strong
    For you then and he's strong for you now.
    He took on all the vampires and spooks
    Who garrotted your Grandads and did for your
        Dads,
1040 Who came swooping and snooping at bedtime,

Till your hair stood on end and you jumped
Out of bed and ran screaming for help.
So our hero defended the state –
And then *last* year he tried something new,
Something dazzling and funny and fresh,
Something novel, original, true,
And you panned it. You let it drop dead.
He insists, hand on heart, it was good.
He was leading the comedy race,
Out of sight of all rivals – and crashed.   1050

If you value his wit
And his dazzling ideas,
If you think he's inspired
You should cherish him, store
What he says, wrap it up
Like a drawerful of fruit
Kept for winter, to fill
All the house, all your lives,
With the sweet smell of wit.

Once we were best,   1060
Carried all before us
In battle, bed and chorus,
Passed every test.
Now we're ancient, blast it,
White-haired and past it –
But better still, we say,
Respectable, elderly vigour
Than the pony-tails, swagger and snigger
Of the youth of today.   1070

Friends, you're sitting there and wondering
'Why wasp-costumes? Why the corsets?
Why the stings?' It's very simple.
Unaccustomed as I am, let me explain.
We're a native species, born here,
Bred here, armed and raised to fight here.
When the Persian hordes invaded,
Mad to burn us, sack us, singe us,   1080

We it was who swarmed against them,
Flew with spear and shield to face them,
Buzzed with fury, flew to fight them.
Clouds of arrows snuffed out daylight;
Persian arrows rained destruction.
All day long we fought; we thrashed them,
Praised the city's gods for helping,
Jabbed those Persians up the backside,
Jangled jaws and knackered kneecaps,
Made those bastards howl for mercy.
Now the whole world knows this saying:
1090 'Wasps from Athens take some swatting.'

We made you free.
It was our exertions
That walloped the Persians
By land and sea.
We'd no time for talking,
Rhetorical tightrope-walking:
Our work was real.
We won the empire, the tribute, the riches
1100 That these yuppie young crooks, sons of bitches,
Now snaffle and steal.

Look at us, you can't deny it:
Wasps by name and wasps by nature.
Always touchy, always testy,
On the warpath, up and at 'em,
Sting the bastards, show no mercy.
Into court we swarm each morning:
Treason, murder, libel, audit,
1110 Packed and bunched along the benches,
Packed like grubs in cells – but watching.
Always watching, always listening,
Stinging hard to earn a living.
Drones? Of course we've drones. You've seen 'em:
Stingless wonders, good for nothing,
Parasites, draft-dodgers, toadies.
We've got battle-scars and blisters,
We worked hard to earn our pension;

All *they* did was strut and swagger.
Now we recommend, in future, 1120
When these bastards claim their wages,
Check 'em. NO WASP STING, NO HANDOUT.

Music. Dance. Then PHILOKLEON *and* BDELYKLEON
come out, followed by SOSIAS, *who is carrying*
fancy clothes. PHILOKLEON *is refusing to strip.*

PHILOKLEON.
I won't. I'd rather die. This dear old friend!
He's stood between me and many a howling gale.
We're part of each other. I won't desert him now.

BDELYKLEON.
You're turning down a treat.

PHILOKLEON.
Of course I am.
I hate treats. Look what happened last time:
I stuffed myself with grilled sardines, and spent
A whole day's pay on cleaning bills.

BDELYKLEON.
Go on. You said I could look after you.
Let yourself be pampered. 1130

PHILOKLEON.
By doing what?

BDELYKLEON.
First, take off that coat and slip into...this.

PHILOKLEON.
Why do we do it? Why go to all that trouble?
Raising children – just so they can smother us!

BDELYKLEON.
Stop moaning. Put it on.

PHILOKLEON.
Gods almighty, what *is* it?

BDELYKLEON.
A Persian.

PHILOKLEON.
  I thought it felt like a carpet.

BDELYKLEON.
  You would. You've never been abroad.
  What do you know of fashion from abroad?

PHILOKLEON.
1140 I've seen Morychos, haven't I? He's brought
  Some very funny fashions from abroad.

BDELYKLEON.
  'Hand-woven in Ekbatana': look.

PHILOKLEON.
  It's still a rug.

BDELYKLEON.
  Don't be silly. This is a luxury garment.
  It took the wool of thirteen sheep.

PHILOKLEON.
  You mean, just so that I wear this,
  Thirteen sheep are running round stark naked?
  Is that what goes on in Ekbatana?

BDELYKLEON.
  Stand still and put it on.

PHILOKLEON.
1150 Talk about the Golden Fleece...

BDELYKLEON.
  Put it *on*.

PHILOKLEON.
  I won't. It's far too hot.
  Just put me in the oven, why don't you?

BDELYKLEON.
  I'll help you. There.

PHILOKLEON.
  You've forgotten the fork.

BDELYKLEON.
  What fork?

PHILOKLEON.
  To fish me out before I melt.

BDELYKLEON.
  Feet next. Get rid of those disgusting slippers
  And put on these Spartans.

PHILOKLEON.
  Spartans?
  Enemy footwear? I won't, I won't.   1160

BDELYKLEON.
  You will. Put this one on.

PHILOKLEON.
  Hob-nobbing with the enemy.
  What next?

BDELYKLEON.
  Next, this one.

PHILKLEON.
  Gods, not that as well!
  This toe's a patriot. He won't wear that.

BDELYKLEON.
  He'll wear it and like it. On!

PHILOKLEON.
  Ahaah! Ahaaaaaah!
  To mock a poor old man with shoes that...fit.

BDELYKLEON.
  Get on with it. Walk up and down. Think rich.
  Strut about a bit. Mince if you like. Like this.

PHILOKLEON.
  There. Hey, I could get used to this.   1170
  Just a minute. There. What do I look like now?

BDELYKLEON.
  A boil in a poultice.

PHILOKLEON.
The wiggle needs work?
There wasn't quite enough? More fanny-flaunt?

BDELYKLEON.
Ah. That reminds me. You're going to be meeting
Gentlemen: educated, respectable:
I need a sample of your table talk.

PHILOKLEON.
No problem.

BDELYKLEON.
I'm listening.

PHILOKLEON.
I'll start with the one about the farting squid.
Or there's Kardopion and his mummy: you know,
Where he –

BDELYKLEON.
No thanks. Keep off mythology.
I mean ordinary stuff, the sort of thing
1180   Ordinary people say.

PHILOKLEON.
Ah. Got you.
'Why did the mouse go looking for pussy...'?

BDELYKLEON.
You idiot! You filthy-minded freak –
As Theagenes said to the dung-cart driver –
You can't start talking of pussy *there*.

PHILOKLEON.
Well, what then?

BDELYKLEON.
Important things. Your fact-finding trip
With Androkles and Kleisthenes.

PHILOKLEON.
What trip?

I went on a day-trip once...to Paros,
And even then I had to row the boat.

BDELYKLEON.
Tell them about that wrestling match – the one
You're always on about. Age versus youth.
White-haired Ephoudion, and how he thumped   1190
Askondas. What a chest! What arms! What wind!

PHILOKLEON.
If he'd had wind, he couldn't have fought at all.

BDELYKLEON.
Gents like that sort of talk. I'm telling you.
Another thing: you're sitting there, at ease,
Drinking with strangers. They ask you
To tell them a little bit about yourself.
Your exploits. That kind of thing. What would you
    say?

PHILOKLEON.
I'd say, I'd say, my greatest exploit   1200
Was nicking those vineprops from old Ergasion.

BDELYKLEON.
You're doing this on purpose. You can't say that.
Can't you talk about hunting, fishing,
Some other sport?

PHILOKLEON.
There was that runner, Phaÿllos,
When I was just so high. *He* was quite a sport.
I had him in court. My first case. One to me.

BDELYKLEON.
That's enough of that. Come here. Lie back.
Let's see some party manners.

PHILOKLEON.
Lie back? How?

BDELYKLEON.
With grace.   1210

PHILOKLEON.
You mean like this?

BDELYKLEON.
Of course not.

PHILOKLEON.
How, then?

BDELYKLEON.
Start like this.
Legs straight. Then flow into position,
Like an athlete, like water from a jug.
Good. Now make flattering remarks about
The plates, the rugs, the pictures on the wall.
They bring us fingerbowls. We dip our hands.
They fetch the food. We eat. We dip. Give thanks.

PHILOKLEON.
We've finished already? I'm dreaming here.

BDELYKLEON.
A flute-girl plays. The after-dinner drinks
Arrive. Your fellow-guests are Aischines,
1220   Theoros, Phanos, Kleon, and beside you, there,
That foreign gentleman. They suggest a song.

PHILOKLEON.
I like this bit. I'm good at songs.

BDELYKLEON.
I start.
I'm Kleon. How about 'Good old Harmodios'?
'Good old Harmodios, so good, so true' –

PHILOKLEON.
'A skunk, a cheat, a bastard, just like you.'

BDELYKLEON.
You won't get far with that. He'll rant and roar,
He'll bluster and huff, and show you the door.

PHILOKLEON.
    I've seen his door. I've heard him roar. I'll sing,   1230
    'Sit down, you're rocking the boat.'

BDELYKLEON.
    What if Theoros lies at Kleon's feet
    And makes sheep's eyes at him, and sings,
    'Night and day...'?

PHILOKLEON.
    'Why don't you go away...'
    What? What? It rhymes.   1240

BDELYKLEON.
    Don't forget Aischines. A trained musician,
    An intellectual. He gives you 'Hallelujah!' –

PHILOKLEON.
    And *I* give *him* 'I see throughyah!'

BDELYKLEON.
    You've got it. By Zeus, I think you've got it,
    As someone nearly said. And it's time to go.
    We're lunching with Philoktemon today.   1250
    Hey, Sosias, bring sandwiches. It's best
    To go prepared: we'll be drinking half the night.

PHILOKLEON.
    Oh no we won't. I don't approve of drink.
    What does it lead to? Assault and battery,
    Breaking and entering, hangovers, fines...

BDELYKLEON.
    But not with *gentlemen*. They'll make it right,
    A word in someone's ear – or you can make
    It right yourself: throw in a joke or two
    From Aesop, a crack about the Cretans –
    Something you heard at the party. Make 'em laugh,   1260
    Hahaha, get away with anything you like.

PHILOKLEON.
    Aesop...the Cretans...hahaha...what a lot to learn.
    Still, if it means I get away with it...
    Come on then, son. What are we waiting for?

Exeunt, with SOSIAS.

CHORUS.
> I'm not a fool, I'm a man of parts,
> But I'm lost when it comes to the social arts.
> Remember Amynias, that snob,
> That pigtailed wonder? Used to hobnob
> With Leogoras? You get the point.
> Lost all his money in a game.
1270
> Nose out of joint.
> No contacts. Friends all dropped him. Shame!
> Then – and *this* is the point –
> He set up as a hermit in the empty interior.
> No more problems: no people, no need to feel
>   inferior.

> Automenes, congratulations!
> What sons you have, what incredible relations!
> A guitarist, loved by all who meet him;
> A brilliant actor, none to beat him –
> And then Ariphrades. You won't believe
> His filthy, disgusting trick –
1280
> Well, it makes my stomach heave.
> One minute he's fluting and tonguing and trilling
> For some chorus or other,
> Then, in some whorehouse or other,
> He's kissing and cooing and billing
> And giving his lady friends a lick.

> What was that? Lost my nerve? Gone yellow?
> Scared of Kleon? Afraid to bellow
> When he jumps on me,
> Dumps on me,
> Skins me alive? Don't help!
> Just watch to see what jokes I'll yelp.
1290
> Well, never mind. He's not so bright.
> He thinks I'm tamed. But watch me bite.

Enter SOSIAS, *fast.*[12]

SOSIAS.

    Ladies and gentlemen, any turtles in the house?
    Any tiled roofs? I envy you: dressed for it,
    Dressed to keep out the blows. I'm black and blue.

CHORUS.

    What's the matter, sonny?
    Someone smacked you and made you cry?

SOSIAS.

    It's that daft old man. He's drunk.
    There's none of them drunker,   1300
    And there was plenty of competition:
    Hippyllos, Antiphon, Lysistratos,
    Theophrastos, Lykon, all that gang.
    Not one of them could touch him. Lovely spread –
    And as soon as he'd lined his guts
    He went wild, like a flea in a dogs' home:
    Leaping about, farting, cackling,
    Banging me with his stick and shouting,
    'Howzat? Howzat for starters?' Lysistratos said
    (I think it was a joke), 'You're like
    A frog in a frenzy, a bee in a breadbin'.   1310
    'And what about you?' the old man said.
    'Lop-sided locust! Cutprice craphound!'
    No one knew what he meant, but it was very loud.
    They clapped and cheered – except Theophrastos.
    He was frowning. You know Theophrastos:
    'I don't quite follow...perhaps you could explain...'
    'Yah, you're jealous,' the old man said.
    'No one famous to flatter here, no stars to suck.'
    He went round the whole table, insulting them,
    Doing farmyard impressions, telling jokes –   1320
    I've never heard such language. Then he got up,
    Him and his skinful, and staggered off for home,
    Waving his stick, bashing everyone he met.
    Look out, he's here. I know those fairy footsteps.
    Who needs another beating? I'm going in.

He goes into the house. Enter PHILOKLEON, *with*
DARDANIS. *He has a blazing torch in one hand,*
and is using it to fend off the angry CITIZEN.

PHILOKLEON.
Back! Hahah! Back, you swine!
Still coming, are you?
1330   Come on then, try me.
You *want* to be shish kebab?

CITIZEN.
You'll pay for this tomorrow. We'll *all* be round.
Senile delinquent! Who d'you think you are?
Assault and battery. You'll pay for this, in court.

PHILOKLEON.
Wa-ha! Hee-hee! In court!
You're out of date.
I think that lawsuits stink.
Fuah! Ptu-ah!
You stuff your urns,
I'll stick to stuffing...these.
1340   Get out of it. Go on.
I'm not in. Get stuffed.

Exit CITIZEN.

Up this way, my lil apple-dumpling.
Pull yourself up by this. Grab hold.
What d'you mean, it's worn? There's years
Of use in that. Years of wear, no problem.
WasnI clever, sneaking you away from them?
Right under their noses. What was that game
You were playing? Suckitansee? Show me.
Go on, you owe me. What d'you mean, you can't?
What're you laughing at? This is no joke.
1350   Is this the way you behave to all the boys?
Look, be a good lil girl, good lil piggywig,
When my son dies, I'll buy your freedom,
Make you First Official BitoFluff.
I can't just now. I'm not 'of age'. I'm loaded

But I'm not allowed to touch it. That sonomine's
A stingy bastard. Eyes like a hedgehog.
Keeps me under observation. Doesn't want me spoiled.
And quite right too. I am his only Daddy.
Sh! He's here. Running. Safterus.   1360
Here. Take the torch. Stand there.
Don't move. I'll play a lil trick on him,
Pay him back for what he did to me. Before.

Enter BDELYKLEON.

BDELYKLEON.
   You daft old fart! You just can't give it up!
   You've done it this time. Really screwed yourself.
   Can't you go on a diet? What's wrong with you?

PHILOKLEON.
   You look peaky, son. Want a really saucy case?

BDELYKLEON.
   You'll be the saucy case. You can't go round
   Stealing dancing-girls at parties.

PHILOKLEON.
   Dancing-girl?
   What dancing-girl? You're babbling. You're past it. 1370

BDELYKLEON.
   This dancing-girl. This...Dardanis. Her, here.

PHILOKLEON.
   That's not a dancing-girl. It's a torch-holder.

BDELYKLEON.
   A torch-holder?

PHILOKLEON.
   A torch-holder. Latest model.

BDELYKLEON.
   So what's that black bit, there?

PHILOKLEON.
   That's where you stick it in.

BDELYKLEON.
  And these bumpy bits, up here?

PHILOKLEON.
  Bumpy bits?
  Oh, those. All torch-holders have bumpy bits.

BDELYKLEON.
  You're joking.

  (*to* DARDANIS)

  And you're coming with me.

PHILOKLEON.
  Hey! Hey!
  What're you doing?

BDELYKLEON.
  I'm taking her away.
1380 She's no good to you, anyway. You're past it, Dad.
  You've forgotten how it's done.

PHILOKLEON.
  I remember one thing.
  I was at the Olympic Games...state business...
  And I saw Ephoudion fight Askondas. He was old,
  But he was good. He feinted with his left, like this,
  Then landed a right, smack in the eye, like this.

  He wallops BDELYKLEON. DARDANIS *runs for it.*

  And the moral is, you're never too young to learn.

BDELYKLEON.
  I wish I'd never started this.

  Enter BREAD-WOMAN, *with* WITNESS.

BREAD-WOMAN.
  Come on. Over here. This is the man.
  Came out of nowhere, bashed me with his torch,
1390 Knocked over my tray, scattered my buns,
  Ten obols worth, and scarpered.

BDELYKLEON.
  You drunken old –
  Fines, lawsuits, you can't go anywhere.

PHILOKLEON.
  Don't panic. These things can be sorted out.
  An Aesop story, a joke or two, hahaha –
  You told me so yourself. I'll handle her.

BREAD-WOMAN.
  Well? What are you going to do about it?
  My name is Myrtle. I'm a citizen,
  I know my rights. You ruined all my stock.

PHILOKLEON.
  If you don't mind, madam. Let me speak.
  I've a tale to tell. You'll like it.

BREAD-WOMAN.
  I bet you have. I bet I won't.   1400

PHILOKLEON.
  It seems that Aesop was walking home one night.
  Been out to dinner. Suddenly, set upon.
  Some rat-arsed bitch...well gone, you know what I mean.
  Well, *he* said, *he* said, 'Down! Good doggy! Down!
  Instead of bapping and snarking...snapping and
      barking...
  Why don't you bake some more, you stupid bitch?'

BREAD-WOMAN.
  That does it! Insult me now? I don't know who
  You are, but I'll see you in court tomorrow.
  Bun-molester! Where's that witness? Oi!

PHILOKLEON.
  Look, madam, in the immortal words of Lasos,
  When he found he was up against Simonides   1410
  For the poetry prize, 'Stuff this for a lark.
  I'm going home.'

BREAD-WOMAN.
  Oh no you're not.

PHILOKLEON (*grabbing the* WITNESS).
  And as for *you*... Good God, it's Chairephon!
  What are you playing at? This isn't Euripides:
  You can't wear a dress like that, and do that here!

BDELYKLEON.
　Here's someone else. He's looking very cross.
　He's got a witness too.

Enter CITIZEN *and his* WITNESS.

CITIZEN.
　Ah, there you are.
　I warned you. Daft old fool. I summons you
　For assault and battery.

BDELYKLEON.
　Don't summons him.
　Can't we settle out of court? Name your figure.
1420　I'll be very grateful.

PHILOKLEON.
　Just a minute, son.
　I'll deal with this. I bashed him, after all.
　Psst. Can't we shettle out of court? Go on.
　You name your figure. Lesh be friends.

CITIZEN.
　You name yours.
　I haven't got time to waste in court.

PHILOKLEON.
　Reminds me of the story about that Cretan.
　Fell out of his chariot and bashed his bonce.
　Well, he would. He just couldn't handle horshes.
1430　His friend said, 'Frightfully hard cheese, old fruit,
　But a man's got to do what a mansh gottadoo.'
　And what *you've* gottadoo is FALL DOWN A DRAIN.

BDELYKLEON.
　He's doing it again. He'll never change.

CITIZEN (*to the* WITNESS).
　You heard him. Don't just stand there. Write it down.

PHILOKLEON.
　Hang on, there's more. I think you ought to know
　What the Cretan said when his missus broke a jug.
1440　'Don't try to mend it, idiot. HAMMER IT!'

He hammers the CITIZEN.

CITIZEN.
That does it. We'll see how loud you are – in court.

Exeunt CITIZEN, BREAD-WOMAN *and* WITNESSES.

BDELYKLEON.
Now look what you've done. Come here. I said come here.

PHILOKLEON.
Whatsh going on?

BDELYKLEON.
I'm taking you inside,
Before anyone else arrives with witnesses.

PHILOKLEON.
That reminds me: Aesop said –

BDELYKLEON.
Stuff this for a lark.
We're going in.

PHILOKLEON.
No no. 'The grapes are sour' –
Remember?

BDELYKLEON.
I'll sour your grapes. Get IN!

He takes him inside.

CHORUS.
That dear old man's in clover.   1450
His troubles are over.
He's comfortable at last.
He's learning fast.
Not an easy task, but he did it,
To do as they ask, but he did it,
To rearrange,   1460
To change – and he did it.

You've got to praise his son, too,
For his 'Do as you would be done to',
His sense and sobriety,

His filial piety.
Who else would you find, apart from him,   1470
So patient and kind, apart from him,
So tirelessly bent
On making his Dad a gent?

XANTHIAS *comes out of the house.*

XANTHIAS.
Ye gods, will he never stop?
Will there always be more, and more, and more?
One sip of a drink, one whiff of a flute,
And he's off. 'I'll dance,' he says,
'I'll dance the night away.
But none of your modern rubbish,
1480 Out of date before it even hits the street:
Let's have some Thespis: some of the good old tunes.'

PHILOKLEON *comes out.*

PHILOKLEON.
Gotta dance...

XANTHIAS.
Oh god, here we go.

PHILOKLEON.
I'm singin' in the rain...

XANTHIAS.
Like a pig in pain.

PHILOKLEON.
You've got something there.
My ribs are revolting,
My kisses are dribbly,
My hooter's all hazy.

XANTHIAS.
You're crazy.

PHILOKLEON.
1490 *There's a song to be sung...*

XANTHIAS.
They're coming for you.

PHILOKLEON.
There's a fling to be flung...

XANTHIAS.
You'll do yourself a mischief.

PHILOKLEON.
I'm too well put together, mate.
The hip-bone's connected to the neck-bone...

XANTHIAS.
That figures. Calm down.

PHILOKLEON.
I'll take them all on. All of you.

(to the audience)

Any fancy dancers out there?
Fancy yourself as dancers? Eh? Eh? Eh?

Enter FIRST DANCER[13].

XANTHIAS.
Here's one.

PHILOKLEON.
Where? Silly bugger. Who?

XANTHIAS.
That son of Karkinos. The middle one.   1500

PHILOKLEON.
Well, he can stuff himself before he starts.
I'll fancy-footwork him. The old one-two...
He can't keep time.

Enter SECOND DANCER.

XANTHIAS.
Don't get excited. Here's another.
His brother.

PHILOKLEON.
I'll eat them both for lunch.

Enter THIRD DANCER.

XANTHIAS.
You'll get indigestion. There's him as well.

PHILOKLEON.
What's *he* doing? What *does* he think he is?

XANTHIAS.
1510   He's the last. The baby of the family.

PHILOKLEON.
All here, then, are we? Karkinos' little crabbiewabs?
Serious business, is it? A major contest?
Clear the floor, then. And lay the table –
It's mincemeat time!

Music. Dancing.

CHORUS.
Stand back. Go over there. Get in!
They need more room. They're going to spin.
Sea children, dance.
Hand in hand
1520   Up and down the sand
Pirouette and prance.

Do twiddly bits,
Wave your arms,
Show your charms,
Do the kick, the splits.

Jump! Slap your belly, flick your wrist.
1530   Jump! Kick your legs out, twirl and twist.

Enter KARKINOS, *the master dancer.*

Here's Crabmaster Karkinos. Watch this now!
He'll show you a thing or two. He'll show you how.
Ladies and gentlemen, what more can I say?
We're going to join in, so there's no more play.

General dance, to end the play.

CLOUDS

Characters

STREPSIADES
PHEIDIPPIDES
SLAVE
STUDENT
SOKRATES
RIGHT
WRONG
PASIAS
PASIAS' FRIEND
AMYNIAS

silent parts:

STREPSIADES' SLAVES
STUDENTS

CHORUS OF CLOUDS

Two housefronts. By STREPSIADES' door, on a stand,
is a small statue of the god of the household: Hermes
the Trickster. By the entrance of the Thinkery, the
stand carries a large earthenware pot (called in Greek
Dinos, which means both 'pot' and 'whirlwind'). It is
the middle of the night. STREPSIADES and PHEIDIPPIDES
are asleep, on single beds. STREPSIADES tosses and
turns, and finally sits up.

STREPSIADES.

    Eeoo eeoo! Zeus almighty, what a night!
    It's going on forever. Will daylight never come?
    I heard the cock crow hours ago. Where are
    The slaves? Still snoring? Times have changed.
    Something else to blame on this confounded war:
    A man can't thrash his own slaves any more,
    In case they run off and fight. And look at *him* –
    My son and heir. Nothing's going to get *him* up.
    He's all right, parcelled in five blankets,   10
    Farting away. Perhaps I should try it myself.
    Wrap up tight...lie down...start snoring...

    He tries.

    Ah, it's no good. I'm being bitten to death
    By debts and bills and stable fees.
    And it's all his fault – him and his long hair
    And his chariot teams and racing curricles.
    Horses! He even dreams of horses.
    It's me that suffers: I'm worn to a thread
    By the end of the month, when the bills come in.
    Slave! Light the lamp, and bring
    My account book. I'll do the sums this minute:
    See who I owe, and what the totals are.   20

    A SLAVE brings a lamp and a sheaf of bills.

    Now then, where are we? 'To Pasias,
    Twelve hundred drachs.' What was that for?
    Oh, I remember. When I bought that thoroughbred.
    I ought to have saddled myself instead.

PHEIDIPPIDES (*in his sleep*).
    Philon, you're cheating. Keep to your own lane.

STREPSIADES.
There you are. It's eating me alive. Horses!
Night and day he thinks of nothing but horses.

PHEIDIPPIDES (*in his sleep*).
How many bends in the four-in-hand?

STREPSIADES.
You're driving your father round the bend.
30   Now, what's the next bill, after Pasias?
'To Ameinias, for chariot and wheels, three
    hundred –'

PHEIDIPPIDES (*in his sleep*).
Unbridle the grey, and rub him down.

STREPSIADES.
And what about me? You're rubbing me *out*
With debts and lawsuits and summonses.
Every time I go to court, I lose.

PHEIDIPPIDES (*half awake*).
What's the matter, Dad? Why can't you lie still?

STREPSIADES.
Lie still? This mattress is alive – with bills!

PHEIDIPPIDES.
Be quiet, for heaven's sake. I'm trying to sleep.

STREPSIADES.
Oh, sleep! Go on. All this will be yours one day:
40   All this worry, all these debts. Sleep while you can.
Oooooh, damn the man who introduced us,
Your mother and me! Why did I marry her?
There I was, blissfully happy on my own farm,
Shabby and shaggy and take-life-as-it-comes,
A paradise of bees and olives and sheep –
And then I married your mother. Me, a yokel,
And the niece of Megakles son of Megakles
(A big name in the city) – a real lady,
Stuck-up and how-de-do and lah-di-dah.
Think of the wedding! Think of us going to bed –

Me smelling of wine and fig-boards and greasy wool, 50
And her smothered in saffrons and silks
And fancy kisses, nothing but the best.
Mind you, I'll say this for her: she worked hard.
In and out, day and night. The loom! I told her,
'You're wearing it thin. It won't stand the strain.'

SLAVE.

Sir, the lamp's run dry. There's no more oil.

STREPSIADES.

Why did you choose that one? You know
It's a drunkard. Come here: you'll be sorry.

SLAVE.

What have I done?

STREPSIADES.

You put in a too thick wick, that's what.
The problem began when *he* was born. 60
That really started us arguing, me
And my lady wife. It was about his name.
She wanted something with *Hippos* in,
Hippos for horse, to show he was upper class:
Xanthippos or Charippos or Kallippides.
I wanted to call him Pheidonides
After his grandad. We settled it at last:
We mixed the two and called him Pheidippides.
Well, she was always picking him up
And cuddling him and saying, 'Dere's a good boy!
When 'oo grows up, 'oo's going to have
A horsy of his own to drive in processions
In a purple cloak, just like Uncle Megakles.' 70
I used to say, 'Drive a herd of goats, more like,
In a shepherd's smock, just like his Dad.'
Well, of course, he didn't listen to *me:*
As soon as he was old enough, him
And his horses, he galloped away with all my cash.
I've been up all night, trying to work it out.
There's only one way, one tiny chink of light.
If I can just persuade him, I'll be saved.

The first thing to do is to wake him up.
Now, what's the *nicest* way to wake someone up?
Pheidippides...Pheidippides... Oo-oo, Pheidippi-
dippides...

PHEIDIPPIDES.
80   What *is* it, Dad?

STREPSIADES.
Give me a kiss, and hold my hand.

PHEIDIPPIDES.
What? Oh, there.

STREPSIADES.
Tell me: do you really love me?

PHEIDIPPIDES.
Yes – by Poseidon the Horselord.

STREPSIADES.
Not him! Anyone else but him!
It's all his fault: it's him that ruined me.
Now, if you love me, truly, with all your heart,
Will you do me a favour?

PHEIDIPPIDES.
Depends what it is.

STREPSIADES.
Will you change your whole way of life,
And do as I ask?

PHEIDIPPIDES.
What *do* you ask?

STREPSIADES.
First, promise.

PHEIDIPPIDES.
90   Oh...cross my heart.

STREPSIADES.
Good. Now, look over that way.
D'you see that door, that funny little house?

PHEIDIPPIDES.
   Yes. What of it? What *is* it, Dad?

STREPSIADES.
   That's the Thinkery, where the professors live.
   They're so clever, they can show you the sky
   And convince you it's really a chimney
   All round you and you're lumps of coal inside.
   Pay them enough, and they'll teach you ways
   To win any case in court, guilty or innocent.

PHEIDIPPIDES.
   Who are they?

STREPSIADES.
   I don't know *what* they call themselves: 100
   Gentlemen-scholars, scientists of the mind...

PHEIDIPPIDES.
   Frauds and cheats! I know who you mean.
   Bare feet, pale faces – we know all about *them!*
   You're talking about Chairephon, and that Sokrates.

STREPSIADES.
   Shut up! You don't know what you're saying.
   It's perfectly simple: if you don't want us all to starve,
   Forget your horses and learn with them.

PHEIDIPPIDES.
   Never! Not if you gave me all
   The racing-stables in the world.

STREPSIADES.
   Oh please...there's a good boy...please,   110
   For Daddy's sake...go and learn from them.

PHEIDIPPIDES.
   Learn what?

STREPSIADES.
   They're supposed to have two kinds of argument,
   Ones you can use anywhere: Right and Wrong.
   I want you to learn Wrong, the second one,

    The one that wins in court. That way,
    I won't have to pay a penny of the debts
    I owe because of you.

PHEIDIPPIDES.
    I'm not going in there. Me, a student?
120   One of *those*? What would I tell my friends?

STREPSIADES.
    Out, then! Out of my house! You, and all
    Your stable! Get stuffed, the lot of you!

PHEIDIPPIDES.
    I'll go and see Uncle Megakles.
    He'll keep me in horses. To hell with you!

    Exit.

STREPSIADES.
    Ha! I'm not finished yet. Two can play that game.
    I'll say a little prayer, and join the Thinkery
      myself.
    Me, a student? An old man, slow,
    With a memory like mine? How will I learn
130   Hair-splitting and needling and argument?
    Well, I've got to. No point in hanging around.
    I'll go over there, and knock.

    He knocks on the door of the Thinkery.

    Anyone at home?

    A STUDENT opens the door.

STUDENT.
    For heaven's sake, who's that hammering on the
      door?

STREPSIADES.
    Er...Strepsiades son of Pheidon, from Kikynna.

STUDENT.
    A yokel. I might have guessed, from the way
    You nearly kicked the door down. My mind

Was pregnant with thought – and now it's
miscarried[14].

STREPSIADES.
I'm sorry. It's different in the country.
How do you mean, miscarried? *What* miscarried?

STUDENT.
Ah, that's private, to anyone but students.   140

STREPSIADES.
Well, you can tell *me*. I've come to sign on.

STUDENT.
Oh. All right. Here's a brilliant thought –
And mind you keep it to yourself.
Just a minute ago, Sokrates asked Charephon
How many of its own feet a flea could jump.
It had just bitten Chairephon's eyebrow, you see,
And then hopped over to Sokrates' head.

STREPSIADES.
How did he measure it?

STUDENT.
It was very clever. He caught the flea,
And dipped its feet in some melted wax...   150
Gave it a pair of slippers. When they cooled,
He took them off and measured them.

STREPSIADES.
Almighty Zeus, what a brilliant brain!

STUDENT.
That's nothing, compared to what he said
The other day.

STREPSIADES.
Tell me. What did he say?

STUDENT.
Chairephon asked him his opinion on gnats:
Do they buzz from the front end, or the back?

STREPSIADES.
And what was his opinion concerning gnats?

STUDENT.
160   He explained that the guts of a gnat
Are hollow, a sort of narrow tube. The air
Is sucked in at the front, and forced
Under pressure down and out the back.
It's the narrowness of the hole that makes the
    noise.

STREPSIADES.
It's a kind of trumpet then, a gnat's behind?
What a brilliant man he must be,
What an expert on agnatomy!
Compared to that, it's child's play to win in court.

STUDENT.
Last night...last night he lost a whole thought
Because of a lizard.

STREPSIADES.
170   Pardon? I don't follow.

STUDENT.
He was investigating the Moon, studying
Its path through the heavens. Well,
To do that, he had to keep looking up.
In the dark. The lizard was on the roof.
Suddenly...*bim, bam!*...Sokrates gets
An eyeful of droppings...end of thought.

STREPSIADES.
A lizard dropping on Sokrates! I like that.

STUDENT.
And then, yesterday, we'd nothing for dinner.

STREPSIADES.
You don't say! How did he conjure up some food?

STUDENT.
Easy. You take two sprinkles of dust, or ash,

A spit and a bent pair of compasses.
You...*loaf* around...and there you are.

STREPSIADES.
Fantastic! Quick, open the Thinkery,   180
Let me in and show me Sokrates.
I can't wait, I've got to go inside
And study. Open the door! Open the door!

*The doors are opened[15], and the inside of the
Thinkery is revealed. There are two groups of
STUDENTS. The first stand motionless, staring at
the ground. The second are bent double, with
their bottoms in the air.*

Herakles! What on Earth are those?

STUDENT.
What do they look like?

STREPSIADES.
Prisoners from Pylos?
Why are they staring at the ground like that?

STUDENT.
To work out what's underneath, of course.

STREPSIADES.
I see: looking for beetroot. It's all right,
I'll show you some fat and juicy ones.   190
What are *they* doing, bent over like that?

STUDENT.
Geology: they're examining the Underworld.

STREPSIADES.
Why are their bottoms stuck in the air?

STUDENT.
They're doing a course of their own:
Fundamental ass-tronomy.

(to the STUDENTS)

All right, go inside now, out of the fresh air.
D'you want the Prof to catch you out here?

STREPSIADES.
No, no. Let them stay.
I've something to show them – all my own.

STUDENT.
Impossible. It's forbidden. Too much fresh air.

He shoos the STUDENTS *away.* STREPSIADES
wanders about looking at different charts and gadgets.

STREPSIADES.
200   For heaven's sake, what's that for?

STUDENT.
Astronomy.

STREPSIADES.
And this?

STUDENT.
Geometry.

STREPSIADES.
What about this?

STUDENT.
Measuring land.

STREPSIADES.
Ah yes – for allotments.

STUDENT.
No, no: all the land on Earth.

STREPSIADES.
Isn't that clever?
An allotment of all the land on Earth.

STUDENT.
This is a map of the world. Look:
Here's Athens.

STREPSIADES.
  Don't be daft! How can that be Athens?
  Where are the lawcourts and the jurymen?

STUDENT.
  I tell you it's Athens: Athens and neighbourhood.

STREPSIADES.
  I still don't believe you. Where's my village,   210
    Kikynna?

STUDENT.
  It's on there somewhere. That's Euboia there,
  That bit lying down the coast.

STREPSIADES.
  I believe that. They're the biggest liars
  In the world. But where's Sparta?

STUDENT.
  Here.

STREPSIADES.
  It's too close! Don't just stand there,
  Move it further away!

STUDENT.
  Can't be done.

STREPSIADES.
  You'll be sorry, then. Good lord.
  Who's that up there, on that pulley affair?

  He points overhead, where SOKRATES *has been swung
  into view on the theatre crane.*

STUDENT.
  That's the Prof.

STREPSIADES.
  What Prof?

STUDENT.
  Sokrates.

STREPSIADES.
Ah, Sokrates.
Go on then, call him down. Give him a shout.

STUDENT.
220   Give him a shout yourself. I'm busy.

Exit.

STREPSIADES.
O Sok-rates...
So-o-okrates...Sok-kee...

SOKRATES.
What is it...mortal?

STREPSIADES.
First tell me what you're doing.

SOKRATES.
I ride the air and ponder on the Sun.

STREPSIADES.
Oh, sneering at the gods. I suppose it's easier
From a flying rug than down here on the ground.

SOKRATES.
Exactly. My investigation, my plane of thought.
Is elevated, airy, almost out of sight.
I find it best to hoist my mind up here,
230   And think lofty thoughts in a lofty atmosphere.
If I'd stayed on the ground looking up,
I'd have got nowhere. It's all to do
With attraction. The Earth, d'you see, attracts
The pure essence of the mind. It's just the same
With watercress.

STREPSIADES.
Of course.
The essence of the mind is watercress.
O Sokrates, Sokkee, hurry and come down.
Come down and teach me what I came to learn.

SOKRATES *is lowered slowly to the ground.*

SOKRATES.
  Now then. You came to learn...?

STREPSIADES.
  Yes. To learn to argue.
  I'm being eaten alive by creditors.   240
  They're coming at me from all sides,
  Hounding me, threatening to get the bailiffs in.

SOKRATES.
  Bailiffs, eh? But how could you fall into debt
  Without noticing?

STREPSIADES.
  It was a horse-fever...
  Galloping consumption, I think it's called.
  I want to learn your second argument,
  The one that means you don't have to pay.
  Charge any fee you like, I will pay *you*.
  I promise, I swear it by the gods.

SOKRATES.
  Gods? What gods? We don't deal in gods in here.

STREPSIADES.
  Don't deal in gods? Whatever do you use
  For oaths? Iron bars, like the Byzantines?

SOKRATES.
  You really want to know? You want the truth
  About the gods, and all that sort of thing?   250

STREPSIADES.
  By god, yes! I mean, if there *is* a god.

SOKRATES.
  You'd like to hold a conversation, face to face
  With *our* gods, the Clouds?

STREPSIADES.
  Ooh, yes.

SOKRATES.
  Sit down, then, on that sacred garden-seat.

STREPSIADES.
All right. There.

SOKRATES.
Put on this wreath.

STREPSIADES.
Wreath? *Wreath?*
What are you going to do? Sacrifice me –
Like Athamas, in that play by Sophocles?

SOKRATES.
No, no. We do this to all our applicants.

STREPSIADES.
What do I get out of it?

SOKRATES (*sprinkling him with flour*).
What you asked for: we turn you into
260   A neat, sharp, slippery master-arguer,
The flower of orators. Keep *still!*

STREPSIADES.
The flour of orators? I see what you mean.

SOKRATES.
Hush now, old man, and hear our prayer.
O lord! O god! O boundless Space,
Ether that glows around the Earth!
O Clouds, goddesses of lightning and thunder,
Gather above us, in majesty and power,
High-soaring, hovering above our heads.

STREPSIADES.
Just a minute. Let me get under cover first.
What a fool! I knew I should have brought a hat.

SOKRATES.
Majestic Clouds, come down, appear.
From your haunts on Olympos' peaks
270   Flurried with snow,
From grave sarabands of water-nymphs
In the gardens of the sea,

From the Egyptian Nile, where water-jugs
Of gold are filled,
From Lake Maiotis and the snowy tip
Of Mimas, answer our prayer,
Accept our offering and come to us.

CHORUS (*offstage*).
Rise up and come, immortal Clouds.
In a sparkle of raindrops, rise
From the swollen sea; rise up
To the peaks of the high hills
Shaggy with trees; look down   280
On the distant view,
Meadows and water-gardens,
Rippling streams,
The booming sea.
The Sun's unblinking eye
Sparkles with light:
Shake free
A mantle of rain all over the Earth.
Immortal Clouds, rise up and come.   290

SOKRATES.
Great goddesses, Holy Ones,
You've heard and answered.

(*to* STREPSIADES)

Did you hear the singing?
The sacred thunder growling?

STREPSIADES.
I heard it all right. Holy Clouds! I heard it.
Didn't you hear me fart with fright? It's turned me
To jelly. It's no use; I've got to...
Quick! Show me the way to the...

SOKRATES.
Sit *still!* Keep *quiet!* Where d'you think you are?
This isn't a farce. They're humming and swarming
    again.

CHORUS (*offstage*).
Rain-bearing maidens, rise up and come
300   To the lovely land of Pallas,
To Athens, home of the brave –
Where holy processions make their way
To secret Eleusis to share
The Mysteries; where temples
Stand high, stand rich,
Blessed with banquets
And festivals
310   Through all the year;
And in spring,
For Dionysos,
A festival of singing, dancing
And the whistle and throb of flutes.

STREPSIADES.
Oh heavens, Sokrates, tell me,
Who are those ladies who sang just now?
Heroes' wives, out of the old stories?

SOKRATES.
No; the Clouds, the Heavenly Ones
Who look after layabouts.
320   They give us brains, judgment, wit,
Big talk, garbling, quibbling, hectoring –

STREPSIADES
I know what you mean. When I heard them singing
I got goosepimples all over. All I want to do now
Is split hairs, fight over shadows,
Blow soap bubbles of argument and burst them
    with a word.
O Sokrates, where are the ladies? Let me see
    them.

SOKRATES.
Over there, floating down beside Mount Parnes.

STREPSIADES.
Where? Show me.

SOKRATES.
Like a thick, soft blanket, over all
The hills and woods.

STREPSIADES.
I can't see them. What's wrong with me?

SOKRATES.
Look, there: just by the door.

STREPSIADES.
Oh, yes.

SOKRATES.
You'd have to be blind to miss them now.

STREPSIADES.
I see them. They're wonderful.
They're everywhere.

SOKRATES.
Of course they are.
They're goddesses. Didn't you know?

STREPSIADES.
I always thought they were mist, and dew, and fog.   330

SOKRATES.
No, no. They look after all of us: philosophers,
Prophets, miracle-doctors, intellectuals,
Quacks and poets. Especially poets. Polish off
A verse or two, walk with your head in the clouds,
Write them a sonnet – you need never work again.

STREPSIADES.
Ah, that explains it. I read a poem once.
Cloud-puffball, torn tufts, tossed pillows
flaunt forth, then chevy on an air-
borne thoroughfare...
Or was it *I wandered lonely as a...?*
And for that, they gorge themselves for life
On fillets of sole, and pheasant, and thrush?

SOKRATES.
What d'you think?

STREPSIADES.
340 But look, if these are clouds, real clouds,
Why do they look like women? Other clouds don't.

SOKRATES.
What do you mean?

STREPSIADES.
Well, those up there.
They look like...oh, I don't know.
Fluffed up fleeces, not women at all.
In any case, yours have got noses.

SOKRATES.
I see what you mean. Tell me...

STREPSIADES.
What?

SOKRATES.
Have you ever looked up and seen a cloud
Shaped like a centaur? A leopard? A wolf? A bull?

STREPSIADES.
Often. What of it?

SOKRATES.
Well there you are. They look like what they like.
I mean, suppose they see a dirty, hairy beast –
You know, like Xenophantes? They turn
    themselves
350 Into hairy monsters and laugh at him.

STREPSIADES.
What about a scrounger...like Simon?

SOKRATES.
Easy: for him they turn into hungry wolves.

STREPSIADES.
Yes – and if they see a coward,
Running away, they turn into deer.

SOKRATES.

They must have seen that what's-it today...you know,
Kleonymos. That's why they look so...so *butch*.

Music. The CHORUS *begins to move in.*

STREPSIADES.

Goddesses, welcome. O Ladies, queens of the Sky,
If you sing all day, please sing for me.

CHORUS

Greetings, old man, old sniffer-out of thought.
And you, Sokrates high priest of windy words,
What do you want of us? We honour you
And no one else, no other professor of air   360
But Prodikos (a man of bulging brain).
You swagger in the streets; we honour you
For beady eyes and arrogance and dirty feet.

SOKRATES.

Oh listen to that! It's beautiful. It's just
Like being in church. I'm tingling from head to foot.

STREPSIADES.

What? Even almighty Zeus?

SOKRATES.

Don't talk nonsense. He doesn't exist.

STREPSIADES.

Zeus doesn't exist? All right, then,
Who makes it rain?

SOKRATES.

They do. Have you ever seen it rain
When there isn't a cloud in the sky?   370
If it's Zeus, let him rain when it's sunny.

STREPSIADES.

Apollo, that's clever. I always thought rain
Was almighty Zeus peeing through a sieve.
What about thunder, though? Who sends us that?
It makes me shiver just to think of it.

SOKRATES.
They do. By linear attraction.

STREPSIADES.
Oh. Eh?

SOKRATES.
When they're full of water, and blown along.
Just think of it: great soggy bags of rain
Bundling along, crashing and bumping by force –

STREPSIADES.
Force, of course. Who forces them? That must be
Zeus.

SOKRATES.
No, no. It's Dinos.

STREPSIADES.
Pardon?

SOKRATES.
Dinos. The Great Wind.

STREPSIADES.
380 I'm sorry. I didn't know. Zeus has gone,
And Dinos rules. But you still haven't explained
What causes the thunder, what makes the noise.

SOKRATES.
Of course I have. I said the Clouds were full
Of water, didn't I, jostling and crowding along?
That's what makes the rumbling.

STREPSIADES.
Prove it.

SOKRATES.
All right. Think about it yourself. You know
That goulash you always buy at festivals?
You stuff yourself with that, and right away
It sloshes and gurgles round your guts inside...

STREPSIADES.
Apollo, yes! My belly starts to churn,
And boils and rumbles. Quietly at first...
Pa-pax, pa-pax...then a bit louder...
Pa-pa-PAX!...and it always ends
With a real eruption...PA-PA-PA-PAX! PA-PA-PAX! 390
Thunder, just like them.

SOKRATES.
You see? If your little fart makes all that noise,
Just think of the thunder the sky can make.

STREPSIADES.
I suppose you could call it a thunder-crap.
But what about lightning, flashing from the sky?
Some get sizzled up, others are left alive.
That must be Zeus, burning up liars and cheats.

SOKRATES.
You idiot! You stone-age freak! If Zeus
Burns up liars and cheats, what about him...

He points into the audience.

And *him*...and *him*? Has he forgotten *them*? 400
And lightning hits temples – *his* temples, too! –
And hills and oaks. Why? What's an oak tree done?

STREPSIADES.
I don't know. You put it very well. But look,
What *is* lightning, if it doesn't come from Zeus?

STREPSIADES.
When a dry wind is sucked up off the Earth,
It fills up a cloud like a toy balloon.
The pressure rises, in the narrow space,
And then, *pfff!* It explodes in a hiss of wind.

STREPSIADES.
I know exactly what you mean.
I was frying a sausage the other day,
At the feast for my relations. I forgot
To prick the skin. It began to swell and bulge, 410

And then *pow! Splat!* It exploded in my eye.
You should have seen the mess.

CHORUS.
Ah! How eager he is to learn our mysteries.
Old man, you'll be the envy of the whole of Greece
(Including Athens), if you study hard with us.
You'll need a good memory, a capacious brain,
The strength of an athlete, untiring day and night.
Can you stand the cold? Can you do without your
    lunch?
Can you give up wine, and exercise, and sex?
Have you got what it takes to join our school,
To quibble and garble and niggle and twist?

STREPSIADES.
420   Is that all it takes? Sleepless nights, hard work,
A will of iron, the constitution of an ox
And the guts of an ostrich? Take me: here I am.

SOKRATES.
You have to give up the other gods, and believe
In ours: Chaos and Clouds and Argument.

STREPSIADES.
If I meet the others in the street, I'll cut them
    dead.
They'll get no more sacrifices out of me.

CHORUS.
All right, you're accepted. What can we do for you?
Worship us, learn argument – you can't go wrong.

STREPSIADES.
Ladies, I ask only one thing: to be
430   The best talker in Greece by a hundred miles.

CHORUS.
Your wish is granted. From now on, no one else
Has any say in politics. Your word is law.

STREPSIADES.
> No, no, no. I'm not interested in politics.
> It's *little* talk I want: to wriggle out of debt.

CHORUS.
> Your wish is our command. Such self-restraint!
> Now, join the school. Our agents will see to you.

STREPSIADES.
> I'm in your hands. What else can I do,
> When I'm trampled by horses and sons and wives?
> Take me; I'm yours: 440
> Beat me, starve me, boil me,
> Freeze me, skin me alive –
> But get me out of debt.
> I'll make a name for myself:
> Twister, wriggler, squealer, snake,
> Windbag, rat,
> Liar, conman, twister, fake,
> Vampire bat,
> Louse, mouse, missing link,
> Punk, skunk, toady, fink,
> Vermin, bum,
> Dungheap, scum,
> Even greasebag, dirty-face –   450
> Sticks and stones!
> I don't care what they do to me
> Once I've cheated them:
> Not if they chop me into sausagemeat
> And serve me up to the boys for tea.

CHORUS.
> Very impressive. He *has* got what it takes.
> Now then, old man, have you any idea
> Of the benefits you'll get if you learn
> From us? The fame reaching to the sky?   460

STREPSIADES.
> Give me an example.

CHORUS.
> For the rest of your life, you'll live
> The most envied man on Earth.

STREPSIADES.
> How d'you mean?

CHORUS.
> They'll be queuing up outside your door,
470 Wanting to meet you, to meet, and talk,
> And ask your advice and pay (yes, pay!)
> For your help in court. Just use your loaf,
> You'll soon be a millionaire.
> He's all yours, Sokrates. Examine him,
> Dig into his mind and probe his thoughts.

SOKRATES.
> All right. One or two questions first:
> I need to know what sort of man you are,
480 Before I really set the wheels in motion.

STREPSIADES.
> Wheels? Are we going for a ride?

SOKRATES.
> No, no. I've got to get this form filled in.
> What's your memory like?

STREPSIADES.
> It's good, and not so good.
> If someone owes me money, I remember that.
> But if I owe someone else, my mind goes blank.

SOKRATES.
> Are you quick to pick things up?

STREPSIADES.
> That depends. If they don't belong to me...

SOKRATES.
> I'm not too sure if you're going to cope.

STREPSIADES.
> Of course I'll cope.

SOKRATES.
What if I tossed you a sudden thought,
An idea to chew on – would you pick it up?   490

STREPSIADES.
What next? D'you want me to sit up and beg?

SOKRATES.
He's hopeless. A dunce. Thick as two short planks.
Old man, I'm afraid you're going to need the cane.
H'm...good question. If someone thrashes you,
What do you do?

STREPSIADES.
I let them get on with it.
Then I find a witness, I wait a bit,
And I summons them for assault and battery.

SOKRATES.
All right. Get undressed.

STREPSIADES.
Pardon? What have I done?

SOKRATES.
Nothing. All students have to get undressed.

STREPSIADES.
I've got nothing to hide. Do I have to strip?

SOKRATES.
Shut up and take them off.

STREPSIADES.
Just one thing first:
Suppose I study really well, learn all
There is to know: which student will I be like?   500

SOKRATES.
Work hard, you'll be another Chairephon.

STREPSIADES.
What? Chairephon? That walking corpse? No thanks!

SOKRATES.
That's enough. Hurry up and get inside.

STREPSIADES.
Oh dear. I don't like it at all. It's like
A lion's den...a monkey house. Give me a bun.

SOKRATES.
Go on, go on! Stop lurking around the door.

They go in.

CHORUS[16].

510   In you go. Good luck to you.
You deserve to do really well,
Crossing, in dim old age,
The frontiers of youth,
Basking in
The suntan of the mind.

Dance.

Ladies and gentlemen, now, with the help
Of Dionysos (who has always guided me)
I intend to be perfectly frank.
What is it I want? I want the first prize,
520   And a name for sharp comments and wit.
I know *you're* quite bright, and I think
That the *Clouds* is my wittiest play
(And the hardest to write) up to now.
I went in for the prize – and I lost,
I came third to incompetent oafs.
Quite unfairly. The judges were fools:
All my efforts were wasted on *them*.
But this audience is different. You're bright,
And I trust you, I won't let you down.
When you saw my first play, how you cheered
At my characters *Nasty* and *Nice!*
You remember? My Muse was a blushing young
     girl,
530   Too young to have children and call them her own.
But she bore me a play, in another man's name,

And you loved it, adored it, and gave it a prize.
I know you're on *my* side: that's clear from the start.
So, just like Elektra, who found
What she wanted at last, here's a play
Come in search of spectators with brains.
Just look at her. Isn't she nice?
She's no need to come holding a prick
With a red leather tip, to get laughs
From little boys; she's no need
To make jokes about bald-heads, or dance
Belly-dances; she doesn't rush out   540
With a torch, like a tragedy queen,
Going 'Ooh, hoo-hoo-hoo!'; and we don't
Prefer slapstick to brilliance and wit.

You know me; I'm a man of ideas,
Not a long-haired freak. I don't serve
The same plots up in play after play:
Mine are clever and sparkling and new.
Remember Kleon? How I dealt with him?
And once he was down, how I left him alone?   550
Not like *them* – just look what they did
To Hyperbolos. Standing joke, right?
But they squeezed him and flogged him to death –
Him and his mother. First Eupolis came
With his *Marikas* (cribbed from my *Knights*):
Gave us Mother Hyperbolos drunk,
Belly-dancing – like Phrynichos did
Years ago...that old woman the sea-monster ate.
Hermippos came next – oh, they all had a go
At Hyperbolos, stealing the point of my *Eels*.
If you find their plays funny, then don't laugh at
        mine;   560
Laugh at me, you'll be famous for thousands of years.

Come down, almighty Zeus,
King of the gods, come down
And join the dance.
Poseidon, trident lord,

Great heaver-up of Earth
And the salty sea, come down.
570   Father of all, majestic Air,
Sustainer of life, come down.
Bright Sun, who rides the sky
In a chariot of circling fire,
Blessed of mortals and gods,
Come down and join the dance.

Ladies and gentlemen, your attention please.
We've a bone to pick with you, face to face.
We're the Clouds. We do you more good
Than all the other gods. We look after you
Day and night – and what do *you* do for *us*?
Nothing. Sacrifice...offerings? Not a sniff.
If you step out of line, right away
580   We send thunder and drizzle and hail.
When that man was elected...you know,
Old pain-in-the-neck, old cursed-of-the-gods...
The general, the tanner!...we frowned on you then,
We thundered and lightninged and made a great
    fuss.
And the Moon went on strike, and the Sun
Turned his wick down and sulked: 'No more
    warmth,
No more light: I'm not shining for *him!*'
But what good did it do? You elected the man.
And it's always the same: you're always quite sure
That the spirit of Athens will win in the end.
590   Why not help it along? Why not take
That impostor to court, and convict
Him of bribery and throw him in jail?
You know it makes sense. You know it's quite true:
The spirit of Athens *does* win in the end.

Phoebus Apollo, lord
Of the rocky slopes
Of Delos, come, join the dance.
Artemis, throned in gold

Where Lydian maidens sing   600
Your praise, come down to us.
Protectress of Athens, come:
Athene, mistress, queen.
Lord Dionysos, leave
The hills, where torches gleam
In the sacred dance;
Come down, come down to us.

We were just setting out when the Moon came round,
With a message she asked us to bring down here.
'To the people of Athens, STOP. Hope this finds you
As it leaves me, STOP. Furious, STOP.'   610
Well, that's how it is. When she helps you out,
You ignore her, the same as us.
First of all, she must save you a drachma a day
In lighting bills. 'Yes, I know it's got dark,
But we don't need a torch – use the Moon!'
There are other things too. Just look at the way
You keep fiddling the calendar, cheating the gods.
They turn up for a sacrifice, banquet or feast –
And find it was yesterday. Festivals too:
You're so busy in court, day after day,
Grilling the witnesses, cooking the books,   620
You forget about feast-days and feeding the gods.
Then, when *we're* deep in mourning, holding a wake
For the death of some hero of old,
You're having a party, with laughter and song.
Well, the gods are fed up, and the Moon gets the blame.
Just remember: Hyperbolos fiddled the dates,
And what happened to him? Oh, it's easy enough:
Get the calendar sorted, and follow the Moon.

Dance. As it ends, SOKRATES *comes out of the*
Thinkery.

SOKRATES.
Breath of Life! Chaos! Outer Space!
In all my life I've not met such a fool,
Such a yokel, such a forgetful oaf!

630   He pokes his way into a tiny chink
    Of knowledge – and by the time he to gets the end,
    He's forgotten the beginning. Oh, come out here!
    Into the light. Bring your mattress with you!

    STREPSIADES *struggles in with a mattress.*

STREPSIADES.
    I can't, can I? The bugs want to stay inside.

SOKRATES.
    Come out here. Put it down. Now *concentrate!*

STREPSIADES.
    Oh...there.

SOKRATES.
    Now, listen. What's the first thing you want to
      learn?
    With what you know now, there's plenty of choice.
    Would you like measure, or metre, or words?

STREPSIADES.
    Measure. There's a grocer down the road
640   Always gives short measure, up to fifty grams.

SOKRATES.
    Not measure...*measure!* Poetry...in verse...
    Lines and feet. Which metre do you prefer?

STREPSIADES.
    I think I like the kilometre best.

SOKRATES.
    That doesn't make sense.

STREPSIADES.
    It makes more sense
    Than feet and yards. Are *your* feet in a yard?

SOKRATES.
    Idiot! Numskull! You haven't a clue!
    You'll be wanting to tackle grammar next.

STREPSIADES.
    Would it help at the grocer's, with all those grams?

SOKRATES.
　These things are important. Don't you want to talk
　Like a man of good taste, a connoisseur,　　　　　650
　About rhythm, and fingering, and tone?

STREPSIADES.
　Fingering? I know all about that.

SOKRATES.
　What?

STREPSIADES (*gesturing*).
　Everyone fingers this way nowadays.

　He fingers his phallus.

　The fingering was different when I was young.

SOKRATES.
　You're hopeless.

STREPSIADES.
　It isn't me, it's you.
　I didn't come to learn all *that*.

SOKRATES.
　Well, what?

STREPSIADES.
　I want to learn that argument...you know,
　The one called Wrong.

SOKRATES.
　You can't begin with that.
　There are other things first. Tell me the names
　Of some male animals.

STREPSIADES.
　Huh! Is that all?
　Male and female? If I didn't know that,　　　　　660
　There'd be something wrong. Ram, goat, chicken,
　　　dog...

SOKRATES.
Stop! Chicken? You've gone wrong already.
Chicken? You're mixing up male and female.

STREPSIADES.
How do you mean?

SOKRATES.
Obvious: chicken, and...chicken.

STREPSIADES.
Good lord, you're right. What should I call them,
then?

SOKRATES.
Simple: chicken, and chickeness.

STREPSIADES.
Chickeness? By Outer Space, that's nice!
That's worth a basket of chickenfeed any day.

SOKRATES.
670 There you go again. Basket. Is that male
Or female?

STREPSIADES.
How can a *basket* be male?

SOKRATES.
Easy. It's just like Kleonymos.

STREPSIADES.
I don't understand.

SOKRATES.
The same rule applies. Basket, Kleonymos: male.

STREPSIADES.
But he isn't a male! Have you looked at him
closely?
He's a basket, I'll grant you that,
But he isn't a male. So what do we do?

SOKRATES.
We make up a special word. Basketess.

STREPSIADES.
Of course! Kleonymos the basketess.   680

SOKRATES.
You've got such a lot to learn. First, proper names:
Boys' names and girls' names. Female and male.

STREPSIADES.
I know lots of girls' names.

SOKRATES.
Let's hear some, then.

STREPSIADES.
Doris...Phyllis...Penelope...

SOKRATES.
Yes, yes. Any males?

STREPSIADES.
Thousands! Millions!
Marcus, Jason, Alexander, George...

SOKRATES.
Just a minute. Those aren't all male.

STREPSIADES.
Of course they are. What d'you mean, not male?

SOKRATES.
Just stand there and call them out. Go on:
Just stand there and call them out.

STREPSIADES.
All right.

He calls into the audience.

Coo-ee! Alexander! All-ee! Georgeeee!   690

SOKRATES.
There you are. Ali...Georgie. Not male at all.

STREPSIADES.
I've known some funny Georgies in my time.
We all have. What's to learn in that?

SOKRATES.
Never mind. Just lie down here.

STREPSIADES.
What for?

SOKRATES.
Lie down and turn over your affairs.

STREPSIADES (*shaking the mattress*).
Oh please, not there! If I have to lie down
And turn over, let me do it on the ground.

SOKRATES.
No. Do it on there.

STREPSIADES.
Oh god, I've had it now.
Those bugs have really got it in for me.

Reluctantly, he lies down.

CHORUS.
700   Curl up and ponder,
Don't let your mind wander:
The subject is complex and deep.
When you haven't a notion,
Don't make a commotion:
Start thinking – and DON'T GO TO SLEEP!

STREPSIADES.
Ow-oo, ow-oo, ow!

CHORUS.
What is it? What now?

STREPSIADES.
I'm dying. I'm on the rack.
It's a vicious attack,
710   They're a bloodthirsty bunch
And my ribs are their lunch.
They furrow and fight,
They burrow and bite –
My arse is a mess,

My balls are in distress –
They're killing me!

CHORUS.
No! How can that be?

STREPSIADES.
Just look here, and you'll see.
My money's been plundered,
No shoes on my feet;
I've been robbed and I've blundered,
I'm as white as a sheet –
And worse than that, my time's   720
Spent singing silly rhymes!

SOKRATES (*after a pause*).
What are you doing under there? Pondering?

STREPSIADES.
What else?

SOKRATES.
What are you pondering?

STREPSIADES (*sticking his head out*).
The bugs.
I was wondering what they'll want for tea.

SOKRATES.
I've had enough of this.

STREPSIADES.
I wish *they'd* had enough.

SOKRATES.
You'll have to put up with it. Wrap up
And concentrate, until you find some way
To shake them off.

STREPSIADES.
Shake who off? Bugs or debts?

He covers his head again and lies still. Pause.

SOKRATES.
730   I wonder what he's doing now. I'll take
      A look.

      He prods STREPSIADES' *blanket.*
      Are you asleep?

STREPSIADES ·(*sticking his head out*).
      Of course I'm not asleep.

SOKRATES.
      Have you got hold of something?

STREPSIADES.
      No.

SOKRATES.
      Nothing at all?

STREPSIADES.
      Well, just *this*...if you really want to know.

SOKRATES.
      For heaven's sake, wrap up and concentrate.

STREPSIADES.
      On what? Give me a subject, Sokrates.

SOKRATES.
      It depends on what you want. What *do* you want?

STREPSIADES.
      I've told you a million times. My debts.
      I don't want to pay my debts. That's what I want.

SOKRATES.
740   All right. Get under, and sharpen up your mind.
      Split the problem up into little bits,
      And deal with each one separately.
      Analyse...examine...scrutinise...

STREPSIADES.
      Oh god... Oo!... Owww!

SOKRATES.
      Stop wriggling. If you come to a dead end,

Turn your analysis round, and take it back
To the nearest crossroads of thought. Look round,
Get the new direction right, and start again.

Another pause. Then suddenly STREPSIADES *leaps up,*
full of excitement.

STREPSIADES.
  Yes! Yes! Dear old Sokrates!

SOKRATES.
  What is it...er...friend?

STREPSIADES.
  I've got it. A way out of debt. That's it!

SOKRATES.
  What's it?

STREPSIADES.
  Just listen, and tell me what you think.
  I'll go to the market and hire myself
  A witch. Then, when it's dark, I'll magic down
  The Moon, and put it in a big round box   750
  Like a mirror. I'll polish it...look after it...

SOKRATES.
  Why? What good will that do?

STREPSIADES.
  Don't you see?
  If the Moon isn't there to rise and shine,
  I'll never have to pay my debts again.

SOKRATES.
  Why not?

STREPSIADES.
  The end of the month will never come!

STREPSIADES.
  H'm. Clever. You're getting the idea. Try this.
  Suppose you went to court and lost, and had
  To pay a fine...? Ten thousand, say.
  Could you find some way to get out of *that?*   760

STREPSIADES.
H'm. Let me think.

SOKRATES.
Feel free, relax, don't bottle up your brain.
Let it fly freely. Let it buzz around
In the fresh air, like a beetle on a string.

STREPSIADES.
I've got it! I've got it! The ideal way.
You'll have to agree, this is pretty good.

SOKRATES.
Go on.

STREPSIADES.
You know in a shop...that round thing...clear,
Like a pretty stone you can see right through...
For fires...

SOKRATES.
You mean a magnifying glass?

STREPSIADES.
That's it. I'll take one with me into court...
770   Stand behind the clerk with the wax tablets...
And when he writes down the fine, melt it away.

SOKRATES.
That's clever. I like it.

STREPSIADES.
I like it even better:
I don't have to pay the fine!

SOKRATES.
Here's another. Get your teeth into this.

STREPSIADES.
Go on.

SOKRATES.
You're due in court, on trial. You're bound to lose.
There's no one to help you. What do you do?

STREPSIADES.
Simple...easy.

SOKRATES.
Go on.

STREPSIADES.
It's obvious.
They're bound to try another case before mine.
While they're busy with that, I'll hang myself.   780

SOKRATES.
Ridiculous!

STREPSIADES.
It's not ridiculous at all.
D'you think they'd take a corpse to court?

SOKRATES.
What rubbish! You've failed. Get out of here.

STREPSIADES.
Failed? No, Sokrates! In the name of the gods...

SOKRATES.
You've forgotten every word you ever learned.
What was the first thing? Go on. What was first?

STREPSIADES.
It was...it was...just a minute...what was first?
It was that thing about a grocer's shop...
Don't tell me...

SOKRATES.
I knew it. Silly old fool!
You've forgotten the lot. Get out of here.   790

STREPSIADES.
Oh god! Now what am I going to do?
I've got to learn tongue-wrestling...argument...
Oh Clouds, please help. Please tell me what to do.

CHORUS.
Certainly. Old man, our advice is this.

Have you got a son, a grown-up son?
If you have, send him to learn instead of you.

STREPSIADES.
A son? Oh yes, I've got a son all right.
A stuck-up little... *He* won't come and learn.

CHORUS.
Does what he likes, then?

STREPSIADES.
He's bigger than me...

800   Stronger. He's got class, on his mother's side.
Still, I can try. And if he won't, I'll...I'll...
Well, he can pack his bags. Wait here. You'll see.

He hurries into his house.

CHORUS (*to* SOKRATES).
He's your bird in the hand,
He's your cash in the bank –
And it's us you should thank,
The best gods in the land.

810   He's jolly impressed:
While you've got him, invest
In his dimness, and hook him today
Before he gets clever and wriggles away.

STREPSIADES *storms out of his house, driving*
PHEIDIPPIDES.

STREPSIADES.
Go on! Get out! By Fog, you're not staying here.
Go on! Eat your uncle out of house and home.

PHEIDIPPIDES.
Dad! What's the matter, Dad? Have you gone mad?
Almighty Zeus, I think he's off his head.

STREPSIADES.
Almighty Zeus! Almighty Zeus! You fool!
A man your age – and you still believe in Zeus?

PHEIDIPPIDES.
What are you laughing at?

STREPSIADES.
You, you baby.   820
D'you still believe those old wives' tales? Come here.
It's time I told you the truth, the facts of life.
Promise one thing: you'll keep it to yourself.

PHEIDIPPIDES.
I promise.

STREPSIADES.
Swear, in the name of Zeus.

PHEIDIPPIDES.
In the name of Zeus.

STREPSIADES.
That's the way. Isn't education wonderful?
Pheidippides...
There's no such thing as Zeus.

PHEIDIPPIDES.
What is there, then?

STREPSIADES.
The Great Wind rules. He put an end to Zeus.

PHEIDIPPIDES.
You've gone raving mad.

STREPSIADES.
I'm telling you, it's true.

PHEIDIPPIDES.
Who says it's true?

STREPSIADES.
Well, Sokrates for one –   830
And Chairephon, the expert on fleas' feet.

PHEIDIPPIDES.
You're crazy, Dad! You really believe those freaks?

STREPSIADES.
Hey, less of that. Don't you insult the Prof.
They're really bright. They're not the same as you:
Don't waste their time in baths and barber's shops.
You're always taking me to the cleaner's.
No, you go there and learn.

PHEIDIPPIDES.
840   What earthly good can I learn in there?

STREPSIADES.
You're really asking? You really want to know?
They'll teach you all the knowledge in the world.
Look: stay here. I'll show you how thick you are.

He hurries into his house.

PHEIDIPPIDES.
Now what am I going to do? He's off his head.
Round the bend. Potty. Who shall I send for?
A coffin...? The doctor...? The funny farm...?

STREPSIADES *comes out, holding, by the legs,
a cock in one hand, a hen in the other.*

STREPSIADES.
All right. What's this, eh? What would you call
   this?

PHEIDIPPIDES.
A chicken.

STREPSIADES.
Very good. And what about this?

PHEIDIPPIDES.
A chicken.

STREPSIADES.
Both of them chickens? Poor, poor boy.
850   Get it right in future. Listen to me:
This one's a chicken, this one's a chickeness.

PHEIDIPPIDES.

A chickeness? They taught you that in there?
Zeus doesn't exist, and that's a chickeness?

STREPSIADES.

Oh, there was plenty more. But I'm too old –
I learn all right, and then it slips my mind.

PHEIDIPPIDES.

Is that what happened to your wallet too?

STREPSIADES.

Eh? Oh, no. It didn't slip: I let it go.

PHEIDIPPIDES.

Your wallet...your purse...the shirt off your back.
You idiot!

STREPSIADES.

No, those were expenses. Essential expenses.
Come on, I'll take you. Please. Do as I ask,   860
Give in to Daddy. Don't you remember,
When you were six, how I gave in to you?
I spoiled you. Whatever you asked, you got.
That little pushcart, with my first day's pay...?

PHEIDIPPIDES.

All right. But don't be sorry afterwards.

STREPSIADES.

There's a good boy. Come on. O Sokrates...!
Are you at home?

SOKRATES *comes out.*

I've brought my son. He said
He wouldn't come, but I persuaded him.

SOKRATES.

He's just a baby. *He* can't learn the ropes.

PHEIDIPPIDES.

I wish *you'd* learn the ropes, and hang yourself.   870

STREPSIADES.
Don't be so cheeky! Don't insult the Prof!

SOKRATES (*aside to him*).
It won't be easy. Just look at him.
Did you see how he curled his lip, looked down his
nose?
How will *he* convince a jury? How will *he* learn
The Whitewash? The Cover-up? The Little Lie?
Mind you, others have. Hyperbolos, for one.
Yes, I think if my fee's made *large* enough...

STREPSIADES.
Don't worry. He'll manage it. He's very quick.
Even when he was tiny...mm, *this* high...

880   He was always building little houses...boats...
Toy carts (reins and all)...and model frogs
Out of pomegranate peel...oh, you'd have loved
them!
So don't worry. Teach him your arguments,
Right and Wrong, the Wrong that beats the Right.
If he can't manage both, make sure it's Wrong he
learns.

SOKRATES.
All right. Look, I have to go inside. I'll get
The Arguments out themselves, to give him
A demonstration, here. Is that all right?

STREPSIADES.
Whatever you like, so long as he learns
To thumb his nose at all that's just and fair.

SOKRATES *goes in.* SLAVES *bring out chairs for*
STREPSIADES *and* PHEIDIPPIDES. RIGHT *and*
WRONG *are brought in, in wicker cages. They are dressed
as fighting-cocks. The cage doors are flung open,
and they come out and circle each other, looking
for an opening*[17].

RIGHT.
   Come on then. Take a bow.
   Show off to the audience.   890

WRONG.
   Oh, take a running jump...!
   I like a crowd. *I'll* show you.

RIGHT.
   You? Me? Who are *you?*

WRONG.
   I'm Argument.

RIGHT.
   No, you're wrong.

WRONG.
   That's right, I'm Wrong.
   Better than *you* are, any day.
   I'll beat you.

RIGHT.
   How?

WRONG.
   With new ideas.

RIGHT.
   Huh! Compost! Weeds!
   The sort these idiots like.

WRONG.
   They know what's what.

RIGHT.
   You haven't a chance.
   I'll beat you.

WRONG.
   How?

RIGHT.
   With simple justice.   900

WRONG.

   Huh! Justice is dead.

   There's no such thing.

RIGHT.

   There is.

WRONG.

   Where is it, then?

RIGHT.

   In heaven, with Zeus.

WRONG.

   With Zeus? The one who threw his father out

   And stole his throne – *and* got away with it?

RIGHT.

   You make me sick.

   Bring a basin, quick!

WRONG.

   Miserable windbag!

RIGHT.

   Dirty-minded oaf!

WRONG.

   You crown me with roses...

RIGHT.

910   Fairy! Toad!

WRONG.

   ...and lilies...

RIGHT.

   Cesspit! Skunk!

WRONG.

   You sprinkle me with gold.

RIGHT.

   Aren't you ashamed?

WRONG.
I like it.

RIGHT.
You just don't care.

WRONG.
You're out of touch.

RIGHT.
All Athens must know
What you've made of the young:
Lazy scroungers, layabouts,
Ignorant freaks –

WRONG.
You really do stink.   920

RIGHT.
We can't all smell
As sweet as you.
We don't all live
Like a beggar prince.

WRONG.
Knowall!

RIGHT.
We certainly know your tastes. D'you think
We'd trust you with our sons?

WRONG.
There's nothing you can do
For him. You're past it, Dad.

RIGHT (to PHEIDIPPIDES).
Come here to me, boy. Learn   930
With Right. No rubbish here.

WRONG.
Let him drool. Join me.

RIGHT.
Hands off! Unless you want –

CHORUS.
> What good is this fighting and arguing?
> There are two different systems at work.
> *You* begin, and explain how the *old*
> Method worked. Then *you* tell us the *new*.
> *He* can listen, and judge for himself.

RIGHT.
> That makes sense.

WRONG.
> Perfect sense. I agree.

CHORUS.
94 So which one of you wants to go first?

WRONG.
> He can start.
> Whatever he says, I'll smother him
> With newer, subtler lines of thought.
> He can try all he likes: my arguments
> Will be buzzing and stinging his ears
> Just like hornets. He'll soon give in.

CHORUS.
950 Now it's time. Let the fight begin.
> Start talking. May the best man win.
> On guard! Words, razor-edged and new,
> Keen arguments, sharp points of view.
> It's a dangerous duel, a battle to test
> If the Clouds and their worshippers really are
> best.

> First, the Old Generation of thought.
960 We admire you: just how were you taught?

RIGHT.
> Try to cast your minds back to the days
> When good manners and decency ruled,
> And our children were properly taught.
> They were seen, but not heard. In the street,

They went quietly and calmly to school,
With their friends, in an orderly group.
They were manly and tough – it could snow
Like a flourmill, they didn't need coats.
In the classroom, no fooling about:
Sit up staight, and rehearse the old songs –
'Praise Athene...', 'Hurrah for the Fight...' –
Good old songs, in the old-fashioned way.
There was none of this new-fangled beat: 970
If you tried it, they gave you the cane.

When you went to the gym[18], you sat down
In a modest position – and when
You stood up, you smoothed over the sand
Till no traces were left to excite
Any dirty old men. When you bathed,
You anointed yourself down to *here*
And no further. The boys of those days
Were downy as apricots...creamy...soft...
No cooing, flirting, walking like *this*,
Or giving those come-hither looks...   980

...or grabbing and helping themselves
If a grown-up was waiting for food:
No, not even to pickles or salt.
Their diet was simple: good, nourishing food,
No titbits or fancies or wriggling the feet.

WRONG.
    'No titbits or fancies...'! 'The good old songs...'!
    Oh yes, those were the days!

RIGHT.
    Well, they *were:*
    The great days of the heroes of old.
    Your pupils are sissies, and soft:
    When the festival comes, and the dance
    In the nude for Athene, they won't.
    They're embarrassed; they cover themselves
    With their shields – I don't know where to look.

990 So, young fellow, choose me: I'm the best.
Turn your back on street corners and baths;
Don't waste time on crude gossip and jokes.
Be a man! Make the best of yourself.
Be a model of virtue and trust.
Stand up when your elders come in;
Show respect for your parents – and don't
Follow flute-girls: they'll blow you a kiss
And embarrass you out in the street.
Don't be cheeky to Daddy; don't call
Him a silly old fool. You're his chick,
And he's worked hard to give you the best.

WRONG (*mocking*).
1000 No, *young fella!* Be warned: if you choose
Him, they'll call you a worm and a weed.

RIGHT.
You'll be glowing with fitness and health.
While the rest of them snigger and joke
In some bar, till they're summoned to court
By a slippery snake-in-the-grass,
You'll be practising out in the park,
Running races with pure-minded friends...

Oh, the garlands! The holiday flowers!
The whispering poplars! The elms
And the plane-trees! The rustle of spring...!

If you follow me, if you try
1010 To do exactly as I say,
The rewards will be these:
A healthy tan; a manly chest;
Broad shoulders; a modest tongue;
Massive buttocks; standard prick.
Follow *him*, and you'll get
Bird shoulders, a lemon skin,
Chicken ribs, a serpent's tongue,
A camel's behind, an elephant's prick –
And a million admirers.
1020 He'll teach you that good equals bad

And that bad equals good;
He'll stuff you with rottenness, fill you with filth.

CHORUS.
That was brilliant! Such wisdom! Such power!
Like a beautiful garden in flower.
Oh, *that's* education! Oh, those were the days!
It's a fact: you can't beat the old ways.
Now, the moment of truth. Bring the other one in.
With his new-fangled thought, he's not likely to win. 1030
Now the New Generation must fight.
And I warn you: so far we like Right.

WRONG.
At last! I've been busting a gut
With frustration and longing to speak.
Now I'll show you his case is absurd.
For many years now, in the schools,
I've come second to him; I'm called Wrong;
No one likes me. The reason? I prove
That old laws and old customs are dead.   1040
It's the way to make money in court:
Stand up, challenge the system, and win.
Yes, and that's how I'll deal with *him,* now.
First, baths. So we mustn't take baths?
Why is that, pray? What harm do they do?

RIGHT.
They weaken and soften you up.

WRONG.
Ha! You're finished. You needn't go on.
Just tell me: which god...*laboured*...most?
Who was famous for toughness and strength?

RIGHT.
Herakles. No one's tougher than he is.   1050

WRONG.
All right. Just look there, down the road.
'The Herakles Sauna. Hot baths.
Open daily.' What more need I say?

RIGHT.

> Very clever! Young people today!
> They've an answer for everything. None
> Do gymnastics – they're all at the baths!

WRONG.

> You object to discussion: I don't.
> If discussion was banned, there'd be no
> Politicians...no public affairs...
>
> Next, the tongue and its uses: you say
> That it's wrong – well, I say that it's right.
> It's the same thing with women: you say

1060
> Men should leave them alone. But what for?
> Show me one of the heroes of old
> Who did well out of leaving alone.

RIGHT.

> There was Peleus. It won him a knife.

WRONG.

> He left *women* alone, and it won him a *knife?*
> I'm so *pleased!* Does Hyperbolos know?
> He left *nothing* alone. Now he's rich –
> But I don't think it won him a knife.

RIGHT.

> Ah! When *Peleus* avoided temptation,
> He married a goddess as well –

WRONG.

> And she left him as soon as she could!
> He was frigid and useless in bed –
> And no female of spirit likes that,

1070
> As you'd know if you weren't quite so old.
>
> What do *you* think? You're young. Can you give
> Up temptation, excitement, and *fun?*
> Can you do without women, and boys,
> And drinking, and gambling, and..*fun?*
> What good is your life, if you have

To give up all the pleasures of life?
There are some things a man *has* to do.
Just suppose you don't learn what to say
When the husband comes home, and you're caught
In the act? Very nasty... But if
You join *me*, you can do what you like.
If he finds you in bed with his wife,
You'll know just what to say. 'It's all right,
There's no harm in it. Think about Zeus.   1080
What a lover! He couldn't resist.
And if *he* couldn't help it – can I?'

RIGHT.

   That argument won't do you much good
   It he grabs you, and calls you a bugger,
   And stuffs a radish up your arse.

WRONG.

   What's wrong with buggers, anyway?

RIGHT.

   What's wrong? Is there anything worse?

WRONG.

   And supposing I prove that you are wrong?

RIGHT.

   I'll shut up: you'll have won.

WRONG.

   Tell me, then:
   What are lawyers?

RIGHT.

   They're buggers.

WRONG.

   And playwrights?   1090

RIGHT.

   They're buggers.

WRONG.

   Politicians?

RIGHT.
They're buggers.

WRONG.
You see what I mean?
Now then: just look out here,
In the audience. There.

RIGHT.
Well?

WRONG.
Well now, what do you see?

RIGHT.
It's stuffed full of them!
Look: there's that fellow there,
1100   And that other one there,
And that one with the hair –

WRONG.
Now what do you say?

RIGHT.
I'm beaten. What else
Can I say? The whole world's
Full of buggers. Move over!
I'm coming to join you. Make room!

He rushes out. SOKRATES *comes out of the Thinkery.*

SOKRATES.
Well, what's the decision? Will you leave your son
Here to learn argument, or take him home?

STREPSIADES.
Teach him and beat him and sharpen him up:
On the right side for lawsuits and debts,
1110   On the left side for matters of state.

SOKRATES.
Don't worry. He'll be a credit to me yet.

PHEIDIPPIDES.
I'll be a crook, you mean, weedy and pale...

CHORUS.
 Go on inside.
 I think you may change your mind.

 SOKRATES, PHEIDIPPIDES *and* WRONG *go into
 the Thinkery.* STREPSIADES *goes into his own
 house.*

CHORUS (*to the judges, who are in the audience*).
 There are certain advantages coming your way
 If you vote for the *Clouds*, if you give us first prize.
 When the season for ploughing begins, you'll want
     rain.
 We'll water your fields first; the others can wait.
 We'll keep a close eye on your vines as they grow:
 They won't shrivel and die, they won't drown in a
     flood.   1120

 Any mortals who laugh at us, gods that we are,
 Ought to know what the penalties are. Number One:
 Barren acres. No harvest, no produce, no fruit.
 All your olives and vines, when they blossom in spring,
 Will be battered to death by a torrent of rain.

 Number Two: house repairs. When you're up on the roof
 We'll send hailstones like footballs to smash all your
     tiles.
 Number Three: family weddings. You want a nice day?
 You won't get one. The choice is a simple one: move
 To the deserts of Egypt, or give us first prize.   1130

 Dance. When it ends, STREPSIADES *comes out,
 checking off days on a calendar. Under one
 arm, he carries a bundled-up cloak.*

STREPSIADES.
 Twenty-seventh, twenty-eighth, twenty-ninth...
 And then the worst day of all, the day
 That gives me goose-pimples and makes me feel sick:
 The end of the month. They'll all be round,
 My creditors. Every one of them. 'Pay up
 Or go to court' – that'll be their line. I'll try

To persuade them: 'My dear chap, be fair,
Be reasonable...take a little, on account' –
1140 That'll be when they start calling me a crook
And summoning me to court. Well, let them!
They can do what they like, if only Pheidippides
Has learned that argument. We'll soon see.

He knocks on the door of the Thinkery.

Hello! Hello! Anyone in?

SOKRATES *opens the door.*

SOKRATES.
Strepsiades! How *very* nice...!

STREPSIADES.
Oh...same to you. Look: I've brought you this...
A little something to cover your expenses.
Now, what about Pheidippides? Has he learned
That argument, the one that performed just now?

SOKRATES.
Yes.
Passed with honour.

STREPSIADES.
115 Practical crookery! Oh, thank god!

SOKRATES.
Now you can slip out of any court you like.

STREPSIADES.
Even if I borrowed in front of witnesses?

SOKRATES.
The more the merrier. A million, if you like.

STREPSIADES (*dancing*).
Oh joy! Oh joy!
My little boy –
A hammer, a spear
When danger's near.
1160 He'll smack the bad
Men, help his Dad:

My little boy –
Oh joy! Oh joy!

Run inside, and fetch him out.

SOKRATES.
Come out here, lad,
And greet your dad.
He's here! He's come!

PHEIDIPPIDES *comes out.*

STREPSIADES.
My son! My son!   1170

SOKRATES.
Take him, and go.

STREPSIADES.
My baby! Oh!
Let me look at you. Oh, I like it:
The pasty face, the sulky look,
The frown, the don't-give-a-damn,
The thump-someone-else-and-then-complain –
I like it! I like it!
That pale, *Athenian* look!
Well, you've ruined me: now you can put it right.

PHEIDIPPIDES.
What's the matter now?

STREPSIADES.
It's the end of the month.

PHEIDIPPIDES.
So what? It's the end of the month.

STREPSIADES.
Today's the day I've got to pay my debts[19].
It's payday today. They've got to be paid.   1180

PHEIDIPPIDES.
Oh no they haven't. Today isn't payday.
How can one day be two days? Tell me that.

STREPSIADES.
Pardon?

PHEIDIPPIDES.
It's Friday today. Not Payday.
You can't have two names for just one day.
1190   If it's Friday today, it can't be payday too.

STREPSIADES.
But what about the law?

PHEIDIPPIDES.
It's not the law.

STREPSIADES.
Oh no?

PHEIDIPPIDES.
The law's there to help you, not hinder you.

STREPSIADES.
I don't get it. Where do the days come in?

PHEIDIPPIDES.
One after the other: never two at once.
Sometimes we pay on Fridays; sometimes
We fry on paydays. But they're two separate days,
1200   And anyone who says they're not, is wrong.

STREPSIADES.
It's brilliant!

(to the audience)

Isn't it? Oh, you should see
Your faces, sitting out there like rows of sheep,
Broken biscuits, pebbles, washing up!
Don't you understand? We've got you now –
Me and my son, and the other clever men.
I think I'll sing another song: a song
Of good luck, short and witty (just like me).

He sings and dances.

Oh happy man,
Strepsiades!

Who's luckier than
Strepsiades?
What a man! What a mind!
And his son – what a find!
Strepsiades!
Strepsiades!

One day they'll all be singing that: our friends,
Our neighbours. They'll be so jealous! They'll be   1210
So green! Just wait till you see their faces
When you stand up and argue me out of debt.
Come on inside. There's a party waiting for you.
We'll see to that first, and then.... Come on.

He ushers PHEIDIPPIDES *and* SOKRATES *into his
house. Enter* PASIAS *and* FRIEND.

PASIAS.
  What's he want me to do? Kiss my cash goodbye?
  I should have screwed myself up and said no
  In the first place. That would have saved all this.
  All I want is what's rightly mine – and to get it
  I have to drag you along, and make a fuss,
  And quarrel with a neighbour. It's not fair.
  Well, he won't get away with it. I know this
  Is a free country – but it's not *that* free.   1220

He knocks.

  Strepsiades!
  Come out and pay your debts, Strepsiades!

STREPSIADES *comes out.*

STREPSIADES.
  Who is it now?

PASIAS.
  Come on: it's the end of the month.

STREPSIADES.
  So what?

PASIAS.
It's payday.

STREPSIADES (*to the* FRIEND).
He thinks today's called Payday.
Remember that.

(*to* PASIAS)

What's all the fuss about?

PASIAS.
Twelve hundred drachmas you borrowed from me
To buy that bay stallion.

STREPSIADES (*to the* FRIEND)
Everyone knows bay stallions make me sick.

PASIAS.
You promised by the gods you'd pay me back.

STREPSIADES (*to the* FRIEND).
I expect that was before Pheidippides
(My son, you know) went and learned the Way that
Wins.

PASIAS.
1230   You mean you're trying to wriggle out of it?

STREPSIADES.
Why else d'you think I paid for him to learn?

PASIAS.
But you swore, in the name of the gods.

STREPSIADES.
What gods?

PASIAS.
Zeus, Hermes, Poseidon.

STREPSIADES.
Oh, those gods. D'you know,
I'd do the same again. *By Zeus!* It's cheap.

PASIAS.

Ohhh! Mocking the gods! You'll go straight to hell.

STREPSIADES (*to the* FRIEND).

He'd make a good wine-barrel, don't you think?
If we rubbed him down with salt...

PASIAS.

Don't you laugh at *me*...

STREPSIADES.

Six gallons, at least.

PASIAS.

Zeus! Zeus and the other gods! You've had it now!

STREPSIADES.

Zeus and the other gods! To us   1240
Really *clever* men, your Zeus is just a joke.

PASIAS.

Wha-a-at? Blasphemy! You'll pay for that.
But you can pay *me* first. Well? Will you
Or won't you? I expect an answer today.

STREPSIADES.

Calm down. You can have it now. Here and now.

He goes inside.

PASIAS (*to his* FRIEND).

What did he mean by that?

FRIEND.

Perhaps he'll pay.

STREPSIADES *comes out again.*

STREPSIADES.

Where's Moneybags? Ah, there. Now, then: what's this?

PASIAS.

What's what? Oh...a basket.

STREPSIADES.

A basket!

And you have the nerve to ask for money!
1250   I wouldn't give tuppence to a man
Who can't tell a basket from a basketess.

PASIAS.
  You...wouldn't...give...tuppence...?

STREPSIADES.
  Not likely. So,
  Lard-belly, who don't you just melt away?
  Slide off my doorstep.

PASIAS.
  Right! You've done it now.
  I'll have you in court if it's the last thing I do.

He storms out with his FRIEND.

STREPSIADES (*shouting after them*).
  You're throwing good money after bad. That's a
    pity,
  On top of everything else. I mean,
  If you can't tell a basket from a basketess...

Enter AMYNIAS. *He has been in an accident.*

AMYNIAS.
  Oh dear! Alas! Oh woe!

STREPSIADES.
  Oh gods,
1260   Another of them! Who's this one, now?

AMYNIAS.
  You ask my name? You wish to know my name?
  A man of sorrow.

STREPSIADES.
  There now...poor soul...

AMYNIAS.
  O cruel fate! To bite the dust like that!
  In a chariot smash. Athene, how it hurt!

STREPSIADES (*to the audience*).
  I can't think *what* he did to get the part.

AMYNIAS.
  My friend, don't mock me. Tell the boy, your son,
  To pay me back that money. Woe! Oh woe!

STREPSIADES.
  Whoa yourself. Steady, boy. What money?

AMYNIAS.
  The money I lent him. Woe!   1270

STREPSIADES.
  You *are* in a bad way. Worse than I thought.

AMYNIAS.
  I was driving along, minding my own business,
  And *crash! Smash!* The gods had it in for me.

STREPSIADES.
  I wonder if he's fallen on his head.
  Excuse me.... Are you off your head?

AMYNIAS.
  What? Off my head? I want my cash.

STREPSIADES.
  You ought to lie down, you know.

AMYNIAS.
  Why?

STREPSIADES.
  There may be brain damage. Best lie down.

AMYNIAS.
  I won't lie down. Brain damage? Off my head?
  You'll have brain damage, if you don't pay up.

STREPSIADES.
  Tell me one thing. You know when it rains...?
  Is that new water every time, or does the Sun   1280
  Suck it back up, and then recycle it?

AMYNIAS.

What do I care? Don't bother me with that.

STREPSIADES.

Don't bother you? An important question of science?
And you have the nerve to ask for cash?

AMYNIAS.

Look, if you're hard up, give me a little now
On account. The interest, say...

STREPSIADES.

Interest? What's that?

AMYNIAS.

You know what interest is. It grows and grows.
Each month, each day. As time flows by.

STREPSIADES.

I see.
And what about the sea? What do you think –
1290   Is there more of it now than there used to be?

AMYNIAS.

Of course not. It's the same. Always the same.
It's a law of nature.

STREPSIADES.

A law of nature, eh?
With all those rivers pouring in, it stays
The same? And you say your *money* grows?
Get out of here! Leave me alone! Where's that
    whip?

AMYNIAS.

Ladies and gentlemen...HELP!

STREPSIADES.

Go on, gee up! That's it.
1300   Faster! Faster! Want a quick flick?
Out! Trying to run me out of house and home!

He chases AMYNIAS out.

CLOUDS.
    Still, crime doesn't pay.
    That's the lesson
    That wicked old fraud
    Will learn today.

    He's a clever old man;
    Well, he'll soon wish he wasn't.
    And he thought up this plan;
    Well, he'll soon wish he hadn't.   1310

    He had his son trained
    As a master of lies,
    Crooked arguments,
    Cunning and tricks.

    That means triumph and joy;
    Well, he'll soon find out it doesn't.
    He's a good little boy;
    Well, he'll soon find out he isn't.

    He may well come
    To wish him dumb.   1320

    Dance. It ends when STREPSIADES *rushes*
    out of his house, chased by PHEIDIPPIDES.

STREPSIADES.
    Ee-ow! Ee-ow!
    Help! Neighbours...ladies and gentlemen...
    Anyone...help! He's beating me up! He-e-elp!
    Oh, my poor head...my aching jawbone...owww!
    Big bully! Beating your father.

PHEIDIPPIDES.
    That's right, Dad.

STREPSIADES.
    He admits it. Ow! Ooh! Oh!

PHEIDIPPIDES.
    Now then, Dad.

STREPSIADES.
    Thief! Bully! Murderer!

PHEIDIPPIDES.
Go on. I like it.

STREPSIADES.
You...pansy!

PHEIDIPPIDES.
1330   Yes, sprinkle me with flowers.

STREPSIADES.
Fancy beating your Dad.

PHEIDIPPIDES.
I'll prove I'm right.

STREPSIADES.
Right? Did you hear that? *Right?* How
Can it be right to beat your own Dad?

PHEIDIPPIDES.
Shut up, let me prove it. Let me explain.

STREPSIADES.
How can you prove it?

PHEIDIPPIDES.
No problem: with argument.
Now then, which one would you prefer?

STREPSIADES.
Eh?

PHEIDIPPIDES.
Which argument? Would you like Right, or Wrong?

STREPSIADES.
Just a minute. You mean...? Oh, my god!
There'll be no stopping you now. You mean
1340   You can really prove it, really persuade me
That it's right for a son to beat up his own Dad?

PHEIDIPPIDES.
No problem. You'll be eating out of my hand.
You'll agree. You won't have a word to say.

STREPSIADES.
Ha, this'll be good. This I can't wait to hear.

CHORUS.
Old man, you'd better think quickly and hard
How to stop him: he looks pretty sure
Of himself. If he hadn't a case, would he act
So conceited, so puffed up and proud?   1350

First, you have to tell us how the quarrel started.
It's in the script: 'It all began like this...'

STREPSIADES.
All right. Listen. It all began like this.
We went inside for a party, remember?
All I did was ask for a little music.
'Get your lyre,' I said, 'and give us a song.
One of the old songs: they're the best.' 'Rubbish!'
He said. 'No one sings at the table nowadays.
What d'you think I am? A washerwoman?'

PHEIDIPPIDES.
Exactly. You see? You wanted a beating right away.
Singing at table. We're not grasshoppers, you know.   1360

STREPSIADES.
His exact words inside. And that wasn't all.
He started making fun of all my favourite songs.
'Archaic rubbish! Drivel!' Kind remarks like that.
Well, it wasn't easy, but I didn't get cross –
At first. I thought, 'Something classical instead.'
So I asked him to grab a myrtle-twig and sing
A bit of Aeschylus. And *he* said, 'Aeschylus!
The greatest ever. The greatest ever rubbish-spouting
     bore!'
It was touch and go: I nearly had a heart attack.
But I fought it down, and said, 'All right, then, sing
One of your own favourites, with all the clever bits.' 1370
Well, what d'you think he sang? Euripides!
Some rubbish about a brother and sister who went
To bed, and – ah, you know the sort of thing.
That did it. I went right through the roof,
Told him just what I thought of him. And he said...
Well, you can imagine. It was hammer and tongs.

Then all at once, he came at me, grabbed me
And started beating me, hammering me, giving me
hell.

PHEIDIPPIDES.
Well, of course I did. Insulting Euripides,
That pure genius...

STREPSIADES.
Pure genius? He's a load of – no,
I'll get beaten up again.

PHEIDIPPIDES.
You're right. You will.

STREPSIADES.
1380 Big bully! Have you forgotten? I brought you up.
Just look how I spoiled you. You couldn't even talk.
When you said 'Dink!', who was it who understood,
And fetched your bottle? 'Bab-bab!' – who gave you
a rusk?
When you said, 'Po-po, Da-da!', who picked you up
And ran outside and held you out? Who was it? Me!
And just now, when you frightened me
Till I had to go myself,
When I sat there and screamed
And went red in the face –
What good did it do?
Did you let me get out?
1390 No! I suffered and sat.

CHORUS.
The audience is full of young people tonight,
And they're panting to hear what *he* says.
If he answers the charges, and proves he was right,
All you grown-ups, you're not worth a damn.

All right, Mr Clever Dick. Dig deep down, pull up
Your weedy arguments, and make them look like
truth.

PHEIDIPPIDES.

The great thing about being educated is, you know
What everything's about. You've got arguments,   1400
Clever arguments; you can turn things upside-down.
In the old days, when I knew nothing else

But horses, I couldn't harness three words together
Without going off course. But the Prof soon stopped
     that.
I'm a master of thoughts and tricks and arguments.
Give Daddy a thrashing? It's easy to prove that's
     right.

STREPSIADES.

My god, I wish I'd been satisfied with horses!
Far better to be eaten up than beaten up.

PHEIDIPPIDES.

You can't put me off, even with jokes like that.
Tell me this: when I was a boy, did you beat me?

STREPSIADES.

Of course, for your own good. I loved you.   1410

PHEIDIPPIDES.

All right, then.
If I love *you*, if it's for *your* own good,
It must be right for me to beat you now.
I'm a free man, the same as you:
What's right for me is right for you.
I know what you're going to say:
Children have to learn, and they learn by beatings.
'Spare the rod and spoil the child.'
That's easy to answer.
I mean, just look at *you:*
A man in his second childhood,
Who has to learn.
The mistakes are bigger;
So are the beatings too.

STREPSIADES.
But you can't beat your father.
1420 It's against the law.

PHEIDIPPIDES.
Who made the law,
Back there in the good old days?
Ordinary people, like you and me.
And how did they know they were right?
They were persuaded, by argument.
Well, now I want to change the law,
By argument. I want to let sons beat fathers.
Oh, I'll be fair:
All the beatings you gave us
Before the law was changed are cancelled.
You don't need to worry about *them*.
Have you got it? It's nature's way.
Just think of cocks:
All son-cocks fight all father-cocks.
And we're the same – except, of course,
That father-chickens don't make laws.

STREPSIADES.
Nature's way!
1430 If you think chickens are so marvellous,
Why aren't you sleeping on a perch
And pecking dung?

PHEIDIPPIDES.
Ah yes.... That's different.
Sokrates could tell you why.

STREPSIADES.
In any case, you've got it wrong.
You can't beat me.

PHEIDIPPIDES.
Why not?

STREPSIADES.
Look; you're my son, so I beat you.
When *you're* a father, you can beat *your* son.

PHEIDIPPIDES.
　Ah well – but if
　I never *have* a son? I can't beat him, I can't
　Beat you – I'm cheated and robbed.

STREPSIADES (*to the audience*).
　That's a very good point.
　Are there any fathers here? We've got to give in;
　We've got to let them beat us. It's only fair.

PHEIDIPPIDES.
　And there's something else.

STREPSIADES.
　I'm sorry I started this.　　　　　　　　　　1440

PHEIDIPPIDES.
　It might help. It might make it easier to bear.

STREPSIADES.
　I'm all for that. Go on, I'm listening.

PHEIDIPPIDES.
　I can beat up Mummy too.

STREPSIADES.
　What? Did you just say what I thought you said?

PHEIDIPPIDES.
　I said it, and I can prove it.
　It stands to reason.
　Of course it's right to beat –

STREPSIADES.
　Oh no you don't! You take
　Yourself, and Sokrates, and all　　　　　　　1450
　Your arguments, and go to Hell!

　(*to the* CHORUS)

　You got me into this.
　I put myself in your hands...

CHORUS.
> It was your own fault entirely.
> *You* chose dishonesty, not us.

STREPSIADES.
> Why didn't you warn me?
> I'm a simple old man, from the country...

CHORUS.
> That's not our way. Whenever we see
> You mortals falling in love with fraud,
1460 We leave you to it. You suffer,
> And learn to respect the gods.

STREPSIADES.
> What a rotten thing to do!
> But I suppose it's fair enough:
> I shouldn't have tried to cheat.

> (*to* PHEIDIPPIDES)

> No hard feelings, son. Come on:
> We'll settle their hash,
> Sokrates and Chairephon,
> For taking us both for a ride.

PHEIDIPPIDES.
> I can't do that. I must respect the Prof.

STREPSIADES.
> You're joking. What about respect for Zeus?

PHEIDIPPIDES.
> Not Zeus again! You're living in the past.
> Zeus doesn't exist.

STREPSIADES.
> He does.

PHEIDIPPIDES.
1470 He doesn't.
> He's been given the elbow. The Great Wind rules.

STREPSIADES.

The Great Wind! You're potty, all of you.
Potty! You might as well believe in this!
*He picks up the pot from outside the
door of the Thinkery*[20].

Is this a god? It might as well be. Look!

He smashes it.

PHEIDIPPIDES.

I'm going. You're off your head. You're raving mad.

Exit.

STREPSIADES.

What a fool! What a bloody fool I was!
Fancy throwing out the gods, for Sokrates!

*He goes to his own door and picks up the statue of
Hermes.*

Hermes, dear old Hermes, don't be cross.
Don't shrivel me. Please try to understand.
I was dazzled by drivel...turned on by talk.   1480
But what am I going to do now? Please tell me.
Shall I sue them? Shall I take them to court?

He listens.

Eh? Pardon...? Yes...Yes... I've got it.
Don't sue them...burn down their drivel-house.

*He puts the statue back, and flings open the door
of his house.*

Xanthias! Come out here. Quickly! Bring
A ladder, and that big crowbar. Hurry.

SLAVES *bustle about, setting up ladders, bringing
crowbars, axes and torches.*

Yes. Now, get up there and start ripping off
Their tiles. Total demolition. Do what I say!
Give me a torch, someone. I'll pay them back.   1490
I'll show them. They won't wriggle out of this.

*He takes a torch and climbs up to the roof
of the Thinkery. Fire, smoke, noise.*

STUDENTS (*inside*).
Help! Fire!

STREPSIADES.
In you go, torch! Set the whole place on fire.

STUDENTS *rush out.*

FIRST STUDENT.
Hey! What are you doing?

STREPSIADES.
Me? Splitting *hairs...*
Just making...*sure*...your *tiles*...get the *point*...

SECOND STUDENT.
Help! Who's burning the Thinkery?

STREPSIADES.
The man whose cloak you stole. Remember?

THIRD STUDENT.
Oh help! We're done for.

STREPSIADES.
1500   That's right. Just wait till I come down...
Whoops! Not quite so fast. You've had it now.

*SOKRATES comes out, coughing and spluttering.
STREPSIADES is above his head.*

SOKRATES.
Hey! You! What are you doing up there?

STREPSIADES.
I ride the air and ponder on the Sun.

SOKRATES.
I... Grooh!... Ergh!... The smoke... I'm choked.

A STUDENT.
Well, look at *me!* I've been fried to a *crisp!*

STREPSIADES *scrambles down.*

STREPSIADES.
I'll teach you. I'll teach you to laugh at the gods,
And look at the Moon when she's gone to bed!
Bang! Wallop! Smash! Pay them back
For everything... but especially for mocking the gods.

He chases them out. The CHORUS *gathers on the
deserted stage.*

CHORUS.
Lead the way out.
No more dancing today.   1510
It's all done. We've reached...

THE END.

BIRDS

Characters

EUELPIDES
PEITHETAIROS
AIDE
TEREUS
PRIEST
POET
ORACLE-SELLER
METON
INSPECTOR GENERAL
LAW-SELLER
WATCHMAN
MESSENGER
IRIS
YOB
KINESIAS
INFORMER
PROMETHEUS
POSEIDON
HERAKLES
BIGGUN

silent parts:

BIRDS (ruddy-rump, Arabian stork, hairy hoopoe, yellow
   streak)
CHAIRIS (flute-player)
SLAVES (Xanthias, Manodoros, Manes and others
   unnamed)
SOVEREIGNTY
WITNESS

CHORUS OF BIRDS

*The foot of a cliff in the desert. There is a tree at
ground level, and thick undergrowth higher up. Enter
EUELPIDES and PEITHETAIROS. Each has a bird perched on
his arm.*

EUELPIDES (*to his bird*).
What? On? You *do* mean 'On'? To this tree here?

PEITHETAIROS (*to his bird*).
You're asking to get stuffed.

(*to* EUELPIDES)

She's cawing 'Back!'

EUELPIDES (*to his bird*).
Look, birdbrain. I'm telling you: we're lost.
And whichever way we go, we just get loster.

PEITHETAIROS.
I've had enough. I've walked a million miles
To please a bloody crow.

EUELPIDES.
I've worn my toes to stumps,
For this...this raven. I must be. Ravin'.

PEITHETAIROS.
Don't look at *me*. *I* don't know where we are.

EUELPIDES.
You mean you can't get home again from here?   10

PEITHETAIROS.
No. What d'you think I am? A boomerang?

EUELPIDES.
Oh god!

PEITHETAIROS.
Never mind 'Oh god'. Come *on*.

EUELPIDES.
I blame Philokrates. That bastard in the market.
That bird-seller, yesterday. Swore blind these two
Would take us to Tereus, His Hoopoeness,
King of the birds, 'Who used to be a man,
Until, hey presto, he changed into a bird.'

I *thought* it sounded odd.
All he was after was unloading these:
His little feathered friends. Just look at them.
They're rubbish. All they know is bite.

(*to his bird*)

20   Yes? Something else? A message winging through?
On? Not again! How can we? It's solid rock.

PEITHETAIROS.
It's the same this side. There's nothing.

(*to his bird*)

Pardon, darling?

EUELPIDES.
Aha! Sense at last? About the road?

PEITHETAIROS.
Not exactly.

EUELPIDES.
What then?

PEITHETAIROS.
She's peckish. Wants a finger. Now.

EUELPIDES.
Why do I always listen? Why do I never learn?
'Go to the birds,' you said. 'We're unemployed;
We're starving. Let's pack, and flit, and fly.'
Go to the birds! We could have stayed at home,
Stuffed the birds, gone directly to the dogs.

(*to the audience*)

30   Ladies and gentlemen! Haha! I see you came.
We've got a problem here. We're sick – I mean,
We're from Athens, The Cradle of Democracy,
The Glory That Is Greece, and *still* we're sick.
Honest citizens...lifetime of service...
And we want to leave. It's not that we hate the
    place.

It's big, and fine, and free... The trouble is,
Grasshoppers hop in the grass and sing
For a couple of months, and then that's that.
But Athenians perch in the lawcourts and twitter   40
Their whole existences, their lives away.
That's what inspired this little expedition.
We took our basket, our firepot, our bits of twigs,
And set out to find somewhere else to put down roots,
A place where lawyers are a pest unknown.
That's why we need Tereus. His Hoopoeness.
He flies about a lot. He'll tell us where
To find the kind of place we're dreaming of.

PEITHETAIROS.
  Hey.

EUELPIDES.
  What now?

PEITHETAIROS.
  She's off again. Pointing up, this time.

EUELPIDES.
  So's mine.   50

  (*to his bird*)

  It's no use gawping at the sky. What d'you mean,
  'Birds are here. Make a noise. You'll see'?
  What sort of birds? What sort of noise?

PEITHETAIROS.
  You could kick the rock.

EUELPIDES.
  You give it a head-butt.
  Twice the noise.

PEITHETAIROS.
  Oh, knock it with a stone.

EUELPIDES.
  If you really think I should.

He knocks on the rock.

Hello. Hello.

PEITHETAIROS.
> What d'you mean, Hello?
> To call a hoopoe, one says, 'Yoohoo'.

EUELPIDES.
> Yoohoo? One's to knock again, and say 'Yoohoo?'

He does. A door is flung open in the rockface,
and the AIDE-BIRD *comes out.*

AIDE.
60   Who went 'Yoohoo'? Was it you? Was it you?

EUELPIDES.
> Apollo, what a beak.

AIDE.
> Bird-catchers! Aaargh!

EUELPIDES.
> That's not very nice.

AIDE.
> Oh? Tough.

EUELPIDES.
> I see your mistake. You think we're mortals.

AIDE.
> Aren't you?

EUELPIDES.
> Birds. I'm an African Squirtitout.

AIDE.
> There's no such thing.

EUELPIDES.
> Then what's this puddle, here?

AIDE.
70   *He's* not a bird.

PEITHETAIROS.
Of course I am: a Dungyrump.
It's a kind of ousel.

EUELPIDES.
And what are you? In god's name what are you?

AIDE.
A tweenytwink.

EUELPIDES.
We guessed. But apart from that?

AIDE.
When His Hoopoeness undertook the Change,
He went on his knees to me to change as well,
To run his errands, like when he was a man.

EUELPIDES.
So that's what it's for, a tweenytwink.

AIDE.
Despite the Change, he hasn't really changed.
He still gets cravings. 'Sardines!' he says,
And I fetch sardines. Or 'Soup!' he goes,
And I grab a dish and spoon and fetch him soup.

EUELPIDES.
How fetching. Fetch yourself inside, and fetch him
    out.   80

AIDE.
You're joking. He's just had lunch:
Three sunflower seeds and a brace of gnats.
He's having his siesta.

EUELPIDES.
So, wake him.

AIDE.
He won't like that.
But since you ask so nicely...

He goes in.

PEITHETAIROS.
So nicely! We're lucky we survived.

EUELPIDES.
My raven's scarpered. Done a runner. Flown.

PEITHETAIROS.
You let it go, you mean. You were scared
And you let it go.

EUELPIDES.
So where's your crow?

PEITHETAIROS.
Ah.

EUELPIDES.
What d'you mean, ah?

PEITHETAIROS.
90   Her flight came up.

EUELPIDES.
Your fright, you mean.

TEREUS (*inside*).
Unbar the bushes. Sir will take the air.

The upper undergrowth is moved aside,
revealing TEREUS, the hoopoe, on his nest.

EUELPIDES.
Good god, what's that? A duster? An eiderdown?
A flying jumble sale?

TEREUS.
Speak up!
Who ist who summoneth?

EUELPIDES.
Good question. Here's another:
Who ist who plucketh you?

TEREUS.
That's not my fault. *I once was mortal too.*

EUELPIDES.
> Your feathers aren't the joke.
> No joke at all.

TEREUS.
> What then?

EUELPIDES.
> Your beak.

TEREUS.
> You can't blame me. Blame Sophocles.   100
> He put me in that tragedy. *Tereus.* Ever so sad.
> Made me change from human being to bird – and here I
>   am.

EUELPIDES.
> You *are* His Hoopoeness! You *are* a bird!

TEREUS.
> Did I say I wasn't?

EUELPIDES.
> Those feathers...

TEREUS.
> I'm moulting.

EUELPIDES.
> You've not been well?

TEREUS.
> No, dummy. It's the time of year.
> We all moult now. New feathers grow.
> So, I'm a bird. So, what are you?

EUELPIDES.
> We're mortals.

TEREUS.
> Ah.

EUELPIDES.
> Athenians.

TEREUS.
Lawyers.

EUELPIDES.
Anti-lawyers.

TEREUS.
110   They don't grow anti-lawyers there.

EUELPIDES.
We're special. Endangered species. Rare.

TEREUS.
But why come here?

EUELPIDES.
To talk to you.

TEREUS.
What about?

EUELPIDES.
You used to be a man. Like us.
You had your little debts. Like us.
You hated paying up. Like us.
Then you changed. You turned from man to bird.
You flew...everywhere. Sky, sea,
You've seen it all, you know it all.
There's no human being alive, no bird, like you.
120   So we've come to ask: have you ever seen
A city, warm, soft, snug, like a blanket
We can wrap ourselves up in, and live in peace?

TEREUS.
Somewhere better than Athens?

EUELPIDES.
Not better. More *comfortable*.

TEREUS.
A nanny state?

EUELPIDES.
That gets my goat.

TEREUS.
Be more specific. Spell it out.

EUELPIDES.
The sort of place where nothing's ever worse
Than when a friend comes knocking at your door
And says, 'Get up, get washed, come round at once,   130
You and the kids. We're having a wedding feast.
Don't fail me now – or if you do, don't try
Crawling round when my luck is...bad.' That sort of
     place.

TEREUS.
You certainly know how to suffer. What about you?

PEITHETAIROS.
Same sort of thing.

TEREUS.
For example?

PEITHETAIROS.
I'm minding my own business. This chap turns up.
He's a father. Really hunky son. Dad's furious.
'You bastard!' he says. 'Just exactly what's going on?
You meet my laddie here outside the baths,   140
And you don't kiss him or cuddle him or bounce his
     balls –
What kind of friend are you, anyway?'

TEREUS.
He may well ask.
There is one place. Fits every requirement.
Beside the Red Sea.

EUELPIDES.
No, no, no, no. Far too much beach.[21]
Have you nowhere in Greece?

TEREUS.
There's Lepreos.

EUELPIDES.

150   Is that a town or a tropical disease?
It always makes me think of Melanthios.
I can't think why.

TEREUS.

Opous?

EUELPIDES.

Sounds much too classical. Opus what?
Hang on. What's life like here?
What sort of life do birds lead?
You should know.

TEREUS.

Pretty cosy. No money, for a start.

EUELPIDES.

I bet that cuts the crime rate.

TEREUS.

We take what comes. This garden or that garden.
We seek out seeds, we banquet on berries,
160   We nibble nuts.

EUELPIDES.

Nibble nuts? Sounds painful.

PEITHETAIROS.

Got it! This is great!
It's brilliant! You birds have got it made
If you listen to me, do exactly as I say.

TEREUS.

Do what?

PEITHETAIROS.

Shut your beaks for a start. Stop twittering.
You've got a dreadful reputation. In Athens,
We're always talking about people swanning about,
Being hen-pecked, rooking their neighbours –
170   Not to mention 'Aren't you the flighty one?"

TEREUS.
 Don't go on. What else should we do?

PEITHETAIROS.
 Build one single state.

TEREUS.
 One bird-state. Why?

PEITHETAIROS.
 It's obvious, fool. Look down.

TEREUS.
 Yes.

PEITHETAIROS.
 Up.

TEREUS.
 Yes.

PEITHETAIROS.
 Round. No, round.

TEREUS.
 What's the good of looking round if I crick my neck?

PEITHETAIROS.
 What d'you see?

TEREUS.
 Clouds. Sky.

PEITHETAIROS.
 Precisely. Your sphere.

TEREUS.
 Pardon?

PEITHETAIROS.
 Your sphere. Here. This is all your sphere.   180
 It goes round and round, doesn't it, round and round
 And round? That's why it's called a sphere.
 So all you have to do is build a wall.
 Surround it. One fortified, enormous nest.

Who do you lord it over now? Grasshoppers, flies.
Then, it'll be the whole human race. Lock, stock
And barrel. Not to mention starving out the gods.
It worked with the Melians[22].

TEREUS.

I don't quite follow.

PEITHETAIROS.

Look: mortals are *there*,
The gods are *there*, and the birds are here,
Right in the middle. When we take a trip
From Athens to Delphi, we go past Thebes.
We have to get a visa. We have to pay.
190   This is just the same. When mortals sacrifice
To the gods down *there*, it has to pass through *here*
To get up *there*. You tax it on the way.
No tax, no food. The gods fork out, or starve.

TEREUS.

Ee-oo! Ee-oo!
Nets, traps and snares, it's brilliant!
Build state...boss human race...starve gods...
We'll do it. That is, we'll put it to the vote.
We'll gather the birds, and put it to the vote.

PEITHETAIROS.

Who'll explain it?

TEREUS.

You will.

PEITHETAIROS.

But I don't speak –

TEREUS.

No problem: I've taught them Greek.
200   They're far more cultured than they were before.

PEITHETAIROS.

But how will you call them?

TEREUS.
    No problem. I step in here,
    Behind this bush, and wake my nightingale.
    She plays; I sing; they flock to hear.

PEITHETAIROS.
    You feathery genius! Beak of beaks! Well done!
    Well, don't just stand there. Step and wake and sing.

TEREUS.
    Up, darling, come, wake up.
    Weep now for Itys,
    Our dear son, weep for him,   210
    Pure sounds from tawny throat
    Throbbing, echoing,
    Echoing in the woods,
    High, high to the throne of Zeus
    Where red-haired Apollo hears,
    Takes his golden lyre,
    Fretted with ivory,
    Plucks chords to answer you,
    And the gods dance, dance for Itys,
    Weep immortal tears
    Singing for Itys,   220
    For Itys.

    A flute is heard.

PEITHETAIROS.
    Lord Zeus, what a pretty sound!
    Hear how it honeys all the wood.

EUELPIDES.
    Hey.

PEITHETAIROS.
    Shh!

EUELPIDES.
    Why?

PEITHETAIROS.
    He hasn't finished.

TEREUS.
    E-po-po-ee, po-po-po-po-po-po-po-ee,
    Ee-oh, ee-oh, ku-ku-ku-ku-ku-ku-
    Come, all of you: come and hear me now.
230   Birds of rich farmland,
    Swooping, soaring behind the plough,
    Pecking up corn-seed, barley,
    Darting, settling in the furrows,
    Calling, soft voices calling:
    Tiou, tiou, tiou, tiou, tiou, tiou, tiou, tiou[23].
    Garden-birds, feasting on berries,
    Swooping to secret nests
    Where ivy tendrils curl;
    Birds of the hills,
240   Whose banquets are olives, arbutus,
    Hurry, fly and hear:
    Triotou, triotou, totobrinx.
    Marsh-birds, birds of ditch and fen,
    Who plane after midges, snapping, snapping;
    Birds of the water-meadows, cool and green;
    Kingfisher, godwit, francolin.
    Birds whose pastures are the sea,
250   The endless, swelling sea,
    Gulls, terns, cormorants,
    Fly to me, hurry, hear.
    Hear what he has to say,
    This shrewd old man
    With his sharp new plan
    And his big idea.
    Hurry now and hear,
    Come, come, come, come, come, come, come.
260   Toro-toro-toro-toro-tinx,
    Kikka-baou, kikka-baou,
    Toro-toro-toro-toro-lili-linx.

PEITHETAIROS.
    See anything?

EUELPIDES.
    Not a bloody thing. I'm standing here

With my eyes on stalks, and...nothing.
After all that hopping into thickets,
All those bird-impressions, all that hoopoeing –
What a waste of time.

FIRST BIRD.
Torotinx, torotinx.

PEITHETAIROS.
Just a minute. Isn't that a bird?

EUELPIDES.
Of course it's a bird.

Enter FIRST BIRD.

Or is it?

PEITHETAIROS.
What is it?

EUELPIDES.
His Hoopoeness will tell us. Oi. What's that?   270

TEREUS.
That's one of our rarer species. A migrant.
Salt-pan habitat.

EUELPIDES.
Never mind its habit, look at its tail.
What a ruddy marvel!

TEREUS.
It *is* a ruddy-rump.

Enter SECOND BIRD.

EUELPIDES.
Look, look, look!

PEITHETAIROS.
Stop shouting. What?

EUELPIDES.
Another one.
What is it? A ladder? A drainpipe? A man on stilts?

TEREUS.
An Arabian stork.

EUELPIDES.
You're joking. Arabian?
It can't be. No camel.

Enter THIRD BIRD.

PEITHETAIROS.
Hey!
Another one. I've seen that sort before.
280   Well, almost. It's not...? I thought you were unique.

TEREUS.
Not quite. This is my cousin. My distant cousin.
The Hairy Hoopoe. We try to keep it quiet.

PEITHETAIROS.
It must be hell to pluck.

TEREUS.
Don't use that word!
You've done it now. He'll not come out for weeks.

Enter FOURTH BIRD.

EUELPIDES.
Gods, not another one! What's this one called?

TEREUS.
The yellow streak.

EUELPIDES.
There can't be two of them.
We've got Kleonymos.

TEREUS.
290   That's not Kleonymos. No shield to shed.

PEITHETAIROS.
I wish I followed this. Do birds shed shields?
I wish I could say that.

EUELPIDES.
Don't bother now.

They're all here. A swarm, a stageful: look!
Fluttering and flapping. No room! No room!

Enter CHORUS.

TEREUS.
Partridge, francolin, mallard, kingfisher,
Pansy –

EUELPIDES.
Pansies are flowers, not birds.

TEREUS.
Take another look.   300
Swallow. Second swallow.

EUELPIDES.
I suppose they're trying to make a summer[24].

TEREUS.
Wheatear, reed-warbler, cuckoo, nuthatch, lark,
Pelican, cormorant, albatross, sea-eagle, wren,
Parrot, canary, ostrich, sparrow, stork,
Falcon, kestrel, merlin, buzzard, kite,
Woodpecker – [25]

EUELPIDES.
Birds! Birds! Twittering, whirling, diving...
Just a minute. Diving? Are they friendly?
Their beaks are open. They're coming this way.

PEITHETAIROS.
Get down!

CHORUS.
Hoo-hoo-hoo-hoo-hoo-hoo-hoo-hoo-hoo   310
Who-hoo-hoo ko-ko-ko-ko-ko-called?
Where is he?

TEREUS.
Here. I called. This way.

CHORUS.
Dee-fe-dee-fe-dee-fe dear friend,

Te-te-te-te-te-te-te-te tell us,
Tell us why.

TEREUS.
I've news to share: fat, juicy news.
Two mortals have come, with bulging brains –

CHORUS.
Who? Where? Why?

TEREUS.
320   Two brilliant, wise old men,
With a mighty, magnificent idea.

CHORUS.
Traitor! I've never heard of such a thing!
Since I was a chick in arms...

TEREUS.
No need to panic.

CHORUS.
What have you done?

TEREUS.
Two strangers came, asking for asylum.
I welcomed them.

CHORUS.
Welcomed them?

TEREUS.
Welcomed them.

CHORUS.
You mean they're here, now? *Here?*

TEREUS.
As here as I am.

CHORUS.
Ee-ah, ee-ah,
Betrayed and cheated,
Tricked, defeated.
330   He grew with us,
Flew with us,

Gave us his word
He was truly a bird –
And then, and then,
Handed us to men:
Our enemy, our curse.
What could be worse?

We'll deal with him later. First, for *them*.
May I suggest – kill them? Peck them to pieces?

PEITHETAIROS.
  We've had it.

EUELPIDES.
  It's all your fault.

PEITHETAIROS.
  You wanted to come.   340

EUELPIDES.
  But not to come to grief.
  We'll be crying for mercy.

PEITHETAIROS.
  Of course we won't.
  How will we cry, with our eyes pecked out?

CHORUS.
  Ee-oh, ee-oh.
  Charge them, barge them,
  Peck them, wreck them.
  Diminish them,
  Then finish them.
  Don't let them hide,
  Peck your prey with pride.
  No peak, no wave
  Their lives will save.
  If they try to fly   350
  Make 'em cry, make 'em die.

Why are we waiting? Action stations!
Poking and pecking. Where's the wing commander?

EUELPIDES.
Oh well, that's that. 'Scuse me.

PEITHETAIROS.
What is it now? Stand still.

EUELPIDES.
And be torn to bits? No thanks.

PEITHETAIROS.
So where are you going to run?

EUELPIDES.
How should I know?

PEITHETAIROS.
No running. Stay and fight. Take this.

EUELPIDES.
A ladle?

PEITHETAIROS.
An owl-club. Look. If those owls
Come closer, bop them. *Make* them 'owl.

EUELPIDES.
Never mind owls. There's eagles.

PEITHETAIROS.
Kebab-sticks. Ha! On guard!

EUELPIDES.
360   What about my eyes?

PEITHETAIROS.
Here. Wear this sieve.

EUELPIDES.
And what d'you suggest I do with *this*, or *this?*

CHORUS.
Chocks away, chaps. Take the air.
Rip, rend, bite, beak, tear.

TEREUS.
Hang on. What's *wrong* with you?

You can't do that. These are Athenians,
Her Ladyship's cousins. You can't beak them.

CHORUS.
Athenians? The worst. They're cats,
They're ferrets. Of course we'll beak them.   370

TEREUS.
Not ferrets. *Friends.*
They've come to help, with good advice.

CHORUS.
Good advice? You're joking.
My feathered father's fearsome foes?

TEREUS.
Exactly. All of that. If you've any sense.
Don't people keep telling you, 'Be prepared'?
Well, who d'you prepare against, friends or foes?
Do cities build watchtowers because of friends or foes?
Not to mention warfleets and long, long walls,
To protect their wives, their children, all they own.   380

CHORUS.
'Be prepared', you say. 'Learn from your foes.'
'Wives, children, all they own.' All right. We'll listen.

PEITHETAIROS (*to* EUELPIDES).
They're calming down. Relax a bit.

TEREUS.
That's better. You'll thank me later.

CHORUS.
Don't we always? Whatever you suggest?

PEITHETAIROS.
They're calm at last. Take off the sieve.
Put the saucers down.
Hang on to your spear,
Your kebab-stick, here.
Patrol the pots,   390
Peer over the pans.

'On guard!' Be hard.
Don't flinch. Don't give an inch.

EUELPIDES.
But if we die,
Where will we lie?

PEITHETAIROS.
Where d'you think?
We're bold and brave.
In a hero's grave
By the kitchen sink.

CHORUS.
400   OK, chaps. Down!
Don't frown.
Be cool, be calm.
Break out the charm.
Let's get it plain.
Let's hear them explain.
Suggestions, questions...
Your Hoopoeness, please speak.

TEREUS.
First question, then.

CHORUS.
Who are these men?

TEREUS.
They're wise. They're Greek.

CHORUS.
410   So why come here?

TEREUS.
That's very clear.
They're in love, they *care:*
Your little ways,
How you spend your days...
They want to share –

CHORUS.
  You can't be serious.
  They told you *that?*

TEREUS.
  Much more than that.
  It *is* mysterious.

CHORUS.
  Say that again.
  Two *men?*
  Just ask yourself: what
  Has bird-life got   420
  For *them?* Yummies for chummies
  Or woes for foes?

TEREUS.
  You've got it wrong. It's this:
  He's offering you bliss
  Beyond belief, beyond compare.
  You're lords, he says, of there,
  And *there*, and over *there* –
  Of everywhere.

CHORUS.
  A loony.

TEREUS.
  Sane as sane.

CHORUS.
  A bulging brain?

TEREUS.
  Not puny.   430
  He's nifty, shifty,
  Fly, dry, sly,
  And as for bright –
  Quite out of sight.

CHORUS.
  You've done it now. I'm weak
  At the knees, I'm shaking;

I'm quivering, I'm aching
To hear him speak.

TEREUS (*to* SLAVES).
You...you...take this hardware
And hang it in the kitchen.
On the what's-it, yes. Now, you:
Tell them what we summoned them to hear.

PEITHETAIROS.
Not a chance.
440   I want a treaty first. Like the marriage contract
That knife-grinder made with his great big wife:
No biting, no tearing, no scratching,
No pecking the pectorals,
Tearing the testicles,
Shoving sharp objects up the –

CHORUS.
Stop!

PEITHETAIROS.
Nose, I was going to say.

CHORUS.
We wouldn't *dream* –

PEITHETAIROS.
So swear.

CHORUS.
We swear. On one condition: you guarantee
That we win first prize. Unanimous.

PEITHETAIROS.
I guarantee.

CHORUS.
And that if we break our word, we lose –
Nothing. One vote's enough to win.

TEREUS.
ALL FIGHTING BIRDS, STAND DOWN.
ALL WEAPONS TO THE STORES. GO HOME.

PERCH BY FOR FURTHER ORDERS.
   MESSAGE ENDS.   450

Bustle as the military formation disintegrates.
Meanwhile:

CHORUS.
  Who trusts the human race?
  They're an absolute disgrace.
  None the less, speak out,
  With your wit surprise us.
  What have we missed?
  Give us the gist.
  Say what it's all about.
  What is this news? Advise us.
  What's on your mind? This is your moment:
    take it.   460
  We gave our word to be good, and we won't break it.

PEITHETAIROS.
  I'm bursting to start. I've kneaded the dough,
  And it's rising, rising. Fetch me an ivy-wreath,
  And some water to wash my hands.

EUELPIDES.
  Going to have dinner, are we?

PEITHETAIROS.
  Dinner, no. A feast of words, fat and sumptuous.
  It'll knock them for six. Aherrm. My friends,
  How I grieve for you. Once you were kings –

CHORUS.
  Us? Kings? Who of?

PEITHETAIROS.
  Everyone. Me, him, Zeus himself.
  You were here before the gods, before the giants,
  Before the Titans, before Mother Earth –

CHORUS.
  Mother Earth?

PEITHETAIROS.
Mother Earth.

CHORUS.
470   Impossible.

PEITHETAIROS.
Oh, I'm sorry. You never went to school.
Never learned to think. Never heard of Aesop.
Don't you remember his Fable of Miss Lark?
'Once upon a time, before time began,
Before Mother Earth existed, there was Miss Lark.
Her poor old Daddy died. No Mother Earth,
No place to dig a grave. She laid him out,
She thought about it for four long days,
Then she dreamed of a grave, and buried him
Inside her head.'

EUELPIDES.
Isn't it clever? What a lark!

PEITHETAIROS.
The point is, if you were here before the gods,
You're older than they are, and you should rule.

EUELPIDES.
Beak-sharpeners, that's all you need.
Lord Zeus won't like you perching on his throne.
Mind you: two woodpeckers, he won't have a
480   throne.

PEITHETAIROS.
In the good old days, birds ruled the human race.
Not gods: you birds. I'll give you an example.
In Persia, who used to be King of Kings?
Darius? Xerxes? Megabates? Mr Cock.
He strutted up and down, he swished his tail, he
crowed.

EUELPIDES.
And he still has that red thing on his head,
And keeps a harem. They're all the same.

PEITHETAIROS.
　He was Beak of Beaks, the Voice Supreme.
　When he spoke, they jumped. And we still do.
　Every morning, he opens his beak and we're off:
　Blacksmiths, potters, tanners, armourers,　　　　　490
　Bakers, carpenters, cobblers – we grab our shoes,
　We're off.

EUELPIDES.
　You're telling me. It's all his fault.
　I used to have a cloak, a woolly cloak,
　But thanks to him... I'd been to a party,
　Wet the baby's head, know what I mean,
　And I was dozing off, when out of the blue
　He started crowing. The Voice Supreme!
　It wasn't even dinner-time. But up I jumped,
　Stuck my nose outside, and *bam!* Mugged, stripped,
　Decloaked – and all because of *him:*
　Mr Beak of Beaks who never could tell the time.

PEITHETAIROS.
　When Cock retired, a buzzard ruled the Greeks.

CHORUS.
　A buzzard?

PEITHETAIROS.
　He taught them that song. You know:
　'Let's all sing like the birdies sing...'　　　　　500

EUELPIDES.
　Don't remind me. I once knew all the words:
　'Tweet-tweet-tweet', all the actions.
　I was walking home. No purse. Coins in my mouth,
　For safety. Buzzard appears. 'Tweet-tweet-tweet'.
　Swallow the lot. No dinner.

PEITHETAIROS.
　The Egyptians were cuckoo for cuckoos.
　Whenever a cuckoo went 'Cuckoo!', they rushed
　To the paddy-fields and grabbed their tools and –

EUELPIDES.
This *is* a family show.

PEITHETAIROS.
You've heard of Agamemnon? Menelaus? Names
like that?
Warlords. Sceptre-swingers. In battle, big.
And what was always on the end of their sceptres?
Birds, keeping watch on Their Majesties' greasy
510   palms.

EUELPIDES.
We should give Lysikrates one of those.

PEITHETAIROS.
It's exactly the same with gods.
Zeus is a king – and who guards him?
An eagle. Athene has an owl; Apollo has a hawk.

EUELPIDES.
So they have. I've always wondered why.

PEITHETAIROS.
Ancestral custom, idiot. Sacrificial custom.
Well, *someone* has be to on guard to snatch the
meat.
Another thing: in the good old days, no one swore
520   By gods, they always swore by birds.

EUELPIDES.
Like Lampon now. Not 'by Zeus': 'by Goose'.

PEITHETAIROS.
Ah, the good old days! When you were kings,
Respected as you deserved,
Not like idiots or slaves.
Now they pelt you with stones,
Now they net you and trap you and snare you –
Protected species? Don't make me laugh.
They sell you in bundles, by dozens.
530   They poke you, they pluck you,
They spit you, they roast you,

They stuff you with herbs,
They serve you in sauce,
In sweet-and-sour sauce,
Wine, vinegar, oil,
Smothering, scalding,
As though you'd no rights,
No rights at all.

CHORUS.
What a distressing story!
To lose such ancient glory!   540
Thank goodness fate
Has sent you here to lead us.
It's up to you.
Tell us what to do.
Only you can make us great:
Instruct us, guide us, feed us.
Tell us what to do. What do you suggest?
If I can't be king again, I'll be *so* depressed.

PEITHETAIROS.
First, build one single city for all the birds.   550
Then stick up a wall, right in the middle of the sky,
All round. Use huge big bricks, like Babylon.

TEREUS.
Like Babylon! Big bricks! That's what I call a wall.

PEITHETAIROS.
When it's finished, demand that Zeus abdicates.
And if he won't, if he wriggles and sulks,
Declare a holy war, and close the wall. No road.
No more pussy-hunts down to Earth from Heaven,
No more Alkmenes or Semeles or Alopes:
No more godultery. Penalty for non-observance:
An official bulldog-clip, right where it hurts.   560
Send a second messenger to mortals: BIRDS
    RULE STOP.
NEW ORDER OF SACRIFICE STOP. (1) BIRDS,
    (2) GODS STOP.
Before they honour each god with offerings,

They must honour a bird appropriate in rank and
    function.
Before Aphrodite (ex-sex-goddess): a turtle-dove.
Before Poseidon (washed-up sea-god): an albatross.
Before Herakles (big god, ate anything): an
    ostrich.
Before Zeus On High, Her Majesty the Wren:
He gets a rampant ram; she gets a muscly midge.

EUELPIDES.

570   Old Thunder-guts is going to be *so* cross!

CHORUS.

But how will they know we're gods, not birds,
If we still flap about, if we've still got wings?

PEITHETAIROS.

No problem. Doesn't Hermes flap about? Hasn't *he*
Got wings? They all have. It goes with the job.
Victory, Eros – you must have seen the statues.
Iris, buzzing about like a demented bee.

EUELPIDES.

And Zeus' thunderbolts have wings. I'm scared.

CHORUS.

Suppose they're too stupid to *see* we're gods?
Suppose they prefer Zeus, Demeter and the rest?

PEITHETAIROS.

Send seed-gatherers to strip their cornfields.

580   *Then* let them ask Demeter for a free delivery.

EUELPIDES.

Too corny. She'd never take the call.

PEITHETAIROS.

Send crows to peck out the eyes of their oxen,
Their sheep, their cattle – then let them beg
Apollo the Healer to help. Can they afford vet
    fees?

EUELPIDES (*to the audience*).
That reminds me: cows for sale.

PEITHETAIROS.
On the other hand, if they *do* bow down,
If they put *you* up there with Mother Earth,
Old Father Time, Poseidon, what blessings will be
  theirs!

CHORUS.
What blessings?

PEITHETAIROS.
No more locusts guzzling their grapelets:
One squadron of owls, and that's the end of them.
No more blowflies filching their figlets: 590
We'll have a battalion of thrushes on pest control.

TEREUS.
But how can we give them wealth? That's what they
  want.

PEITHETAIROS.
Aerial surveys. Tell 'em where the goldmines are.
Map out their trade routes in advance. Thanks to you,
They'll never lose a ship.

TEREUS.
Why not?

PEITHETAIROS.
Weather forecasting.
'It's stormy ahead; don't sail.' 'Fair winds today:
You should do very nicely.'

EUELPIDES (*to the audience*).
Wanted: a merchant ship.

PEITHETAIROS.
All over the world, there are treasure-hoards,
Buried by their ancestors. Only you know where.   600
And, as you *also* know, 'A little bird told me...'
You can spill the beans.

EUELPIDES (*to the audience*).
   Stuff merchant ships. Who's got a spade?

TEREUS.
   What about good health? Only gods grant that.

PEITHETAIROS.
   No problem. If they're wealthy, they're healthy.

EUELPIDES.
   No cash: that's what really makes them sick.

TEREUS.
   But they die so *young*. We can't extend their lives.

PEITHETAIROS.
   Of course you can. Three hundred years each.

TEREUS.
   Where from?

PEITHETAIROS.
   You live much faster lives than they do.
   One of your years equals dozens of theirs.
   So hand a few over. It's in all the books.

EUELPIDES.
610   They'll be far better kings than Zeus.

PEITHETAIROS.
   Exactly.
   You won't have to build
   Huge stone temples
   With gorgeous golden gates.
   Birds live in thickets, shrubs:
   To them, an olive-twig's a shrine.
   You won't have to make
   Pilgrimages
   To Delphi or Ammon to sacrifice –
   Make offerings wherever you are:
   A handful of barley,
620   Chucked in the bushes,
   A word or two of prayer
   And whatever you want is yours.

Goodies for barley-seeds:
That has to be a bargain.

CHORUS.
What a master-plan!
What a wise old man!
How did we ever misjudge him?
I give you my word –
That's my word as a bird –   630
That we'll do as you say,
That we'll do things your way:

We'll tackle Lord Zeus and we'll budge him.
We'll hustle and bustle,
We'll shoulder the strain.
We'll supply all the muscle,
If you bring the brain.

TEREUS.
Right. No more wittering and twittering.
Nikias can see to that.   640
It's time for action. Step inside my nest –
A few twigs and branches, but it's home to me.
Wait a minute: we haven't been introduced.

PEITHETAIROS.
I'm Peithetairos –

EUELPIDES.
Persuader.

PEITHETAIROS.
And he's Euelpides –

EUELPIDES.
Optimist.

TEREUS.
You honour my humble home.

PEITHETAIROS.
How kind.

TEREUS.
Step this way, would you?

PEITHETAIROS.
After you.

TEREUS.
No, no, I insist.

EUELPIDES.
Hang on. Just a minute. What I mean is,
650 How can we live with you? We don't have wings.

TEREUS.
No problem.

EUELPIDES.
You're joking. Don't you know
What happened to the fox that tried to fly?

TEREUS.
It's easy. Wing-wort.

EUELPIDES.
Pardon?

TEREUS.
Wing-wort.
Inside. One nibble, you'll be as high as kites.

EUELPIDES.
In *that* case... Xanthias, Manodoros, pick up the
bags.

CHORUS.
Sir, sir, your Hoopoeness, oh sir.

TEREUS.
You called?

CHORUS.
Take these gentlemen inside, and give them lunch.
But send us out our nightingale, our darling,
660 Our own beloved Muse, to play with us.

PEITHETAIROS.
>Please do. The little darling!
>Call inside, and ask her out.

EUELPIDES.
>Oh, please, the nightingale, oh please.
>We're dying to see her, to feast our eyes.

TEREUS.
>All right, if you say so. Prokne, darling,
>We've visitors. Come out and say hello.

>*The flute-player* CHAIRIS *comes out, in*
>*nightingale-mask and costume*[26].

PEITHETAIROS.
>What a gorgeous creature! Those feathers!
>So soft! So fine!

EUELPIDES.
>So ripe for ruffling!

PEITHETAIROS.
>Look at all that gold, like a virgin bride.   670

EUELPIDES.
>I think I'll give her a little kiss.

PEITHETAIROS.
>You fool!
>There's a pecker under there. Beware!

EUELPIDES.
>It's easy, look: just like shelling an egg...

>*He takes off* CHAIRIS' *mask, and kisses him.*

TEREUS.
>Come on, come on.

PEITHETAIROS.
>My dear chap, *after* you.

>*Exeunt* TEREUS, PEITHETAIROS *and* EUELPIDES.

CHORUS.
Oh darling, tawny-throat,
Nightingale,
Beloved, come to us,
680   Come, sing with us.
Melting as honey,
Soft as spring,
Beloved, sing for us,
Play and sing for us.

Flute music. Then, over it:

Listen. You down there. Mortals. Leaves. Dreams.
Shadow-creatures. Mud-puppets. Pay heed
To your masters, the birds of the air,
The immortals, the favoured, the ever-young.
We'll explain. Pay attention, and learn:
690   How the universe came into being:
Birds, gods, rivers, emptiness, dark –
Chuck your schoolbooks away. This is IT.
First of all there was nothing. No light,
No existence. Just emptiness, space.
In that fathomless, featureless dark,
Night mated with Storm, laid an egg,
And began all creation. Desire,
Golden-winged, iridescent, aglow,
Hatched and mated with Emptiness; birds
Were their nestlings, first creatures of light.
700   Soon the rest of the universe hatched:
Mother Earth, Sky, Sea, gods above.
We're the oldest powers, heirs of Desire,
And we'll prove it. Just picture the scene:
Blushing virgin, a little alarmed,
Not quite certain – till lover-boy sends
One of *us*, pigeon, partridge, goose, cock.
We're your friends. We're essential. We *help*.
For example, the seasons. Each year
710   When the cranes start migrating, you know
Winter's coming. No sailing; sow seeds;
Put warm clothes on. When kites fill the sky,

That's a signal it's spring. Shearing-time.
When the swallows of summer appear
Shed those winter clothes, wear something light.
And another thing. Forecasts. Forget
Holy pilgrimages, oracles, shrines:
We'll advise you. Big business, love, sex,
Family problems: we cover them all.
You're besotted with omens and charms:
When you both speak at once, or you sneeze
It's good luck; when a slave sings a song   720
Or a donkey ee-aws, it's good luck.
Well, in future *we're* lucky. Choose us.

We're available, friends,
Not aloof like the gods.
Zeus up there never bends,
Never dozes or nods.
We won't hide in the sky
With a snooty expression;
We'll accept every cry,
We'll make every concession.
Peace, happiness, wealth,
Smiling fortune, long lives
In the pink of good health
For your good selves, your wives   730
And your kids: all you need,
Milk and honey,
Piles of money,
Guaranteed.

Woodland Muse,
Tiou, tiou, tiou, tiou, tiou, tiou, tioutinx[25],
All birds who sing with us
In forests, on hillsides,   740
Tiou, tiou, tiou, tioutinx,
As we perch among the leaves,
Tiou, tiou, tiou, tioutinx,
Singing from tawny throats,
As we weave our songs for Pan,
For Cybele, Mother of All,

Toto, toto, toto, toto, totinx,
Sweet songs, like nectar sipped
By the poets of old,
750   A garland, the good old songs.
Tiou, tiou, tiou, tioutinx.

Ladies and gentlemen, are you *happy?*
Problem-free? If so, good luck. If not,
May I recommend: life with the birds?
For example, in trouble with the law?
You beat up your Daddy? No problem here.
It's *expected* here. Every fighting cock
Must challenge his dear old Dad to win his spurs.
You, over there. You're too conspicuous:
760   Arrow-suits, on humans, give the game away.
But here, who'd notice? You've heard of jailbirds...?

Ah! Spintharos. How are things at home?
Another application for citizenship?
Come to us. We've a twig and a perch for everyone –
I mean, we take Carians, we'd take Exekestides.
Who's that cowering there? Not *Peisias'* little boy?
What d'you say? Scared? Want to run away
Like Daddy did? No need for that: join us.
We know all there is to know about ducks and
    quails.
So once they sang,
770   Tiou, tiou, tiou, tiou, tiou, tiou, tioutinx,
Swans sang for Apollo,
There by the riverside,
Tiou, tiou, tiou, tioutinx,
As they flew on creaking wings,
Tiou, tiou, tiou, tioutinx,
Songs like mist, mist rising;
All creation pricked to hear,
Waves on the shore fell silent,
Toto, toto, toto, toto, totinx,
780   Olympos itself stood still,
Its lords struck dumb, as the Graces,

The Muses, echoed the rising song.
Tiou, tiou, tiou, tioutinx.

There's nothing better than a pair of wings.
If you had wings – yes, you, or you, or you –
And you suddenly felt peckish sitting there,
I mean *really* peckish, you could flap off home,
Fix yourself a sandwich and swoop right back.   790
It's the middle of the play, you're taken short –
Soar up, drop your load, fly down again:
Don't even *think* about clean underwear.
Or say you fancy someone's else's wife.
You see him here: in the posh seats, there,
Wedged in with his party. You spread your wings –
The ones *we* gave you – you flutter off,
Find his old lady, fuck and flutter back.
Wings are *worth* it. Need more proof?
Shall I mention Dieitrephes? Last year?
The basket-maker? Wove wicker wings,
Flew to the polls, got elected –
And's been feathering his own nest ever since.   800

Music, and a short dance. Then PEITHETAIROS
and EUELPIDES *come out. They are now*
equipped with wings.

PEITHETAIROS.
Well, there we are then. My god,
I've never seen anything funnier.

EUELPIDES.
What d'you mean?

PEITHETAIROS.
You and your wonderwings.
What *do* you look like? Old Mother Goose?

EUELPIDES.
What about you? A half-plucked duck?

PEITHETAIROS.
Only a bird in a gilded cage –
Isn't that Aeschylus?

EUELPIDES.
Can we please get on? What's first?

PEITHETAIROS.
First, we give the place a name. A good name,
810   One to roll round the tongue. Then we sacrifice.

EUELPIDES.
Name...sacrifice. OK by me.
What shall we call it, then?
Something impressive...
Sparta!

PEITHETAIROS.
Sparta? *Sparta?*
I wouldn't call a dog-blanket Sparta. I hate that
    word.
You call *Sparta* impressive?

EUELPIDES.
It impresses me.

PEITHETAIROS.
It ought to be something light, airy,
Billowing like clouds –

EUELPIDES.
Deceptively spacious –

PEITHETAIROS.
Cloudcuckooland?

EUELPIDES.
820   That's it! Cloudcuckooland.
Cloudcuckooland, where castles in the air are
    built:
Where Aischines is a financial colossus,
Theagenes a billionaire.

PEITHETAIROS.
Where gods outboasted giants:
Cloudcuckooland, on the Windy Plain of Brag.

EUELPIDES.
It rolls off the tongue: Cloudcuckooland.

PEITHETAIROS.
Now, we need a patron god. Any suggestions?

EUELPIDES.
Athene? She's got the shield.

PEITHETAIROS.
You're joking.
The last time *she* was in charge of a city –
Named after her, it was – you saw what happened.   830
Role-reversal. Think Kleisthenes. Think knitting.

EUELPIDES.
We're going to have battlements, aren't we?
A big stockade? We'll need a patron god.

PEITHETAIROS.
A patron bird, you mean. Storkade, you said.
Well, *I* say cock.

EUELPIDES.
Beg pardon?

PEITHETAIROS.
Cock.

EUELPIDES.
Ah, cock.
Perched high on the city rock: a cock.

PEITHETAIROS.
Good.
It's time, then. You've got to fly. High.
Up there. In the air. Give the builders a hand.
Hump hardcore, mix mortar, bring breezeblocks,
Scale scaffolding, fall,   840
Check the nightwatch,

Bank the brazier,
Take a bell and beat the bounds,
Bed down on the battlements –
Oh, and send off two messengers.
One up *there*, one down *there*.
When they come back, they must see me
    personally.

EUELPIDES (*crossly*).
See you personally in Hell?

PEITHETAIROS.
Don't argue. Don't grumble. Just go.
Who else can I trust? Who else knows all the
    ropes?

Exit EUELPIDES.

Right. Time to sacrifice. To the powers on high,
The new ones. What do we need? We need a priest.
850   But first... Slave! Fetch me a basket, a water-jug.

A SLAVE *sets up an altar and prepares for the
sacrifice. Meanwhile:*

CHORUS.
That's very good.
We think you should.
A sacrifice.
That's *very* nice.
Eeto, eeto, pray for us.
Chairis, Chairis, play for us.

Enter CHAIRIS, *now dressed as a crow, and playing
suitably raucous flute-music.*

PEITHETAIROS.
Hang on, hang on. Stop that. What are you?
A fluty crow? What's the...caws...of that?
860   There has to be a cause.

Enter PRIEST.

Ah, there you are. We want to sacrifice,
To the new powers that be. Can you manage that?

PRIEST.

My son, no problem. Where's the basket-bearer?
Let us pray. Nest-Hestia, O Kite of Might,
Immortal cocks, cockesses everywhere –

PEITHETAIROS.

O Puffin of Piety, fish-faced and water-winged –

PRIEST.

O Sacred Swan of Prophecy, of Delos, of Delphi,   870
O Bunting Artemis, O Leto, Quail-mother –

PEITHETAIROS.

Hail, quail.

PRIEST.

O Winter Finch, O Ostrich Mother of All the World –

PEITHETAIROS.

Especially Kleokritos. Have you *seen* him?

PRIEST.

Grant health, wealth and happiness
To Cloudcuckooland, not to mention the Chians –

PEITHETAIROS.

I won't if you won't. How did *they* get in?   880

PRIEST.

Come hero birds, and the birdlets they begat,
Come pelicans, come shags;
Come coots, come cranes;
Come sparrows, magpies, wrens;
Come gannets, swallows, hens;
Come eagles, hawks,
Come vultures, kites –

PEITHETAIROS.

Hang on! Vultures, kites? Have you *seen* that sheep?   890
One swallow and it's gone, never mind a kite.
Oh, go away. I'll do the job myself.

He shoos the PRIEST *out.*

CHORUS.
    Yes, good idea.
    We'll help. We're here.
    We'll kill the beast,
900   We'll make a feast –
    Hardly, hardly. Take a look.
    Skin and bones. Too small to cook.

PEITHETAIROS.
    As we make this sacrifice, we pray
    To bird-gods one and all –

Enter POET.

POET.
    Haunts of coot and tern! Cuckoo-echoing,
    Lark-charmed, rook-racked!
    Cloudcuckooland! Elysium!

PEITHETAIROS.
    Who the Hell are you?

POET.
    A poet. One of Dame Nature's craftsmen.
910   I flit; I pluck; I serve.

PEITHETAIROS.
    A long-haired freak.

POET.
    No, no, no.
    One of Dame Nature's craftsmen –
    As I think I said.

PEITHETAIROS.
    You've not come *here* to flit, and pluck, and serve?

POET.
    I've composed an ode celebrating your city,
    And a sonnet-sequence, and a limerick
    In the style of Simonides:
    There once was a town in the sky...

PEITHETAIROS.
    All that? Since when?   920

POET.
    Since days of yore, as we poets say.

PEITHETAIROS.
    Days of yore?
    It was only born five minutes ago.

POET.
    Poetic licence. When the Muses come
    It's like horses galloping, galloping.
    Just a moment, something's arriving now.
    He rules the mighty mountains,
    He rules the soggy sea;
    He's generous and kindly
    To artists, such as me –   930

PEITHETAIROS (*to the* SLAVE).
    He'll go on like this all night, unless...
    Look: you don't need *all* that gear.
    Strip off, and make a donation.

    (*to the* POET)

    Oi. Will this do? Warm up your limericks?

POET.
    Ah! *Lineaments of gratified desire.*
    Excuse me: another inspiration.

PEITHETAIROS.
    He *will* go on all night.   940

POET.
    Blow, blow, thou winter wind,
    When icicles hang by the wall,
    A cold coming we had of it...
    Something about *Snow had fallen,*
    *Snow on snow...*you know the one?

PEITHETAIROS.
    I know we're talking underwear.

(to the SLAVE)

Divest. We must all support the arts.

(to the POET)

Take this, and go.

POET.
I will, I will.
'Tis nearly morning; I must needs begone;
Oft have I travell'd in the realms of gold,
950   *Not to mention the forests, the forests of the night –*
Oft in the stilly night...the rest is silence.

Exit.

PEITHETAIROS.
I should think so, under all those clothes.
Who invited him? How did he sniff us out?
Never mind. Time to get on. Pick up
The holy water, and walk round the altar.
In the name of...

Enter ORACLE SELLER, *loaded with scrolls.*

ORACLE SELLER.
STOP! Don't gut that goat.

PEITHETAIROS.
Who are you?

ORACLE SELLER.
The oracle man.

PEITHETAIROS.
960   Bye bye.

ORACLE SELLER.
Don't be like that. Respect the Other Side.

He rummages among his scrolls.

I've a message here from Bakis. An oracle
Directly concerning Cloudcuckooland.

PEITHETAIROS.
Why didn't you say so before?

ORACLE SELLER.
The Powers prevented me.

PEITHETAIROS.
Get on with it.

ORACLE SELLER (*reading*).
WHEN WHITE-HEADED RAVENS AND WOLF-
PACKS
COME TOGETHER 'TWIXT SIKYON AND
CORINTH –

PEITHETAIROS.
Beg pardon. Corinth?

ORACLE SELLER.
It's what they call the air on the Other Side.   970
FIRST OFFER MOTHER EARTH A BAALAMB,
THEN OFFER MY SPOKESMAN THESE PRESENTS:
A NICE NEW CLOAK, A PAIR OF SANDALS –

PEITHETAIROS.
Excuse me. Sandals?

ORACLE SELLER.
See for yourself.
– AND SOME WINE AND A PLACE AT THE
BANQUET.

PEITHETAIROS.
I'm sorry. Banquet?

ORACLE SELLER.
See for yourself.
IF YOU LISTEN AND DO AS I TELL YOU
YOU'LL SOAR IN THE SKY LIKE AN EAGLE.
IF YOU DON'T, THEN YOU WON'T. NOT AN
EAGLE,
NOT EVEN A PIGEON, A SPARROW –

PEITHETAIROS.
That's in there?

ORACLE SELLER.
980   See for yourself.

PEITHETAIROS.
That's funny. Look at *this* one.
A BEGGAR WILL COME OUT OF NOWHERE
DEMANDING A SEAT AT THE BANQUET.
A CONMAN, A PAIN IN THE BUM.
GIVE HIM ALL HE DESERVES –
A KNUCKLE SANDWICH, A BUNCH OF FIVES.

ORACLE SELLER.
Excuse me. Fives?

PEITHETAIROS.
See for yourself.
HE MAY PRATTLE OF BAKIS
OR FUSS ABOUT FAKIS.
IT'S PHONEY, BALONEY –

ORACLE SELLER.
That's in there?

PEITHETAIROS.
See for yourself.

(*hitting him with scrolls*)

See? See? See?

ORACLE SELLER.
990   Ow!

PEITHETAIROS.
Find a home for your Bakises somewhere else.

Exit ORACLE SELLER. *Enter* METON.

METON.
One could begin just here.

PEITHETAIROS.
Another of them!

Excuse me, what can I do for you?
This *is* a professional visit, one assumes.

METON.
Indeed. Project Middle Air. Two priorities:
One: three-dimensional survey;
Two: cubic allocation.

PEITHETAIROS.
But who *are* you?

METON.
Meton, geometer, cartographer,
Estate agent. My card.

PEITHETAIROS.
And what is *that?*

METON.
An air-surveyor. Look.
The concept's simple. Our latest thinking   1000
Is that space is, how shall I put it, *nightcap*-shaped.
I take my instrument, put one leg here,
Another here, and move the arm like *this* –
You see the principle?

PEITHETAIROS.
No.

METON.
If you calibrate with care,
You can square each circle, which simplifies
The whole equation. I'm envisaging
Town centre *here*, streets *here* and *here* and *here:*
It's a radial alignment, patterned on the rays
Of that other celestial sphere, the Sun.

PEITHETAIROS.
Pythagoras rides again! Excuse me.

METON.
Of course.

PEITHETAIROS.
I'm sorry to interrupt. I mean...I like you,
1010 The way you think... But you really ought...

METON.
What?

PEITHETAIROS.
To bugger off.

METON.
Pardon?

PEITHETAIROS.
Before it's too late.

METON.
You mean, there's trouble here?
Some socio-political unrest?

PEITHETAIROS.
Not exactly.

METON.
What then?

PEITHETAIROS.
They just like beaking frauds.

METON.
Beaking?

PEITHETAIROS.
Frauds.

METON.
I think I get it.

PEITHETAIROS.
I think you do. Hey! What was that?
Did *you* hear wing-beats?

METON.
Yike!

Exit.

PEITHETAIROS.
I thought so. Bye.
Make a straight line somewhere else.   1020

Enter INSPECTOR GENERAL.

INSPECTOR GENERAL.
Where's the welcoming committee?

PEITHETAIROS.
A walking tailor's shop!

INSPECTOR GENERAL.
Aren't you ready for inspection?
This *is* Cloudcuckooland?

PEITHETAIROS.
Inspection? Who by?

INSPECTOR GENERAL.
We represent the majesty of the Athenian state.
We were otherwise engaged, but were snatched away –
Emergency proposal, that hothead Teleas...

PEITHETAIROS.
Suppose I slip you something to go away?

INSPECTOR GENERAL.
We'd be grateful. We were halfway through
An *absorbing* piece of work when the summons came.
The Pharnakes file. A motion before the People.

PEITHETAIROS.
I understand. Suppose I slip you...this?

INSPECTOR GENERAL.
Ow! What's that?

PEITHETAIROS (*gesturing at the audience*).
A motion before the people.   1030

INSPECTOR GENERAL.
You can't hit State officials.

PEITHETAIROS.
Can't I? Out!

He chases him out.

What are they doing? Inspectors?
I haven't even sacrificed.

Enter LAW-SELLER.

LAW-SELLER.
PARAGRAPH THREE. TORTS AND
   MISDEMEANOURS.
SUBSECTION FORTY-NINE.

PEITHETAIROS.
Not more paper! Well?

LAW-SELLER.
You're in the market for some laws. Try these.
Full constitution, by-laws...take your pick.

PEITHETAIROS.
Give me an example.

LAW-SELLER.
WEIGHTS, MEASURES, COINS.
CLOUDCUCKOOLANDISH MEASURES WILL
1040   CONFORM
TO THOSE PREVAILING NOW IN OLOPHYXIA.

PEITHETAIROS.
Olo-fix-ya? Not a bad idea.

LAW-SELLER.
What's the matter?

PEITHETAIROS.
Out!
Take your laws and...out!

Enter INSPECTOR GENERAL *with* WITNESS.

INSPECTOR GENERAL.
I summons Peithetairos for assault and battery –

PEITHETAIROS.
That's right. And here's some more.

LAW-SELLER.
  For G.B.H. against an officer of state –   1050

PEITHETAIROS.
  Are you still here?

INSPECTOR GENERAL.
  I demand restitution. Ten thousand drachs.

PEITHETAIROS.
  Ten thousand whacks. Just watch me.

LAW-SELLER.
  WHEREAS LAST NIGHT YOU CRAPPED IN COURT –

PEITHETAIROS.
  Keep him away from me. And you, get out!

He chases them out.

  I've had enough of this. I'm going. Here, goat.
  We'll see to the sacrifice, inside.

He goes in.

CHORUS.
  Soon mortals everywhere
  Will sacrifice to *us*, will pray to *us*,
  All-seeing, all-ruling, the birds of the air.   1060
  Their world is our concern:
  In fields, in orchards,
  We patrol their crops:
  We pick off the pests that swarm there,
  Nibbling, sucking the swelling seeds,
  Buds on the bough.
  Destroyers of sweet-smelling gardens
  We dive-bomb:
  Stingers, creepy-crawlies –
  We swoop from on high; they die.   1070

  Did you hear that announcement the other day?
  WANTED FOR BLASPHEMY: DIAGORAS OF
     MELOS,

DEAD OR ALIVE. REWARD: SIX THOUSAND
DRACHMAS.
Well, we've a counter-announcement of our own.
WANTED FOR BIRD-SELLING: PHILOKRATES
OF MARKET STREET.
SIX THOUSAND FOR HIS CARCASS, TWENTY
THOUSAND
IF YOU BRING HIM IN ALIVE. You want to
know why?
He sells finches on strings, a dozen a drach.
He sells thrushes, blown up to look like grouse
1080 (Not much fun for you, and none at all for them).
He sells blackbirds with straws up their noses,
Stool pigeons, netted and caged, to be decoys.
That's enough about him. But there's this as well.
If anyone here keeps a budgie, let it go
Or be sorry. We'll string you, we'll sell you,
We'll budgie you. D'you want to go cheap?

How lucky we are, we birds,
How blessed in our feathers, in our wings.
1090 We need no winter cloaks to cosset us;
No blazing summer sun
Ever scorches us, stifles us.
We sit in the shade,
In leafy woods, in lush green grass,
While cicadas, drunk on sunshine,
Giggle and shriek.
In the high hills we winter, snug
In dark caves;
In spring we banquet on berries,
1100 White myrtle, the Graces' feast.

A word in the judges' ears. It'll do you no harm
If you give *us* first prize. Remember Paris,
That beauty contest? Peanuts, compared to *this*.
To start with, drachmas: coins in the pocket.
Just have a quick look. Which bird's on the back?
Owls. Exactly. Owls and drachmas go together.
You'd like them swooping round your houses,

Nesting in your purses, hatching little ones?
It could be arranged. Are you ambitious –
A career in politics, perhaps? We'll send you
Eagles to soar overhead and impress the
   neighbours,   1110
Hawks to help anyone who wants to grease your palm.
Going out to dinner? No need for a doggy-bag:
Our friendly local Pelican has a surprise for you.
If, on the other hand, we *don't* win, we suggest
A tin helmet, and never go out in new clothes.

Dance. When it ends, PEITHETAIROS *comes out.*

PEITHETAIROS.
   That's that, then, Birds. One sacrifice.
   I'm surprised we haven't heard what's going on
   Up there. No, here's someone. Heavens!   1120
   What does he think this is, the Olympic Games?

Enter MESSENGER.

MESSENGER.
   Whey pey, whey whey pey, whey whey whey pey,
   Where's Peithetairos? Where's Himself?

PEITHETAIROS.
   I'm here.

MESSENGER.
   The wall's...hoo, arrgh...finished.

PEITHETAIROS.
   Marvellous.

MESSENGER.
   The very word. Marvellous. Hoo. Magnificent.
   Big enough for chariot races, Proxenides
   And Theagenes even, the Trojan Horse.

PEITHETAIROS.
   That's big.

MESSENGER.

1130   And high. Hoo, high. I measured it myself.
Six hundred feet.

PEITHETAIROS.

That's high. Who built it that high?

MESSENGER.

Birds.
No one else. No brickies from Egypt,
No stonecutters, no pyramid-erectors.
Birds, just birds, with their own bare claws.
I stood like this, hoo, haa, and watched.
Thirty thousand cranes flew in from Africa
With cropfuls of stones, and handed them
To stonebills for cornering. Sand martens mixed

1140   Cement, and dippers and waders and spoonbills
Kept the water coming.

PEITHETAIROS.

Six hundred feet...
Who carried the mortar?

MESSENGER.

Herons. In hods.

PEITHETAIROS.

And how did they fill those hods?

MESSENGER.

You'd have liked that.
Geese stuck in their feet like this, and shovelled it.

PEITHETAIROS.

What a feat.

MESSENGER.

A duck-line passed the bricks along.

1150   Swallows darted about like apprentices,
Pecking the cement in place.

PEITHETAIROS.
What a production-line.
Who did the carpentering?

MESSENGER.
Who d'you think? Woodpeckers.
They tapped and split and planed and drilled
Those gates. Tock, tack, thwock, thwack,
It was as noisy as a shipyard. Well, it's done.
It's gated, it's barred, it's bolted.
Watch set, patrols, bells, beacon fires.   1160
It's up to you now. I'm going to have a bath.

Exit.

CHORUS.
What's wrong with you? You're looking sick.
They built a wall, and they built it quick.

PEITHETAIROS.
Exactly. Sounds like castles in the air to me.
Here's someone else. A watchman from the wall.
But why the war-dance? There's something wrong.

Enter WATCHMAN.

WATCHMAN.
Eeoo eeoo, eeoo eeoo, eeoo eeoo.   1170

PEITHETAIROS.
What's wrong with eeoo?

WATCHMAN.
Disaster! On the wall.
Some god, some messenger from Zeus slipped past
The crow-guard. Flew through the gates, flew *here*.

PEITHETAIROS.
The cheeky sod. Which god?

WATCHMAN.
It had wings, that's all we know.

PEITHETAIROS.
Call security. Send out a posse.

WATCHMAN.
> We have already.
> A phalanx of falcons,
> A squadron of sparrowhawks,
1180
> The entire beak-and-hook brigade,
> Every osprey and eagle and kite in sight.
> They're beating bounds, they're combing clouds.
> Wings whirring, beaks banging, claws clattering –
> Can't you hear them? Whatever it is, it's *near*.

PEITHETAIROS.
> Slings, bows, stones! To arms!
> Send the squadron-leaders here.
> Where did I put that catapult?

CHORUS.
> War, war, that dreadful word,
1190
> Between every god and every bird.
> Man the sky,
> On guard!
> Low and high,
> Look hard.
> Don't let immortals through:
> They're fighting *you*.

> The whole air's humming.
> Something's coming.
> Make a circle. Peer.
> There's someone here.

> *Enter* IRIS, *with rainbow wings and elaborate*
> *helmet. She flies in on the theatre crane.*

PEITHETAIROS.
> Hey. Here girl, here girl, here girl.
1200
> Stop flapping. There now. Steady.
> Who are you? You have to say. Where from?

IRIS.
> From high Olympos' halls I come, the gods.

PEITHETAIROS.
What's your name? What are you – messenger
Or sailing boat?

IRIS.
Iris the fleet.

PEITHETAIROS.
The fleet's in, lads!

IRIS.
What's here afoot?

PEITHETAIROS.
Quick, grab her: she's off again.

IRIS.
Unhand me. DON'T DO THAT!

PEITHETAIROS.
You've had it now.

IRIS.
Outrageous.

PEITHETAIROS.
Quite. Which gate did you fly through?

IRIS.
Great Zeus on high! One recognised no gate.   1210

PEITHETAIROS.
'Great Zeus'... 'One recognised no gate'...
You *did* see the customs crow? The visa stork
Did prick your permit?

IRIS.
What impertinence *is* this?

PEITHETAIROS.
They didn't? You didn't?

IRIS.
You're out of your mind.

PEITHETAIROS.

Officially, then, you've not been entered?

IRIS.

Of course not. One would like to see them try.

PEITHETAIROS.

So there we are. Illegal entry...
You force our frontier, violate our air-space –

IRIS.

One *is* an immortal god. One flies where one likes.

PEITHETAIROS.

1220 Not here, one doesn't. One's well out of order.
If we're talking punishment that fits the crime,
Iris or no Iris, you're dead. Quite dead.

IRIS.

But I'm *immortal!*

PEITHETAIROS.

That's no excuse.
There are no exceptions. Why should everyone else
Bow down, and you gods turn up your noses,
And refuse to acknowledge your betters? No
chance.

IRIS *flaps her wings for take-off.*

Now what are you doing? What *is* all this?

IRIS.

1230 One can't stay here all day. One flies
From Zeus on High to mortals. Urgent orders.
YOH!
START SACRIFICE. BASH BULLS, GUT
GOATS, SLAY SHEEP.
LET EVERY HIGHWAY, BYWAY, STEAM WITH
SMOKE.
THE POWERS ON HIGH ARE PECKISH.

PEITHETAIROS.
  Powers on high?
  What powers on high?

IRIS.
  Us. Gods. *The* gods.

PEITHETAIROS.
  Ye gods!

IRIS.
  Who else would you suggest?

PEITHETAIROS.
  I see you haven't heard.
  They sacrifice to birds now. Birds are gods.
  Not gods. Our feather in Heaven. Stuff Zeus.

IRIS.
  Fool! Fool! Rouse not immortal rage,
  Lest Zeus almighty curse thee quite,
  Lest Justice, mattock of the gods,   1240
  With vengeful violence hoe thy house,
  Lest baleful blasts of flaming fire –

PEITHETAIROS.
  Do shut it. Do stand still.
  Just who d'you think you're scaring?
  Vengeful violence? Mattock of the gods?
  It's mumbo-jumbo. Anyone can do it.
  Tell Zeus to put a sock in it –
  Unless he wants his palace purged
  With eagle-fire, a fearsome force
  Of firecrests, zooming up with zest
  To kindle chaos and dish out doom.   1250
  I've got six hundred here, on standby,
  Tawny as leopards, grim as giants –
  That's right, giant trouble, just like he had before.
  And as for you, young lady...Zeusogram...
  Any more out of you, and I'll clap on sail,
  Open up your shipping-lanes, and give you a big
      surprise.

IRIS.
You dirty old man. How dare you?

PEITHETAIROS.
Fly away. Go on. Shoo.

IRIS.
I'll tell my Daddy. He'll see to you.

PEITHETAIROS.
1260   I'm scared. Show some other little boy
Your fireworks. Shoo. Shoo. Shoo.

Exit IRIS, *by crane.*

CHORUS.
This air is closed. No way
For Olympian gods, as from today.
Don't expect
Friends here.
Show respect,
Keep clear.
No sacrifice, no joke:
No holy smoke.

PEITHETAIROS.
I thought I sent a messenger to mortals.
1270   Where is he? Is he ever coming back?

Enter MESSENGER.

MESSENGER.
Peithetairos! Magnificence!
O Excellence, O Wisest of the Wise,
O Thrice Renowned, O Brain of Brains,
Oh ask me what I want.

PEITHETAIROS.
What is it?

MESSENGER.
Mortals.
They want to give you this golden crown,
For bulging brains, for services.

PEITHETAIROS.
I'll take it. What services?

MESSENGER.
You mean you don't know? You founded
   Cloudcuckooland
And you've no idea what it means to them?
They love it. They can't get enough of it.
Until you built Cloudcuckooland   1280
They were mad for all things Spartan:
Spartan haircuts, Spartan diet, Spartan pong
(They saved on baths. Like Sokrates),
Spartan walking-sticks. Now that's all gone.
They're bird-mad. Some even *think* they're birds:
Up with the lark each morning, and flit away
To perch in the lawcourts, to cluck and peck.
The madder ones have even changed their names.   1290
That one-legged stallholder: he's 'Flamingo' now.
Menippos is 'Swift'; Opountios is 'Crow';
Philokles is 'Lark'; Theagenes is 'Stork';
Lykourgos is 'Ibis' and Chairephon is 'Bats'
(I know bats aren't birds, but you know Chairephon);
Syrakosios is 'Popinjay' and Meidias –
He's 'Shite-hawk'. That's right, 'Shite-hawk'.
What d'you mean what's new, you're not surprised?
The good old songs have never been so popular: 1300
'Lullaby of Birdland...', 'A Nightingale Sang...'
'There'll be Blue Birds Over...', 'Swannee...',
'O for the Wings of a...'. That reminds me. Wings.
You'd better get a stock in, fast.
Wings, claws, beaks, all that.
They're flocking here in millions.
To join you. They're on their way.

PEITHETAIROS.
No point standing here, then. You go in,
Stuff all the baskets and boxes you can find   1310
With wings. Manes, help him. Bring them out here.
I'll wait. I'll see these would-be birds myself.

Bustle of preparations.

CHORUS.
Cloudcuckooland, sublime –

PEITHETAIROS.
We're short of time.

CHORUS.
No grief, no worry –

PEITHETAIROS (*to* SLAVE).
Why can't you hurry?

CHORUS.
A lovely land. Desire is here,
1320   Wit, Wisdom, Charm and Grace;
Here Quiet smiles,
And Calm –

PEITHETAIROS (*to* SLAVE).
Come on! Be quick!
You make me sick.

CHORUS.
Here. Put the basket down.

PEITHETAIROS.
Get on, you clown.

CHORUS.
Be strict. Be firm.

PEITHETAIROS.
I'll make him squirm.

CHORUS.
1330   Set out the wings, in proper piles.
They'll choose the kind they want:
Gull, songbird, swift,
Hawk, owl –

PEITHETAIROS (*to* SLAVE).
You'll feel my fist.
I can't resist.

YOB (*offstage*).
    Wings! Wings! Wings!
    Gimme wings!
    I wanna fly.
    High. Inna sky.
    Gimme wings! Wings! Wings!

PEITHETAIROS.
    That messenger was right.   1340
    Here's someone already, eager for eagles.

    Enter YOB.

YOB.
    Whee, wheeeyyy,
    Gimme wings! Wings! Wings!
    You've got new laws here. I like them.
    Make me a bird. You heard.

PEITHETAIROS.
    What laws? We've got a lot of laws.

YOB.
    All of them. Specially the one
    Says you can peck your Daddy's head in.

PEITHETAIROS.
    We *do* think it's natural for a fighting chick
    To challenge his father, test his strength –   1350

YOB.
    And choke him and chuck him out the nest.
    Grab everything. Why else d'you think I came?

PEITHETAIROS.
    But we've another law:
    Older, much older, the Pterodactyl Code.
    WHEN DADDY AND MUMMY HAVE REARED
        THEIR CHICKS,
    BEGAT THEM, HATCHED THEM, FLEDGED
        THEM, FED THEM,

YEA VERILY, THEN SHALL THE ROLES BE
REVERSED:
LOOK-AFTER-TIME BEGINS FOR EVERY
CHICK.

YOB.

Look-after time? Look-*after* bloody time?
I've come to the wrong place after all.

PEITHETAIROS.

1360   No, no. You chose to come. You want to stay.
Why not join our 'A' Team, our Do-the-Business
Firm?
Forget your father. Leave him alone.
I'm telling you. I learned that years ago.
Take these wings, this battle-spur, this crest.
Join the Professionals, Take the Strain,
Rely on Yourself, Look out for Number One,
Leave Daddy alone – and if it's a fight you want,
Fly North. Away match. Tough. They need you
there.

YOB.

1370   'A' Team. Look out for Number One. Fly North.
I'll do it. You're right.

PEITHETAIROS.

I always am.

Exit YOB.

KINESIAS (*offstage*).
Away! Away! For I will fly to thee,
Not charioted by Bacchus and his pards,
But on the viewless wings of Poesy...

PEITHETAIROS.

We'll need a ton of wings for this one.

Enter KINESIAS.

KINESIAS.
Already with thee! Tender is the night,
And haply the Queen-Moon is on her throne...

PEITHETAIROS.
Kinesias. What d'you want? What is it?

KINESIAS.
My heart aches, and a drowsy numbness pains
My sense –   1380

PEITHETAIROS.
Stop quoting and tell us what you want.

KINESIAS.
I want some wings. I want to fly,
Stopping through a fleecy cloud,
Plucking up inspiration on the wing.

PEITHETAIROS.
Inspiration. You pluck it up up *there?*

KINESIAS.
Of course. It hangs there,
On a sort of *heaventree of stars.*
It's all up there:
The fleeting, the darkling, the purple, the plain –
Let me show you.   1390

PEITHETAIROS.
It's all right.

KINESIAS.
No, no.
It's the least I can do. A guided tour.
Look at the stars! Look, look up at the skies!
O look at the fire-folk sitting in the air!

PEITHETAIROS.
Just a minute.

KINESIAS.
My heart in hiding
Stirred for a bird –

PEITHETAIROS.
I think I'll do some stirring of my own.

He selects a wing.

KINESIAS.

The achieve of,
1400 *The mastery of the thing!*
Ow! Critic! That wasn't nice at all.

PEITHETAIROS.

I thought you wanted wings.

KINESIAS.

I don't have to put up with this.
In Athens they queue to hear me.

PEITHETAIROS.

Stay here. We'll queue as well –
To get away.

KINESIAS.

You cheeky devil.
Don't think you've heard the last of this.
I want those wings!

Exit.

INFORMER (*offstage*).
1410 *'Is it weakness of intellect, birdie?' I cried,*
'Or a rather tough worm in your little inside?'...

PEITHETAIROS.

Another warbler. It's a flock, a plague,
A migration. What's the *matter* with them all?

Enter INFORMER.

INFORMER.

O swallow, swallow, flying, flying south,
Ti-tum-ti-tum ti-tum-ti something something eaves,
And tell her, tell her, what I tell to thee...

PEITHETAIROS.

Don't ask her to swallow it, that's all.
Has something been nesting in your cloak?

INFORMER.
There's a free handout of wings going on. Who?
Where?

PEITHETAIROS.
Me. Here. What exactly do you want?

INFORMER.
Wings, fool, wings. Some kind of joker, are you?   1420

PEITHETAIROS.
Don't tell me: you're trading-in that cloak.

INFORMER.
Undercover work. Or ground-cover, rather.
I cover a lot of ground. I go round the islands,
Delivering summonses, collecting evidence,
Sniffing out offenders...

PEITHETAIROS.
Public Benefactor Number One.

INFORMER.
Exactly. The point is, if I had wings,
I could scare them witless twice as fast.

PEITHETAIROS.
Dump them with summonses from up above?

INFORMER.
There are some real crooks out there. Pirates.
I could slip in and out in a flock of cranes,
With a cropful of summonses for ballast.

PEITHETAIROS.
Aren't you a little *spry* for this kind of work?   1430
A little *husky* to be putting the bite on strangers?

INFORMER.
What else d'you suggest? Not...go *legit?*

PEITHETAIROS.
There must be something. Decent, clean –
Well, anything's cleaner than hatching lawsuits.

INFORMER.
Look, pal, I came here for wings, not sermons.

PEITHETAIROS.
I'll give you wings: word-wings.

INFORMER.
What's that mean?

PEITHETAIROS.
Words are wings. Everyone knows that.

INFORMER.
They do?

PEITHETAIROS.
1440   Haven't you heard people talking? Fathers,
  For example, in barber's shops. 'I'll kill
    Dietrephes.
  All that talk of chariots. My boy's flown off
  To learn to drive.' 'With mine, it's poetry.
  One ode and he's off. Head in the clouds. Away.'

INFORMER.
You've lost me, squire.

PEITHETAIROS.
  It's simple. Words inspire.
  They give you uplift, make you rise
  To higher things. In your case, I hope,
  An honest job of work.

INFORMER.
1450   Not interested.

PEITHETAIROS.
  Pardon?

INFORMER.
  It's genetic, what I do. It's in the blood.
  Father, grandad before him. I can't disgrace
  The family. Just give me wings – executive type,
  Hawk's, falcon's, I'm not fussy – so I can zoom

To the islands, deliver the summonses,
Whizz back to Athens, give evidence in court...

PEITHETAIROS.
So that everything's despatched and decided
Before the defendant even gets there?

INFORMER.
That's how it works.

PEITHETAIROS.
So while he's sailing *out,* you're flying *in*
To pick up his goods and chattels.

INFORMER.
That's right.   1460
You need speed in this job, to stay on top.

PEITHETAIROS.
Top. Top. I've got it. Here are some wings.
Try these.

INFORMER.
Those aren't wings, they're whips.

PEITHETAIROS.
That's right.
Words inspire the mind. *You* mentioned tops.

INFORMER.
Ow! Oo!

PEITHETAIROS.
Speed, speed, you said you needed speed.
Get whizzing, then. Get zooming – somewhere else.

He chases him out.

We'll take the rest of the wings inside.

He and the SLAVE *take the wings, and go in.*

CHORUS.
We've been on mystery flights,   1470
And seen some funny sights.
The oddest of all must be

The K-K-Kleonymos-tree.
It's big, and thick, and yellow.
Hear it stammer, lie and bellow.
In spring it never fails:
Its buds are fairy tales.
1480   When autumn comes, it yields
A crop of little shields.

It's the darkest place we know,
Where the Sun's afraid to go,
Where the Moon holds back her light
And it's always dead of night.
Strange creatures wail and moan there.
Don't wander on your own there.
You'll be jumped on, bumped and bashed,
1490   Stripped naked, mugged and mashed.
That's Orestes' cunning plan.
The hero? The highwayman.

Enter PROMETHEUS, *cloaked.*

PROMETHEUS.
Oh dear, I do hope Zeus doesn't see me.

(*to* PEITHETAIROS, *as he passes in and out*)

Psst. Where's Peithetairos?

PEITHETAIROS.
A walking duvet. Who are *you?*

PROMETHEUS.
Are there any gods about? Behind?

PEITHETAIROS.
No. Who *are* you?

PROMETHEUS.
What time is it?

PEITHETAIROS.
Afternoon. Just. *Who* are you?

PROMETHEUS.
1500   How much after noon?

PEITHETAIROS.
I'm getting tired of this.

PROMETHEUS.
What's Zeus doing? Is it dark or sunny?

PEITHETAIROS.
Dear, dear!

PROMETHEUS.
All clear? In that case...there.

He unwraps himself.

PEITHETAIROS (*overjoyed*).
Prometheus!

PROMETHEUS.
Shh! For heaven's sake, not so loud.

PEITHETAIROS.
What's wrong?

PROMETHEUS.
Don't shout my name all over the place.
If Zeus gets to hear I'm here... I've come
To tell you what's going on in Heaven.
I tell you what. Get under this.

He puts up a sunshade.

Hold it up, so the gods can't see us.   1510

PEITHETAIROS.
I do like you.
You always have everything worked out.
Come under. What's going on?

PROMETHEUS.
Listen.

PEITHETAIROS.
I'm listening.

PROMETHEUS.
Zeus is done for.

PEITHETAIROS.
Since when?

PROMETHEUS.
Since you closed the air.
The human race stopped sacrificing, on the spot.
We haven't had a sniff of offering for yonks.
Emergency rations. It's worse than the annual fast.
The Olympian gods are fine: stiff upper lip.
1520 But some of the out-of-towners are turning nasty,
Threatening to chuck Zeus out and start again
If he doesn't reopen the trade-routes
And get the gravy-train on the move again.

PEITHETAIROS.
Out-of-towners? You don't have gods from out-of-
town.

PROMETHEUS.
Of course we do. From beyond the stars.
We've a god for everyone – even Exekestides.

PEITHETAIROS.
And what d'you call these out-of-towners?

PROMETHEUS.
Bigguns.

PEITHETAIROS.
Why Bigguns?

PROMETHEUS.
1530 Because they *are*.
Anyway, they're sending down a mission,
Zeus and the Bigguns. To ask for terms.
And what *I* came to say is, stand your ground.
Don't budge till Zeus agrees to two conditions:
(1) The birds get total, universal power;
(2) You get to marry Sovereignty.

PEITHETAIROS.
Who?

PROMETHEUS.
Sovereignty.
She's a kind of...personal assistant.
Knockout to look at. She polishes
His Nibs' Ultimate Weapon, his thunderbolt.
She's got a bunch of keys *this* big.
You name it, she dishes it out:
Life, Liberty, Pursuit of Happiness,   1540
Naval Bases, Political Debate, the Welfare State –

PEITHETAIROS.
She's got keys to all those?

PROMETHEUS.
Marry her, control the lot.
That's my advice. That's what I came to say.
You know how I dote on the human race.

PEITHETAIROS.
Who gave us the barbecue?

PROMETHEUS.
I never *did* like gods.

PEITHETAIROS.
I think it's mutual.

PROMETHEUS.
There must be a play in there.
Now I really must run. Look, take the sunshade,
And walk in front. That way, if Zeus looks down,   1550
He'll think I'm part of some procession.

PEITHETAIROS.
Good idea. You carry this deckchair:
That'll make it look more natural.

Exeunt.

CHORUS.
In the land of the Darkyfeet
Where shadows flit and bleat,
A man with dirty knees
(They call him Sokrates)

Gives classes to the spooks there.
Peisandros comes and looks there.
'Please help me find my soul.'
1560   'Pour camel-blood: one bowl.
But watch out for Chairephon:
He'll drink it on his own.'

Enter POSEIDON, HERAKLES *and* BIGGUN.

POSEIDON.
This is the place. Cloudcuckooland.
Fancy *us,* ambassadors to a place like this!

(*to* BIGGUN)

What're you *doing?* You don't wear that like that.
Over the *other* shoulder. For heaven's sake,
Who do you think you are, Laispodias?
1570   Is that what advanced democracy means,
That we have to put up with clowns like this?

BIGGUN.
Yarrup.

POSEIDON.
Thanks. Oh thanks. That's very nice.
Gods, what a specimen! I thought I'd seen it all...
Well, Herakles, have you got it straight?
Our plan of campaign?

HERAKLES.
Find the mortal bastard
Who built the wall, and throttle him.

POSEIDON.
No, no, no, no.
We're a *peace* mission.

POSEIDON.
So make peace first, *then* throttle him.

Enter PEITHETAIROS *and* SLAVE. *They bring*
cooking implements, to prepare for a feast.

PEITHETAIROS.
Give me the grater. Where's the garlic?
I've lost the cheese. That fire needs air.   1580

POSEIDON.
You. Mortal. The Embassy from Heaven presents
Credentials. We've come to kiss hands.

PEITHETAIROS.
Better not. I'm grating garlic.

HERAKLES.
What meat is this?

PEITHETAIROS.
Jailbirds.
They plotted High Treason, they paid the price.

HERAKLES.
You garlic them first, then spit them?

PEITHETAIROS.
I *thought* you were Herakles. How's tricks?

POSEIDON.
Harumph. The Embassy from Heaven presents –

PEITHETAIROS.
We're short of oil.

HERAKLES.
That's bad. I like my poultry oily.   1590

POSEIDON.
Our position is: this war is getting us nowhere,
And peace could get *you* somewhere. For example:
Rain-butts full, permanent supply. Summer weather,
Whenever you want. We've full authority,
Full power to negotiate, my colleagues and myself.

PEITHETAIROS.
We didn't start the war. It's not our fault.
We'll make peace gladly, any time you like.
All we ask is our rights. And our rights are these:

1600   Lord Zeus must hand our sceptre back. If that's
Acceptable, I invite the Embassy to lunch.

HERAKLES.
Acceptable? I'll say. That gets my vote.

POSEIDON.
You brainless oaf! You gutbag! Think, for once.
Lord Zeus' sceptre? You can't be serious.

PEITHETAIROS.
You don't understand. Let birds rule here,
You'll be far better off than you were before.
You've had a hell of a time with mortals – up
Till now. It's because of the clouds.
They skulk underneath the clouds. They laugh
At you. They take your names in vain. Not any
1610   more.
Come in with *us*, when mortals swear 'By Jove'
They'll have to add 'By Jay' – and then,
If they break their word, a jackdaw slips down,
And pecks their eye out.

POSEIDON.
Poseidon! Yes! That's clever.

HERAKLES.
I agree.

PEITHETAIROS.
And what do *you* say?

BIGGUN.
Ploog.

PEITHETAIROS.
He's with us all the way.
And there's something else we can do for you.
Suppose a mortal makes a holy promise –
'Grant this wish, and I'll sacrifice a sheep' –
And then delays, thinking 'The Gods are immortal,
1620   They can wait'? We can deal with that.

POSEIDON.
Oh can you? How?

PEITHETAIROS.
We'll wait till he's otherwise engaged,
Counting his money, say, or lying in his bath,
Then *Woof! Shoof!* We'll send a kite
To snaffle you up the price of two fat sheep.

HERAKLES.
Two sheep?

PEITHETAIROS.
Double-dealing, double penalty.

HERAKLES.
That gets my vote. Give them back their power.

PEITHETAIROS.
Right. What does Biggun say?

HERAKLES (*to* BIGGUN).
Oi. Bunch of fives?

BIGGUN.
Sinoffeta snakko. Blap.

HERAKLES.
Yes, he agrees.

POSEIDON.
If that's the majority decision, I accept.   1630
You. Mortal. That sceptre: request agreed.

PEITHETAIROS.
– Which brings me to the second thing I had
To ask. I don't want Hera: Zeus can keep her.
But you must hand Sovereignty, his...handmaiden
To me to marry.

POSEIDON.
Come on, you two.
He doesn't want peace at all.

PEITHETAIROS.
It's all the same to me.

(*to the* SLAVE)

How's the sauce? I told you sweet *and* sour.

HERAKLES.
Poseidon, lovey. I mean, Poseidon, sea-lord,
We're not going to argue over a bit of skirt?

POSEIDON.
What else do you suggest?

HERAKLES.
1640 Make peace, of course.

POSEIDON.
You haven't the brains you were born with. Clown!
They're swindling you. Say yes, it's you that
    suffers.
If Zeus gives these people all his sovereign power,
What's left for you? Your father, right? His son?
When he shuffles off, *you* stand to get the lot.

PEITHETAIROS.
Don't listen to him. It's a three card trick.
Come over here a minute. Let me explain.
Don't listen to uncle. He's got it wrong.
You won't get a penny when your old man dies.
When your old *god* dies. The problem is,
1650 You're a bastard.

HERAKLES.
What did you say?

PEITHETAIROS.
Not me, the law.
Olympian father, yes, but mortal Mum.
Legitimate heirs take precedence –
Athene, in this case. She gets the lot.

HERAKLES.
  Unless he makes a will leaving all to me.
  I could arrange that.

PEITHETAIROS.
  No use. Another law.
  Try anything like that, and *he'll* contest it:
  Your uncle Poseidon, who's so hot for you right now.
  He'll have you up in court: his Lordship's brother.
  Next of kin. He'll grab the lot. You know the law: 1660
  WHEREAS IF THE AFORESAID TESTATOR
    DIETH INTESTATE
  THE ESTATE, TOGETHER WITH ALL
    MESSUAGE, CHATTELS, GOODS
  THERETO APPERTAINING, SHALL PASS,
    DUSTIBUS FUSTIBUS,
  (1) TO LEGITIMATE ISSUE, (2) TO NEXT OF
    KIN.

HERAKLES.
  I don't get a penny?

PEITHETAIROS.
  Dustibus fustibus.
  Unless, of course, he passed a separate law
  Making you legitimate.

HERAKLES.
  He never did. What a bastard!   1670

PEITHETAIROS.
  Like son, like father. Don't grind your teeth.
  Stay here with us, you're made. Captain of Crows,
  Duke of Dodos, throne of your own, best pigeon's
    milk...

HERAKLES.
  I said it before and I say it again,
  She's yours. Hand her over. That's *my* vote.

PEITHETAIROS.
  Poseidon?

POSEIDON.
Never.

PEITHETAIROS.
It's up to Biggun, then.
You've got the casting vote. Well, what d'you say?

BIGGUN.
Sovrankro, burdi handle. Heap.

HERAKLES.
Well, that was clear enough.

POSEIDON.
1680   'Sovrankro'? 'Sov-*ran*-kro'? You call that clear?

HERAKLES.
It seemed clear to me. 'Sovran crow, birdie handle.
    Heap!'

POSEIDON.
Oh, settle it yourselves. I've nothing more to say.

HERAKLES (*to* PEITHETAIROS).
Right, it's agreed. Exactly as you asked.
She's ready and waiting, up in Heaven.
Come along with us, then. Walk this way.

PEITHETAIROS.
Those jailbirds will come in really handy.
Wedding-banquet.

HERAKLES.
Wedding-banquet? Ah.
You three go on. I'll stay and roast the meat.

POSEIDON.
1690   'Stay and roast the meat'... That's all you're fit for!

HERAKLES.
Who's complaining?

POSEIDON.
Walk *this* way.

PEITHETAIROS.
Someone fetch my wedding suit. I won't be long.

Exeunt PEITHETAIROS, POSEIDON, HERAKLES.

CHORUS.
In Lawcourt Land, behind
The water-clock, you'll find
The grimy, slimy nest
Of the Creepy-crawly pest.
It's a tongue on legs. It wriggles,
Slobbers, nudges, niggles.   1700
It tends its crop of lies
Till they tower to the skies.
So before it gets too fat,
Lift a foot and squash it, flat[27].

Enter MESSENGER.

MESSENGER.
Happiness! Happiness! Blissful race,
Flap happy wings, receive your king.
He comes to claim his rightful place,
The golden, the star-bright, wide of wing.
He dazzles the Sun; he rides the sky;   1710
His glory glitters, wide and high.
And at his side, his shining queen,
His lovely lady, and in his hand
Fire-wings, the thunderbolt. Be seen!
Be welcome! Grace this happy land!
He comes. Play music, loud and long.
Burn incense. Sing the wedding song.

Music. Enter PEITHETAIROS *and* SOVEREIGNTY,
in procession.

CHORUS.
Make way! Draw back! Stand clear!   1720
Our king is here.
Fly round his head with pride.
Serenade his bride.

Hymen, Hymenaios, O!
Hymen, Hymenaios, O!
Oh happy man, oh saviour-king,
With pride we sing.
For you, your Queen, our songs we raise,
Our hymns of praise.
Hymen, Hymenaios, O!
1730   Hymen, Hymenaios, O!

As now, so then, the Fates once led
Zeus and his bride to bed,
His lordliness,
Her loveliness.
Hymen, Hymenaios, O!
Hymen, Hymenaios, O!

Young Cupid, golden-winged and fair
With blessings showered the pair,
The king, the queen,
1740   Joy to be seen.
Hymen, Hymenaios, O!
Hymen, Hymenaios, O!

PEITHETAIROS.
Your song is pleasing; sweet your voices.

CHORUS.
Now, while Heaven with Earth rejoices,
Wake Zeus' thunder. Let it roll,
Let it terrify each living soul.
Golden thunder, Heaven-cleaving,
1750   Echoed from the sea-swell's heaving;
It shakes the Earth, makes rain-clouds weep,
It gives all power, on Earth, in Air –
Like Sovereignty, Zeus' consort fair,
That once was his, and now is yours to keep.

Thunder.

Hymen, Hymenaios, O!
Hymen, Hymenaios, O!

PEITHETAIROS.
Birds of the air, salute my royal bride.
Come with us now, inside.

CHORUS.
Hymen, Hymenaios, O!
Hymen, Hymenaios, O!

PEITHETAIROS.
Give me your hand, my love, and wing to wing   1760
We'll lead the way,
To end the play,
While nightingales our wedding-chorus sing.

CHORUS.
Alalala-ee, ee-ay, pay-ohn,
Lead the way,
Sing today,
Sing for the king.
Hymen, Hymenaios, O!
Hymen, Hymenaios, O!

Exeunt omnes.

FESTIVAL TIME

THESMOPHORIAZOUSAI,
'Women at the Thesmophoria'

Characters

MNESILOCHOS
EURIPIDES
AGATHON'S SECRETARY
AGATHON
HERALDESS
KLEISTHENES
MIKKA
MYRTLE-SELLER
KRITYLLA
ORGANISER
CONSTABLE

silent parts:

DANCING GIRL
MANIA
PHILISTA
THRATTA

CHORUS OF WOMEN

A street in Athens. Enter EURIPIDES, *followed by*
MNESILOCHOS.

MNESILOCHOS.
Zeus almighty! Talk about early birds and worms.
He'll be the death of me. He's been lugging me round
Since breakfast time. Oi! Before I collapse entirely,
I'd like to hear where you're taking me, Euripides.

EURIPIDES.
You can't. You mustn't. You can't say *hear*
When what you mean is *see*.

MNESILOCHOS.
Pardon? Say that again.
I can't say *hear* –

EURIPIDES.
For *see*. Not *hear* for *see*.

MNESILOCHOS.
What about *see* for *hear?*

EURIPIDES.
See for *hear?* See, hear? No, no.

MNESILOCHOS.
You put it so well. But what does it mean?
Are you saying I mustn't see *or* hear?   10

EURIPIDES.
They're entirely disjunct phenomena.

MNESILOCHOS.
Not seeing and not hearing?

EURIPIDES.
Precisely.

MNESILOCHOS.
How d'you mean, disjunct?

EURIPIDES.
Like this. When Outer Space first split
And started giving birth to all creation –
This was after the Great Big Bang, of course –
For *seeing* she devised the eye,

A sphere in imitation of the Sun,
And for *hearing* the tube we call the ear.

MNESILOCHOS.
A tube? And that's why I mustn't see or hear?
20   I'm so glad you told me that. What a thing it is
To have a professor all my own.

EURIPIDES.
Stick around; I'll teach you plenty more.

MNESILOCHOS.
Let's stick around *here* a bit. You can teach me
And all these nice ladies and gentlemen
How to play silly beggars. You seem to know.

EURIPIDES.
Come here and pay attention.

MNESILOCHOS.
There.

EURIPIDES.
D'you see that door?

MNESILOCHOS.
Er...I think so.

EURIPIDES.
Keep quiet!

MNESILOCHOS.
Keep quiet about the door?

EURIPIDES.
Listen.

MNESILOCHOS.
Listen, and keep quiet about the door?

EURIPIDES.
Inside that house lives Agathon,
The famous tragic poet.

MNESILOCHOS.
30   Agathon, eh? What's he look like?

EURIPIDES.
How to describe dear Agathon –

MNESILOCHOS.
Suntanned? Ever so strong?

EURIPIDES.
That's someone else. Have you never *seen* him?

MNESILOCHOS.
Big, bushy beard?

EURIPIDES.
You *have* never seen him.

MNESILOCHOS.
Not face to face.

EURIPIDES.
Ah, you've fucked him? No? You can't remember?
Come over here. Crouch down. Someone's coming.
His secretary, with twigs and a firepot.
It'll be a sacrifice. For art. For inspiration.

AGATHON'S SECRETARY *comes out.*

SECRETARY.
Let all the people be silent, not a word
Be heard.   40
Hark how they knock at our window-frame
Again:
Muse-midwives, delivering a brand-new poem
To my master's hoem.
Dame Nature, batten the balmy breeze,
Cease all the sounding seas –

MNESILOCHOS (*bleating*).
Me-e-eh.

EURIPIDES.
Shh.

MNESILOCHOS.
What's he *saying?*

SECRETARY.
> Blest birds, sky-racers, each on your nest
> Now rest.
> Coarse creatures of forest, field and hill,
> Be still.

MNESILOCHOS.
> Me-e-e-e-e-eh.

SECRETARY.
> Hark! Agathon, paragon, paladin of poesy,
> Word-lord –

MNESILOCHOS.
50 Turd-lord.

SECRETARY.
> Who said that?

MNESILOCHOS.
> Dame Nature, dummy.

SECRETARY.
> A plinth he planneth,
> Play-planks he planeth,
> Skimmeth, trimmeth,
> Screweth, glueeth,
> Buffeth –

MNESILOCHOS.
> Stuffeth.

SECRETARY.
> Who *is* this oaf? These are private prayers.

MNESILOCHOS.
> I'll prayer *you*, mate. You *and* your word-lord.
60 See this? If it's screwing you're after,
> And pricking and sticking and poking –

SECRETARY.
> You dirty old man. What a brat *you* must have
> been.

EURIPIDES.
Pay no attention. Don't encourage him.
Go in and tell Agathon I need him, now.

SECRETARY.
No problem. He'll be out directly.
He's moulding odes, and you know what that's like
When the weather's cold. He'll be bringing them out
Any minute, to give them a bit of sun.

He turns to go in.

EURIPIDES.
Just a minute. I –

SECRETARY.
Stay there. He's on his way.   70

Exit.

EURIPIDES.
Oh Zeus! What hast in mind for me this day?

MNESILOCHOS.
I was wondering that myself. What's going on?
Why d'you keep groaning? What *is* it?
Go on, tell uncle. No family secrets here.

EURIPIDES.
I'm snagged in the very warp and weft of woe.

MNESILOCHOS.
Pardon?

EURIPIDES.
To be or not to be. What's in a name?
Euripides! Will they come to bury me or praise me?
What about tomorrow...and tomorrow and tomorrow?
This day decides.

MNESILOCHOS.
Of course it doesn't.
No courts are sitting today, no juries.
It's that women's festival. A holiday.   80

EURIPIDES.
That's it. That's what it's all about.
They're holding a meeting today, the women,
To decide whether I must live or die.

MNESILOCHOS.
Die? Why?

EURIPIDES.
They say my tragedies make fools of them.

MNESILOCHOS.
Well, so they do. You're done for, mate, unless –
Have you something in mind? Some clever plan?

EURIPIDES.
I'm going to ask Agathon, the paladin of poetry,
To go to the festival.

MNESILOCHOS.
What for?

EURIPIDES.
90   He can stand up, among all those women,
And plead my case.

MNESILOCHOS.
As himself, or in disguise?

EURIPIDES.
In disguise. In a dress. What else?

MNESILOCHOS.
Brilliant! I knew you were planning something.
When it comes to sneakiness, we take the cake.

EURIPIDES.
Shh!

MNESILOCHOS.
What now?

EURIPIDES.
He's coming out. The paladin.

MNESILOCHOS.
You're joking. Where?

EURIPIDES.
There. Watch the stage effect.

By means of the ekkuklema, AGATHON *is revealed.*

MNESILOCHOS.
I must be blind. I see no paladin.
No...*man.* Just a kind of custard tart.

EURIPIDES.
Shh! Quiet! He's opening up an ode.

AGATHON *sings a preliminary arpeggio.*

MNESILOCHOS.
He's clearing out the moths.   100

AGATHON *sings, taking both the solo and the
choral parts.*

AGATHON (*solo*).
Lift torches, dance and sing.
Let maiden voices ring.
It's a free country.

(*as chorus*)

Which gods, what song? Name names.
I love these holy strains.
Can't get enough.

(*solo*)

For Apollo of golden bow
Who built Troy long ago –   110
Song number one.

(*as chorus*)

Let lilting voices rise
For Apollo, who gives first prize
In the competition.

(*solo*)

For Artemis next, no urging,
The mountain-queen, the virgin,
Who's very fierce.

(*as chorus*)

You're certainly not wrong.
We dedicate this song
To Artemis, then.

(*solo*)

120   Dance on, for here's another,
For Leto, their lady mother.
A different rhythm.

(*as chorus*)

For Leto, lo!, this lilting lay,
Our lyres we pick and pluck and strum.
Light floods from Phoibos' face this day,
From laughing eyes, a rum-te-tum.
Hail Phoibos, Leto's son, and his sis-
Ter, Leto's daughter, Artemis.

MNESILOCHOS.

130   Ooh. Lovely. Swaying...yielding...
Open-your-mouth-darling...kissy-kissy...
Run your fingers along my...Ooooooh.
Listen, friend, I don't know who you are,
But you remind me of that play, what-was-its-
         name,
You know, that big hit, that thing by Aeschylus:
Lykourgos, Lykourgos, wherefore art thou Lykourgos –
Something like that. Wherefore art thou, anyway?
There's something wrong. Yellow dress, lute,
Hair-net, high heels, oil-bottle, handbag...
It doesn't add up. Why the sword and the makeup
140   box?
Who are you? *What* are you? If you're a man,
There are several bits missing. Boots...cloak...
Dingle-dangle... If you're a woman,

What happened to your tits? What's the matter?
Lost your voice as well? D'you want me to *guess*
What you are? Is that it? From that song?

AGATHON.

Sour grapes, old man. You're jealous. In any case,
It's sticks and stones to me. I have my art,
And I dress to suit my inspiration.
That's how poetry works: one's bent, how shall I put it,
Bent into shape by the Muse of the moment.   150
If one's writing a play about women,
One adjusts one's dress to suit one's theme.
Simple, really.

MNESILOCHOS.

Thank god it's not *Oedipus* you're writing.
Too much of an eyeful.

AGATHON.

I see you understand.
If one's writing about a man, one has to hand,
As it were, hung about one's person, all the bits
And pieces. Otherwise, one improvises.

MNESILOCHOS.

When you get to the dirty part, send for me.
I've all the bits, as it were, hung, here.

AGATHON.

In any case, one has one's standards.
One's an artist, not some kind of hairy beast.
I mean, think about Ibykos, Anakreon, Alkaios: 160
All that refinement, that exquisiteness –
Of *course* they wafted around in grace and silk.
And Phrynichos – you know his work, of course –
Such a *shapely* man, such a lovely mover,
And the same can be said of his effusions:
An ecstasy of taste from first to last.

MNESILOCHOS.

H'm. If what you write depends on who you are,
That explains Philokles, Xenokles, Theognis.

Tough, rough and duff – not to mention the guff
170   they write.

AGATHON.
Exactly. That's why one took oneself in hand.

MNESILOCHOS.
You keep *saying* that. *Show* me.

EURIPIDES.
That's enough.
You're worse than a puppy. Down!

(*to* AGATHON)

I understand.
I was just the same when *I* began to write.

MNESILOCHOS.
'I was just the same'...that explains a lot.

EURIPIDES.
Shut up and let me tell him why we're here.

MNESILOCHOS.
Get on with it.

EURIPIDES.
My dear Agathon, you know what they say:
A stitch in time. A nod and a wink.
I'll cut it short. I've got a problem.
Only you can help.

AGATHON.
180   What problem?

EURIPIDES.
Women. At the festival, today.
They say I make fun of them. They want my blood.

AGATHON.
They want *your* blood. And *you* want *me* to help.

EURIPIDES.
I want you to go to the festival, slip in,
Take part, just as if you were one of them.

They won't even notice. And when the moment comes,
Stand up and speak in my defence. You can,
You must. Only you can do it. You *understand*.

AGATHON.
Why can't you go and make a speech yourself?

EURIPIDES.
I'm too well-known. Too easy to recognise.
In any case, I'm grey... big, bushy beard...   190
Whereas you – you're smooth, and soft, and white.
You've a lovely voice, you move well, you're *neat*...

AGATHON.
Ahem.

EURIPIDES.
What?

AGATHON.
D'you remember that line of yours?
You love your life. Your Daddy loves his too.

EURIPIDES.
That's right.

AGATHON.
And you still want me to help you?
I'm not that daft. You got yourself into this,
You get yourself out. There's another pair of lines:
When storms of troubles blow – and they can, my son –
Don't try to wriggle out, be a man, my son.

MNESILOCHOS (*aside*).
That's easy for *him* to say. 'Be a *man*, my son'?   200

EURIPIDES.
There's more to it than that. What's wrong with you?

AGATHON.
If I went I'd be sorry. Far more than you.

EURIPIDES.
Oh, why?

AGATHON.
> All *you* do is mock them. *I* steal their men.
> Or so they say.

MNESILOCHOS.
> Well, what do you expect
> If you go around like that?

EURIPIDES.
> You're saying no?

AGATHON.
> Yes: no.

EURIPIDES.
> Alack! Oh woe! Where can a poor man go?

MNESILOCHOS.
210
> There, there. Cheer up. Come to uncle.

EURIPIDES.
> But what am I going to do?

MNESILOCHOS.
> Tell him: get stuffed.
> Uncle's here. I'll help. Just tell me what you want.

EURIPIDES.
> You mean, *you?* You'll do...*anything?* All right,
> Take your cloak off.

MNESILOCHOS.
> Easy. There. What for?

EURIPIDES.
> For the shaving scene. The shaving and singeing
>   scene.

MNESILOCHOS.
> Whatever you say. I offered, after all.

EURIPIDES.
> Agathon, you're smooth. As smooth as they come.
> Lend us a razor.

AGATHON.
Of course. There's the case, there.
Choose any you like.

EURIPIDES.
Thank you *so* much. 220

(*to* MNESILOCHOS)

Sit there. Puff out your cheek.

MNESILOCHOS.
Ow.

EURIPIDES.
Stop moaning. Put a sock in it, or I will.

MNESILOCHOS.
Ah-ta-ta-ta-HAH.

EURIPIDES.
Where you are going?

MNESILOCHOS.
To sanctuary. The temple. I'm not staying here
To be sliced to bits.

EURIPIDES.
The temple? With one bare cheek?

MNESILOCHOS.
One's quite enough.

EURIPIDES.
Oh, sit down. *Please.*
Uncle. Stand by me. Sit.

MNESILOCHOS.
I'm done for.

EURIPIDES.
No you're not.
Look up. Sit still. Stop wriggling. 230

MNESILOCHOS.
Mooh. Mooh.

EURIPIDES.
Rubbish. There!

MNESILOCHOS.
My god, there's nothing left.

EURIPIDES.
Nothing but character. Sir would like to see?

MNESILOCHOS.
Show me.

EURIPIDES.
There.

MNESILOCHOS.
Oh no, it's Kleisthenes!

EURIPIDES.
Stand up. It's singeing time. Bend over.

MNESILOCHOS.
What d'you think I am, a sucking pig?

EURIPIDES.
Someone bring a torch. Right, bend.
Keep your tail out of the way.

MNESILOCHOS.
240   Don't worry, I'll – *yeow!* That hurts!
I'm on fire. Ooh-aah. Quick, water it!
It's going up in smoke.

EURIPIDES.
Not long now.

MNESILOCHOS.
What d'you mean, not long?

EURIPIDES.
I'm nearly done.

MNESILOCHOS.
You're nearly done? I'm crisped.
What a stink of soot. You've barbecued my bum.

EURIPIDES.
I'll get a slave to wipe it.

MNESILOCHOS.
Just let him try.

EURIPIDES.
Agathon, I'm sorry to disturb you.
But...a dress, shoulder pads...
It's not as if you're short...   250

AGATHON.
Which d'you fancy? It's all the same to me.

MNESILOCHOS.
H'm. Which suits me best...?

AGATHON.
How about this one? This daffodil silk...

MNESILOCHOS.
Very nice. What's it smell of? Jockstrap.

EURIPIDES.
Just put it on.

AGATHON.
Now the pads.

EURIPIDES.
There.

MNESILOCHOS.
Hey, wrap it round my legs.

EURIPIDES.
Pass the hair-net, the wig.

AGATHON.
What about this one? One uses it after dark.

EURIPIDES.
We guessed.

MNESILOCHOS.
Does it go? Do I look all right?

EURIPIDES.
260   You're beautiful. Now, a shawl.

AGATHON.
There's one there, on the couch.

EURIPIDES.
And shoes.

AGATHON.
Take these. My best pair.

MNESILOCHOS.
Do they fit?

EURIPIDES.
Of course they fit. He *likes* a loose fit.

AGATHON.
Got everything? In that case, excuse me.
Roll back the housefront, someone.

The ekkuklema removes AGATHON *from view.*

EURIPIDES.
Now, madam. You certainly look the part.
But there's still the voice. You've got to sound...
How shall I put it?...demure, alluring.

MNESILOCHOS.
Like this?

EURIPIDES.
Yes. Time to go.

MNESILOCHOS.
There's just one thing. You have to promise...

EURIPIDES.
What?

MNESILOCHOS.
270   To rescue me, if things get out of hand.

EURIPIDES.
By Air I swear, the dwelling-place of Zeus.

MNESILOCHOS.
Not good enough. I can't stand airy-fairy swearing.

EURIPIDES.
By gods' lofty pinnacles on high I swear.

MNESILOCHOS.
That's better. Pinnacles. Now don't forget.
And no uncrossing your fingers, if things get tough.

EURIPIDES.
Get on. They've put the flag up.
The meeting's about to start. I'll leave you to it.

Exit. MNESILOCHOS *minces about, talking to*
THRATTA, *while assorted* WOMEN *take their*
places for the meeting.

MNESILOCHOS.
Do keep up, Thratta. Walk this way.
Just *look* at all the torches.   280
What a lot of smoke! I do hope today goes well.
Mother Earth, Persephone, let today go well.
Put the basket down, Thratta. Take out the biscuit.
That's right, dear. For the offering.
Mother Earth, majesty, darling,
Persephone queen of the Underworld,
Accept my offering a thousand, thousand times –
Or at least this once. Let my little daughter
Piggy-wig find the rich dimwit husband she's
   looking for,   290
Let my darling little Willy grow big and strong.
Amen. Now, where's the best place to sit, I wonder,
To hear the speeches properly? That's right, Thratta,
Off you go. When the speeches start, no slaves allowed.

The CHORUS *has gathered. The* HERALDESS *steps*
forward.

HERALDESS.
Silence, silence.
Pray to the holy Twain:

To Demeter, to Persephone her daughter,
To the lord of Wealth, her consort,
To Loveliness her handmaid,
To Mother Earth who nourisheth,
300   To Hermes, soul-guide,
To the Graces.
Bless this our gathering,
Our festival,
Smile on Athens; smile on us.
Whoever giveth best advice
For the city,
For its women,
Hear her, accept her words.
Gods, hear our prayer.
310   Bless us.
Amen. Let the festival begin!

CHORUS.
Come down, our song inspire,
Lord Zeus, our prayer enhance;
Apollo, take your lyre,
And lead the sacred dance.

Athene, warrior-queen,
Who wields the golden spear;
Fair Artemis, be seen,
320   Come down to us, appear.

Poseidon, sealord, leave
Your throne in booming sea,
While nymphs their dances weave,
Their voices floating free.

Let golden harp resound,
Let minstrels sing and play,
Let dancers tread the ground
330   In our festival today.

HERALDESS.
O gods, Olympians, Pythians, Delians,
All others, hear our prayers.

Whoever here today
Slanders our city...
Slanders our womenfolk...
Favours the Persians...
Favours Euripides...
Plots against women...
Works for dictatorship...
Prattles and gossips...
Finds a young man for you,   340
Then runs to master...
Garbles your messages...
Offers you the Moon, the stars, the Sun,
Then finds someone younger for fun...
Rents a handsome and well-hung young stud
When she's past it, exhausted and dud...
Takes your money then won't give you pleasure –
Oh, and wine-sellers giving short measure –
Bad luck to them all! Tears! Misery! Gloom!
Catastrophe! Disaster! Doom!
Send *us* good luck, we pray,   350
At our festival today.

CHORUS.
O gods above,
Praise moderation;
Praise all who love
This nation.
In your all-powerful way
Keep our secrets today;
If anyone blabs,
Keep tabs.
What possible reason
Could there be for such treason?   360
If you find a defector,
Please don't protect her;
A pain, a perversion,
Far worse than a Persian.
Betraying her gender –
Please don't defend her.

Lord Zeus, hear our prayer,
Spread word to the heavenly powers:
Be fair.

370 Be ours.

HERALDESS.
Attention please. MINUTES OF PREVIOUS
MEETING.
(CHAIR: TIMOKLEIA. SECRETARY: LYSILLA.
SPEAKER: SOSTRATE.) MOTION: THAT
TOMORROW MORNING –
That's today, now, since the meeting was
yesterday –
AS SOON AS A QUORUM HAS GATHERED
FOR THE FESTIVAL –
We thought more people would be able to make it
If we chose today – DISCUSSION BE
COMMENCED
ABOUT JUST PUNISHMENT FOR EURIPIDES,
ALREADY CONDEMNED FOR INSULTING
WOMEN. NEM. CON.
Does anyone want to add anything?

MIKKA.
Yes. Me.

HERALDESS.
380 Put on the garland. Speak.

MIKKA.
Ladies. Listen. Ahem.

CHORUS.
Just hear how she clears her throat.
She's done this sort of thing before.

MIKKA.
I'm not trying to show off or anything.
But I *had* to say something. The point is,
I've had enough, I've really had enough
Of that man's mud-slinging. Euripides.
He just can't leave us alone. Who does he think he is?

You remember his mother: that greengrocer in the
    market.
Anyway, what *hasn't* he accused us of?
Every play of his, in every theatre everywhere,   390
Makes us out to be walking mysteries, shiftless,
Obsessed with sex, drink, lies and gossip,
Beyond saving, a plague to all...*man*kind.
So when they come home from the theatre, our
    husbands,
They give us *very* funny looks, start turning out
All the cupboards and drawers to find our fancy-men.
Thanks to him, spilling the beans to our 'better halves',
We can't do *anything* we did in the good old days.
Draw the curtains late one morning, and it's
'Who's that you've hidden behind the arras?'   400
Put yourself on a diet, and it's
'Yon wife of mine hath a lean and hungry look – who
    for?'
Lose *one* little handkerchief, he's up the wall.
And what if he can't give you a baby?
You *have* to get one somewhere –
And how can you, the way he's watching you?
D'you remember how easy it used to be
To find a rich old man to marry? Not any more.   410
An old man weds a tyrant, not a wife –
Euripides. Put them off wedding-bells forever.
It's all that bigmouth's fault – like those bolts and bars
They put on women's quarters nowadays,
And those huge fanged hounds they breed
To scare the boyfriends away. And that's not all.
Once we were mistresses in our own kitchens:
It was up to us what corn, oil, wine we used.
Not any more. Who keeps the keys these days?   420
His Nibs – great fancy things with triple teeth.
Once, all you needed to get into the pantry
Was a ha'penny ring. Break the seal, open up,
Take what you want, reseal, hey presto.
Now, thanks to our playwright friend,
They've all got seals like spider's webs.

'Leave nothing to chance', he says.
And so do I. He's condemned himself. He's dead.
Shall we poison him, or find some other way? –
430   That's all there is to decide. Thankyou, thankyou...
There's a lot more I *could* say,
But I'll leave it in writing with the clerk.

CHORUS.
Such confidence! So true!
I was convinced. Weren't *you?*
Every word well-placed!
Such power! Such taste!
A speech so neat
Will be hard to beat.
440   Even Xenokles
She'd beat with ease.

The MYRTLE-SELLER *takes the speaker's crown.*

MYRTLE-SELLER.
I haven't much to add, really.
This lady really said it all.
I just want to say what happened to me, personally.
My husband died in Cyprus, leaving me
With five little mouths to feed.
I scraped a living, selling myrtle wreaths[28]
For people to wear at sacrifices.
It wasn't much, but we managed –
450   Until *he* started writing plays
Telling people that the gods don't exist.
Imagine that! My business dropped to half.
I think he ought to pay,
He's done terrible things and he ought to be
    punished.
He stinks, worse than that garlic his mother sells.
Well, excuse me, I've got to go: a rush order,
Twenty gentlemen all clamouring for wreaths.

CHORUS.
Another gem! Where do
460   They find such eloquence?

So simple, and yet so true!
Such common sense!
There's nothing more to say.
He's guilty, and soon he'll pay.

MNESILOCHOS.
   I'm not surprised, ladies. Euripides!
   You've every reason to be annoyed.
   I'd be fuming. As a matter of fact I am,
   After what he did to me.
   But that's not the point.   470
   I mean, let's be reasonable.
   We're all friends here, all sisters here.
   No one to spill *our* beans.
   What I say is, why get so cross about pinpricks,
   The two or three little things he's found out about us,
   When there are thousands more he doesn't know?
   I mean, take me for instance.
   The tricks I've played! The stories I could tell!
   Imagine: I'd been married just three days,
   And I was lying there beside my husband.
   Well, I had this friend, this *close* friend.
   He'd known me really well since I was seven.   480
   Anyway, I'm lying there, and suddenly 'Tap! Tap!'
   At the door. I knew who it was at once,
   And what he wanted. I *inch* out of bed,
   His Nibs stirs and says, 'What's the matter?',
   And *I* say, 'I don't know *what's* got into me,
   Twisting and wriggling and writhing. I'll nip outside
   And see to it'. 'Go on then.' Up he jumps
   And starts pounding and grinding aniseed,
   Juniper, sage to ease my guts, while I
   Pour water on the hinge to stop it creaking,
   And slip outside to lover-boy. Oh, it was lovely,
   Beside the statue, clutching that twisty laurel branch.
   You never see *that* sort of thing in Euripides.   490
   Then there's *The Mistress Hot for the Ballsy Shit-carrier* –
   I don't remember *that* in his list of plays.
   Or chewing garlic the morning after the night before –

And *my*, what a night *that* was! – so that when
    Hubby
Comes home from guard-duty he takes one sniff
    and says
'All quiet on the nooky front!'
Let him write about Phaidras and Medeas – who
    cares?
So long as we never see the one about the woman
Who pirouetted past her husband, holding out her
    skirt
500 ('Isn't it *flattering?* Let me do a twirl')
And smuggling out her lover underneath.
And what about *her?* Moans and groans ten days
Pretending labour, while they try to find a child.
Her husband's buying up every medicine in town,
Every speeder-upper he can find – and while he's
    gone
They bring her a brat in a basket,
With a bung in its gob to stop it bawling.
Sir comes back; the midwife nods; she yells,
'Go away, darling, go away, it's starting!'
Out the idiot hurries;
They open the basket, unbung the brat;
510 It howls;
And that wicked old witch who fetched it
Runs to Daddy with a great big smile:
'It's a lion, a lion, the image of his Dad,
The same darling little pine-cone of a willy –'
Well we *do*, don't we?
And *we're* the ones who blame Euripides!
What for? He doesn't know the half of it.

CHORUS.
520 What impudence! What cheek!
Who is *she* to speak?
Every word's a lie.
Uncalled-for. *Why?*
What a terrible fuss
From one of *us!*

Well, *I* don't know –
It goes to show: 530
When a woman is shameless, really out to risk it,
She'll outsmart all rivals, really take the biscuit.

MIKKA.

Ladies, look at us. We're standing here
Hypnotised, gob-smacked, goggling.
You heard her. You heard her insult us all.
Well, she won't get away with it. Who'll help?
Are me and my maids to see to her on our own?
We'll upend her and pluck her and singe her.
That'll teach the bitch,
Next time she's mixing with ladies,
To mind her tongue. Grab her fanny.

MNESILOCHOS.

Not the fanny. That's not funny.   540
I thought this festival was free for all.
Free speech for all. I spoke as I found.
Just because I said nice things about Euripides,
Do I have to be plucked and singed?

MIKKA.

Of course you do. Who else dared to stand there
And say nice things about that...that...
When did he ever write about decent, honest women?
Phaidras, Medeas, he was first in the queue for *them* –
But when it was Penelope's turn, where was he then?

MNESILOCHOS.

He's not to blame. Look around you:
There, and there. Phaidra...Phaidra...Phaidra...
How many Penelopes do *you* see?   550

MIKKA.

That does it! D'you hear her, ladies?

MNESILOCHOS.

You've heard nothing yet.

MIKKA.

Oh yes we have.

MNESILOCHOS.

There are thousands more. For example,
I don't remember Euripides explaining
How to use one of those back-scrapers from the
    baths
To scrape up corn from the pantry.

MIKKA.

Ohhh!

MNESILOCHOS.

Or snitching meat
From the family altar to give your fancy-man,
And blaming the cat –

MIKKA.

You *saw!*

MNESILOCHOS.

560   Remember that woman who did her old man in
With his own chopper? The one who put poison
In Sir's porridge? The one who buried her dear old
    Dad
Under the copper in the garden –?

MIKKA.

She didn't.

MNESILOCHOS.

She did. She was from Acharnai.

MIKKA.

Is there *more* of this?

MNESILOCHOS.

What about the time your maid
Had a little boy, and you had a girl –
And you swapped them over and said nothing?

MIKKA.

You bitch! I'll tear your hair.

MNESILOCHOS.
Just try.

MIKKA.
Philiste, hold my cloak.

MNESILOCHOS.
Keep back, by Artemis, or else I'll –

MIKKA.
Yes?

MNESILOCHOS.
You'll be sorry you ate those figs.   570

CHORUS.
Stop, stop. There's someone coming.
Look how she's running. Put your dresses straight.
Be dignified. See what she has to say.

Enter KLEISTHENES.

KLEISTHENES.
My dears, you know I'm one of you at heart.
I've got the cheeks to prove it. Look.
I've never hidden the way I feel for you –
And that's why I'm here today. It's big.
They were saying in the market... *Do* be careful...
It could be nasty...big and nasty...*do* watch out.   580

CHORUS.
What's the matter, sonny? You don't mind
If I call you sonny? Those downy cheeks...

KLEISTHENES.
They say Euripides has smuggled a relative
In here, some dirty old man –

CHORUS.
Whatever for?

KLEISTHENES.
To spy on your festival.
To listen to your discussions. To find out
Exactly what you have in mind for him.

CHORUS.
But how could he? A man? We'd notice.

KLEISTHENES.
590   Euripides has plucked him and singed him
And dressed him in women's clothes. *You* know.

MNESILOCHOS.
Rubbish! What sort of man would let himself
Be plucked and singed? I know I wouldn't.

KLEISTHENES.
You know nothing about it. It's *true*.
If it wasn't true, why else would I have come?

CHORUS.
This is serious. He must be lurking somewhere.
Quickly, ladies. Turn everything upside-down
600   Until you find him. Is he up *there?* Down *there?*
Kleisthenes, darling, do lend a hand.

KLEISTHENES.
Of course.

(*to* MIKKA)

You, madam. Who are you?

MNESILOCHOS (*aside*).
Now what can I do?

KLEISTHENES (*to* MIKKA).
I have to question everyone.

MNESILOCHOS (*aside*).
I knew it.

MIKKA.
If you must know, I'm Kleonymos' wife.

KLEISTHENES.
Do any of these ladies vouch for you?

CHORUS.
Of course we do. Move on, move on.

KLEISTHENES.
Who's this young lady with the baby?

MIKKA.
That's nanny. My baby's nanny.

MNESILOCHOS (*aside*).
I'll try to slip away.

KLEISTHENES.
Just a minute. Who are *you?*
Stand still.   610

MNESILOCHOS.
Cheeky monkey! I have to pass water.
Kindly let me pass.

KLEISTHENES.
All right. Pass over there. I'll wait.

CHORUS.
Yes, wait – and then take a very close look.
No one recognises that one. She's very strange.

KLEISTHENES.
You're not *still* peeing, are you?

MNESILOCHOS.
Won't be long, darling. It's just...I can't...
I should never have eaten all that cress.

KLEISTHENES.
What's cress to do with it? Come here.

MNESILOCHOS.
Put me down. You brute.

KLEISTHENES.
What's your husband's name?

MNESILOCHOS.
You know, surely. Everyone knows.
Him up the road.   620

KLEISTHENES.
Him up the road? Which him up the road?

MNESILOCHOS.
That's right. Whichhim. Uptheroad. My husband.

KLEISTHENES.
You're babbling. Have you been here before?

MNESILOCHOS.
Every year, you silly boy.

KLEISTHENES.
Who did you come with?

MNESILOCHOS.
That's right. Whod'yecome.

KLEISTHENES.
You're not making sense.

MIKKA.
Excuse me, darling. Let me have a go.
There are questions I can ask...*women's* stuff...
You wouldn't think of them, being, er, male.
Stand back, out of earshot. That's it.
Now, you. What was the first thing we did
When we arrived for the festival this morning?

MNESILOCHOS.
630   What was the first thing...? H'm. We had a drink.

MIKKA.
And the second thing?

MNESILOCHOS.
A second drink.

MIKKA.
Someone's been talking. What happened next?

MNESILOCHOS.
Xenylla ran for the bushes. There wasn't a potty.

MIKKA.
Got you! She didn't. Kleisthenes, come here.
This is the one.

KLEISTHENES.
What shall I do with her?

MIKKA.
Strip her. You should hear what she's been saying.

MNESILOCHOS.
Strip me? A mother of nine?

KLEISTHENES.
Take off that bra. Don't argue.

MNESILOCHOS.
Cow.

MIKKA.
There's something wrong here. Look: no tits.   640

MNESILOCHOS.
I'm barren. I never had a child.

MIKKA.
A moment ago you'd nine.

KLEISTHENES.
Stand properly. Where have you stuffed your willy?

MIKKA.
Through here. Isn't it *sweet?* It's blushing, look.

KLEISTHENES.
I can't see it.

MIKKA.
He's popped it round in front again.

KLEISTHENES.
No he hasn't.

MIKKA.
It's back behind again.

KLEISTHENES.
It's a shuttle service. In, out, in, out,
You'd think he was tatting a mat.

MIKKA.

This is the one all right: likes Euripides...
Said all those *wicked* things about us.

MNESILOCHOS (*aside*).

650   Whoops.

MIKKA.

What shall we do with him?

KLEISTHENES.

Keep him here. Don't let him get away.
I'll fetch a policeman. Won't be long!

Exit.

CHORUS.

Gather round. Hitch up your skirts.
One man got in. Are there *others* here?
Search everywhere: the wings,
The stage, behind the scenes.
Quickly, carefully,
660   Check all around.
Cautiously, silently,
Don't make a sound.
They're sneaky,
They're cheeky,
They could be lurking,
And smirking.
Search far and near.
Leave nothing to chance,
Make it into a dance.
Over here. Over here.

Dance.

Catch them! Blasphemers,
Atheists, schemers,
They pollute this place.
Punish the swine! Make them kneel,   670
Make them howl, make them squeal,
Make them pay for this disgrace.

Make them cry
To the sky,
Make them beg for god's blessing,
Confessing.
If they fight,
If they bite,
If they're mad, if they're manic,   680
Don't panic.
The gods are on guard.
They'll hit them hard –
Yes, and anyone else
Who rebelse.
They'll use this play to reach 'em,
They'll use this play to teach 'em –
Through pity and terror –
To steer clear of error.
We've looked everywhere. It's clear.
There's no one here.

MNESILOCHOS *snatches* MIKKA's *bundle and*
clambers up the altar out of reach.

MIKKA.
Aah! Where are you going? Come down!
Help! He's stolen Diddums,   690
Snatched him from Mummy's arms.

MNESILOCHOS.
Shout all you like. Take one more step,
You won't see Diddums' fat little face again.
With a single slice of this nice sharp knife
I'll butcher the brat and that'll be that.
We're talking blood, big blood.

MIKKA.
Oh no. Help! Help!
Sing a song. Raise a shout. Do something wild.
In a trice he'll slice Diddums, my only child.

CHORUS.
Ee-ah! Ee-ah!

700   O woe is me,
What a sight to see.
You shameless, wicked one,
What horror have you done?

MNESILOCHOS.
I've made you think, and I don't mean maybe.

CHORUS.
You plague, you curse.
Could anything be worse?

MIKKA.
Of course it could. HE'S GOT MY BABY.

CHORUS.
Who could believe it?
Who could conceive it?

MIKKA.
You kidnapping clown.
710   Oh, you won't get away.
You'll be sorry. You'll pay.

MNESILOCHOS.
But I'm not coming down.

MIKKA.
Give him back!
You'll be black,
You'll be blue, dancing agony's dance –

MNESILOCHOS.
Not a chance.

CHORUS.
You're alone.
Weep and moan.
You're a villain, a rascal, a rabble –

MNESILOCHOS.
Don't babble.
He's here, and here he stays.

CHORUS.
In a thousand ways
You'll be sorry for this. You'll regret it.

MNESILOCHOS.
Forget it.

CHORUS.
You use a child to block us,
You dance about and mock us –   720
You boaster, you bluffer,
You're certain to suffer.
Bring firewood. Bring torches.
Let's see if he scorches.

MIKKA.
Come on, Mania. We'll gather sticks.

(*to* MNESILOCHOS)

We'll make a barbecue – of you.

Exit with MANIA.

MNESILOCHOS.
I'm *so* scared. Come on, little Diddums,   730
Let's see what you look like. *Aren't* you wrapped?
What sweet little tootsies. Doomed, poor brat –
And it's all oo's Mummy's fault... Just a minute.
Where's the rest of you? Where's Diddums gone?
A skin of wine. That explains the wrapping.
Not to mention the tootsies. Ladies and gentlemen,
Just look at this. Ah, women, god bless 'em,
They're all the same. 'Drink to me only',
'I don't mind if I do', 'There's a tavern in the town' –
And they do such a *profitable* Ladies' Night.

Enter MIKKA *and* MANIA.

MIKKA.
Put the sticks here, Mania. Pile them high.

MNESILOCHOS.

740   Yeah, Mania, pile. And you, madam, tell me:
Is this little Diddums? Your pride and joy?

MIKKA.
I carried that Diddums for nine long months.

MNESILOCHOS.
Nine months? You carried this?

MIKKA.
Exactly.

MNESILOCHOS.
How big would you say – two pints?

MIKKA.
You dirty old man. You've interfered with
Diddums.
Poor ickle darling.

MNESILOCHOS.
Ickle?

MIKKA.
Ickle.

MNESILOCHOS.
Looks big enough to me.
A good year, was it?

MIKKA.
What d'you mean, good year?
Put Diddums down.

MNESILOCHOS.
No.

MIKKA.
We'll crisp you.

MNESILOCHOS.

750   Crisp away. Just wait while I bare my blade.

MIKKA.

No, please. Oh please. Do what you like with me,
But spare my child.

MNESILOCHOS.

She really loves her Diddums.
Isn't that sad? Now shut up and let me slice.

He stabs the wineskin and drinks.

MIKKA.

Aah-aah! Quick, Mania, a bowl, a basin –
Anything to catch that baby's blood.

MNESILOCHOS.

Hold it out. I don't mind sharing. Careful!

MIKKA.

You bastard! There's nothing left.
How can you bear to see me so deprived?

MNESILOCHOS.

Depraved, you mean. Here. Have this.

He throws the skin at her.

MIKKA.

What's that for?

MNESILOCHOS.

I got the skinful, and you get the skin.
Now go away.

Enter KRITYLLA.

KRITYLLA.

O Mikka, Mikka, why are you sobbing so?   760
Good grief, who's done for Diddums?

MIKKA.

That swine up there.
Stay here, keep watch, while I fetch Kleisthenes
And that hunky policeman.

(*to* MNESILOCHOS)

I'm going to *tell.*

Exit.

MNESILOCHOS.
   What next? There has to be some cunning plan,
   Some subtle stratagem. It's all his fault.
   Euripides. He got me into this –
   Where is he when I need him, now?
   A message. I'll send him a message.
   Like in that play of his, *Palamedes,*

770   When the chap wrote 'Help' on bits of oar
   And threw them overboard. Bits of oar...
   Bits of oar... Ah! Votive plaques. The very thing.
   What d'you mean, pardon? Votive plaques. These,
      here.
   They're made of wood. They look like bits of oar.
   I write on them, I throw them overboard –
   What more d'you want? Come, hands, to work.
   Fingers be nimble, thumbs be quick.
   This is a rather clever trick.
   Wise wood, come here and let me whittle.
   Here's a good one. This little bit'll

780   Do nicely. HUH...EH...ULL...p – OW!
   That's a terrible pee,
   Looks more like a tree,
   But it'll do for now.

   He skims the plaque away like a frisbee.

   Fly, fly, with grace and ease
   To Euripides.
   If he doesn't come soon, his dear old unc
   Will be entirely sunk.

   He subsides and waits. The CHORUS *dances.*
   Then:

CHORUS.
   What comes next is a speech on behalf
   Of the feminine sex – or 'those pests',
   As you gentlemen call us: the root

Of all wrangles and quarrels and fights.
Inconsistency rules. If we're pests,
Then why marry us? Why keep us shut   790
In at home, why forbid us to peep
Through the windows, why rumble and roar
If we take just one step out of doors?
If we're pests, you should fall on your knees,
Thank the gods that we're out of the house.
If we go to a party and then
Spend the night with a girl-friend, you sulk
Till your 'pest' comes back home. If we're bold,
If we smile from our balconies, how
You adore it – and then, if we're coy,
If we blush and retire, how you shout,
Stamp and whistle for more. Which are best,   800
Men or women? We'll have to name names.
What it means is, Charminos is matched
With Nausimache, queen of the seas.
Kleophon, Salambaccho. Need I mention
Aristomache, First Lady of Marathon?
Stratonike? Euboule, who gave up her life
For her city? – you've all seen the statue.
I needn't go on. It's no contest.   810
Which woman embezzles state funds
To buy horses, then gallops round town
With her nose in the air? If we snitch
It's the price of a loaf from the housekeeping –
Yes, and it's made up the very same day.

Who needs argument? Men
Are inferior: vulgar
And greedy and sly.
Women manage their lives
With a sure sense of thrift –   820
For example, we use
Granny's shuttle and shaft:
Just as good as they were
When she plied them herself –
And her sunshade still wards off the sun.

Whereas *Grandad's* old spear
And his sheltering shield –
Where are *they?* What d'you mean,
You abandoned them, dropped them and ran?

Discrimination.
830   We could mention a thousand things.
Mothers of heroes, for example.
If a man does patriotic service,
By land or sea, serves the state well –
Don't you think it's right for his mother
To be honoured, to take a front seat
At festivals and feasts?
Then there's the other kind:
Mothers of cowards, losers, traitors –
Shouldn't their heads be shorn,
Shouldn't they be given hard wooden benches
Behind the heroes' Mums? I mean, was it *ever* right
For Hyperbolos' mother,
840   In a dress like that, with *hair* like that,
To sit up there with the mother of...well, *Lamachos?*
Hyperbolos' mother! The money-lender,
    remember?
'Gather all your debts into one convenient parcel' –
What about that inconvenient parcel *she* produced?

Dance.

MNESILOCHOS.
    Strain, strain, strain, I still can't see him.
    I'll go cross-eyed. Where *is* he?
    Was it something I said? Was it *Palamedes?*
    Not *juicy* enough? Try something else...
850   Got it! *Helen.* His latest masterpiece.
    Mm. Helen of Troy. I even look the part.

KRITYLLA.
    What are you wriggling for? What are you staring
      at?
    Be good till the policeman comes. I'll Helen you.

MNESILOCHOS.
Beside these banks Nile's virgin waters flow,
Stand in for rain, and water both the plain
And Egypt's hordes, who feast on senna pods.

KRITYLLA.
You're up to something. Senna pods? Sit still.

MNESILOCHOS.
My native land and parentage I'll tell:
My country Sparta, my father Tyndareus.

KRITYLLA.
Your father was no-damn-use. *Sit still!*   860

MNESILOCHOS.
They call me: Helen.

KRITYLLA.
Another woman, now!
You still haven't paid for the last time. Sit!

MNESILOCHOS.
For my sake, many thousands bit the dust
By the topless towers of Troy.

KRITYLLA.
And *you* survived?

MNESILOCHOS.
My wand'ring steps led hither. Woe is me!
No sign of him, Menelaos my wedded lord.
I wish I were dead, stone dead.

KRITYLLA.
Oh, so do I.

MNESILOCHOS.
But soft, what light up yonder pathway breaks?
Be still, my pounding heart. Is't he? Is't he?   870

Enter EURIPIDES, *armoured like Menelaos,
with a sprig of green vegetable leaves for
helmet-crest.*

EURIPIDES.
Who lords it here, in this stupendous pile?
And will he welcome wanderers, I wonder,
Storm-tossed, ship-shattered, saved from salty
sea?

MNESILOCHOS.
This place is Proteus' palace.

EURIPIDES.
Tell me more.

KRITYLLA.
Don't listen to a word he says. Such lies!
This isn't Proteus' place, it's somewhere else.

EURIPIDES.
Say whither, whither have we steered our course?

MNESILOCHOS.
To Egypt.

EURIPIDES.
Ah! So far! So far from home!

KRITYLLA.
He's doing it again. Don't you be taken in.
880   This is Athens, the temple of The Twain.

EURIPIDES.
You mean, not Proteus' place? Not *Proteus'* place?

KRITYLLA.
You've been too long at sea, darling.
I'm telling you, this isn't Proteus' place.
Whoever Proteus is, he's somewhere else.

EURIPIDES.
You don't mean...shuffled off this mortal coil?
I beg you, show me where his body lies.

MNESILOCHOS.
His tomb's up here. I'm sitting on it now.

KRITYLLA.

How dare you? That's the altar of the Twain.
Don't listen to him. That's an altar, not a tomb.

EURIPIDES.

You sit like Patience on a monument,
In your dreamy dress, fair maid. Why so?

MNESILOCHOS.

Alas!   890
They force me, sir, to bed with Proteus' son.

KRITYLLA.

Why do you tell this strange old man such *lies?*
He's a crook, your worship, a gang of one.
Snuck into our Festival to heist our handbags.

MNESILOCHOS.

Ooh! Well, see if I care. Sticks and stones.

EURIPIDES.

Young woman, who is this crone who slandereth
You so?

MNESILOCHOS.

One of Proteus' *older* daughters.

KRITYLLA.

I am not. My father's name was Antitheos,
And mine's Kritylla. Who *is* this Proteus?

MNESILOCHOS.

Protest how you like. I'll never wed him, no,   900
Never wed your brother, betray my wedded lord,
Red-haired Menelaos, my wedded, absent lord.

EURIPIDES.

Soft, what was that you said? Oh, raise those
    cheeks.

MNESILOCHOS.

I blush to raise these cheeks – and you know why.

EURIPIDES.
Good grief! I shake so much I scarce can speak.
Ye gods, who is it? Who are you, lady? Who?

MNESILOCHOS.
I, too, astonished stand. Sir, who are you?

EURIPIDES.
Art thou Hellenic or Egyptian? Speak.

MNESILOCHOS.
Hellenic. Got it in one. Now *who* are *you?*

EURIPIDES.
Hellenic...Hellenic...Helen! You're she!

MNESILOCHOS.
910   You're he! Menelaos. Of course: the greens.

EURIPIDES.
That's right, I'm he – the wretchedest of men.

MNESILOCHOS.
At last! You're here. You're he. The gods be
   praised.
So take me, take me, husband, hold me tight,
Give us a kiss, and take me, take me, take me,
Away from here. Get on with it.

KRITYLLA.
Stay there.
Put him down, or you'll feel this torch.·

EURIPIDES.
How dare you, madam? My lawful, wedded wife.
Helen of Sparta. I'll take her home again.

KRITYLLA.
920   You're another of them. You're in his gang.
Pretending to be Egyptians! You don't fool me.
He's for it now. He's *really* for it now.
Here comes the organiser, and that policeman.

EURIPIDES.
Ah. Pardon me. I really ought to go.

MNESILOCHOS.
But what about me?

EURIPIDES.
Stay there. Don't move.
Don't panic. I'll think of something.
I'll save you. I've a million more ideas.

MNESILOCHOS.
As many as that? I can hardly wait.

Exit EURIPIDES. *Enter* ORGANISER *and*
CONSTABLE.

ORGANISER.
Here he is. Just as Kleisthenes described.
You, stand up straight. Take him inside;   930
Tie him to a plank; then bring him back and watch
    him.
If anyone comes near him, use your whip.

KRITYLLA.
We've just had someone, a travelling story-teller,
Gave me some real old flannel.

MNESILOCHOS (*to the* ORGANISER).
Madam, I'm on my knees.
I beg you, by your own right hand – the one
That rakes in the money – grant me one favour.
I know I'm doomed, I'm doomed, but still I beg.

ORGANISER.
What is it?

MNESILOCHOS.
Don't let him plank me in this dress.
Please. I'm a poor old man.   940
Don't leave me in a yellow dress to die.
D'you want the crows to laugh as they pick my bones?

ORGANISER.
Request denied. By order. The dress stays on,
To show all passers-by what a swine you are.

MNESILOCHOS.
>Ahahahaah! In a yellow dress, ahaah!
>What can I hope for now? I'm doomed. I'm
>doomed.

The CONSTABLE *and* ORGANISER *take him out.*
Exit KRITYLLA.

CHORUS.
>It's time to dance,
>Time to honour the Twain.
>You remember the words?
950 (Pauson does. Always here,
>Always greedy for more.)

>Make a circle.
>Hold hands. Listen for the tune.
>Twirl, whirl,
>Watch each other,
>Keep the circle, keep the beat.

>Raise voices,
>Hymn
960 The Olympian powers supreme.

>(No satire,
>None!
>Just solemn, sacred joy.)

>Dance, now, dance,
>Sing,
>Renew the sacred strains.

Round dance.

>For Apollo, dance,
>For Artemis,
970 The minstrel, the archer,
>The ever-pure.
>Holy powers, look down,
>Grant victory.
>Queen of Heaven, Hera,
>Your praise we sing.

You love the sacred dance,
You keep the nuptial keys.

For Hermes, dance,
The shepherd;
Pan and his laughing nymphs
Hear our song,
Hear the throb of our dancing,
Be with us now.
Smile on us, smile again;   980
Your praise we sing;
In solemn festival,
We dance your sacred dance.

*The circle breaks; the dancing grows more
frenzied.*

Faster! Faster!
Pick up the beat.
Dionysos, come,
Ivy-crowned.
Lord of the dance,
Lead us, lead us,
Your praise we sing.

Yoo-o-ee!   990
For Dionysos, dance.
Sing in the hills,
In the high hills,
Yoo-o-ee, o-ee, o-ee!

Echoes, bounce,
Sing, mountain-slopes,
Sing caves, sing woods,
For Dionysos,
Ivy-crowned, o-ee, o-ee!   1000

As the dance ends, the CONSTABLE[29] *returns with*
MNESILOCHOS *tied to a plank: a kind of pillory.*

CONSTABLE.
So, now. Be moaning here outside.

MNESILOCHOS.
   Please, constable. I'm desperate.

CONSTABLE.
   No desperate.

MNESILOCHOS.
   A little looser.

CONSTABLE.
   Loser. Yes.

MNESILOCHOS.
   Ye-ow-oo. You're pulling it TIGHTER.

CONSTABLE.
   Tighter. Yes.

MNESILOCHOS.
   Bastard. A-haa-aah-aah.

CONSTABLE.
   I go now. Rug I fetch. Then cosy watch.

   Exit.

MNESILOCHOS.
   Well, *thanks*, Euripides. Wherever you are.

   EURIPIDES *flies overhead on the stage crane.*
   The crane is mocked up as Pegasos, the flying
   horse, and EURIPIDES *is dressed as the*
   myth-hero Perseus. He flies in, waves, and
   flies out.

   Aha! Gods, Zeus above, a ray of hope.
1010 This must mean rescue. Why else
   Would he whizz in and out as Perseus?
   Perseus, eh? That makes me Andromeda.
   I certainly *am* a damsel in distress.
   Not to mention this dress. He's coming
   To rescue me. He must be. He wouldn't just fly by.

   (*partly as Andromeda, partly as himself*)

Fair sea-nymphs, hear,
Be near.
Let me get away
Today.
(Won't someone stop
That cop?)
I want my life
(My wife).
Oh Echo, hear me, let your answering word   1020
Be heard.

EURIPIDES (*offstage, as Echo*).
Be-urd, be-urd.

MNESILOCHOS.
I wail and moan.
That heart of stone
Has pulled this chain
To give me pain.
(The hag was tougher,
But I knew how to bluff her.)
Weep for me, weep.
Shed tears in a heap.
No more bright youth,
No dancing days,
Entrancing days –
(And that's the truth).   1030
In chains I lie, poor sinner,
A monster's dinner.
(I've a nasty hunch
I'll be Glauketes' lunch.)
Poor kidnapped bride,
Nowhere to hide.
Oh weep and groan,
Oh mope and moan,
Sing mournful songs,
Bewail my wrongs.
Oh gods above,
Plucked from all I love,   1040
Chained to this rock

(In this daft frock),
In this dreadful place,
(By the female race).
Oh, no more woe,
I'm doomed, I know.
Don't envy me:
It'll hurt, you'll see.
1050   Oh Zeus, send thunder,
(Split that cop asunder).
What joy remains
Amid these pains?
I'm doomed. What more can I say?
I must leave the light of day,
The Sun's bright, cheery glow,
For the dark, dank depths below.

Enter EURIPIDES, *disguised as Echo.*

EURIPIDES.
All hail to thee, young woman. Goodness me,
God curse the man who pinioned you so sore.

MNESILOCHOS.
And who are you who so bemoans my woe?

EURIPIDES.
I'm Echo, the mythical mocking-bird.
1060   Speciality: repeats. You must remember.
My triumph, last year, with Euripides,
Here on this very spot. Ahem. Dear child,
You know what you have to do. Make moan. Make
   moan.

MNESILOCHOS.
I'll only make moan if you make moan.

EURIPIDES.
I know my lines. Get on with it.

MNESILOCHOS.
Oh holy night,
In chariot bright

With stars, you fly
In the darkling sky.

EURIPIDES.
Kling sky.

MNESILOCHOS.
How can human brain
Such grievous pain –

1070

EURIPIDES.
Vous pain.

MNESILOCHOS.
Conceive.

EURIPIDES.
Onceive.

MNESILOCHOS.
Not yet. Give over.

EURIPIDES.
Vover.

MNESILOCHOS.
Wait for your cue.

EURIPIDES.
Yoocue.

MNESILOCHOS.
Oh shut it.

EURIPIDES.
Utit.

MNESILOCHOS.
Hush!

EURIPIDES.
Ushhhh.

MNESILOCHOS.
What's eating you?

EURIPIDES.
Tingyou.

MNESILOCHOS.
We haven't time.

EURIPIDES.
1080   T-time.

MNESILOCHOS.
I'm warning you.

EURIPIDES.
Ningyou.

MNESILOCHOS.
Come over here.

EURIPIDES.
Verere.

Enter CONSTABLE. EURIPIDES hides.

CONSTABLE.
WHY SHOUTING?

EURIPIDES.
Outing.

CONSTABLE.
I SEND FOR BACKUP?

EURIPIDES.
Ackup.

CONSTABLE.
Hello, hello.

EURIPIDES.
Ello.

CONSTABLE.
You throw your voice?

EURIPIDES.
Oorvoice.

CONSTABLE.
You cheeky.

EURIPIDES.
Eeky.

CONSTABLE.
Whip you want?

EURIPIDES.
Oowant.

CONSTABLE.
YOU MAKE FUN WITH ME?

EURIPIDES.
Ithme.

MNESILOCHOS.
It isn't me, it's her.   1090

EURIPIDES.
Tsher.

CONSTABLE.
Little cheeky one. Come out.
Where you are?

EURIPIDES.
Ooar.

CONSTABLE.
I find you.

EURIPIDES.
Behind you.

CONSTABLE.
Keep talking.

EURIPIDES.
Keep walking.

CONSTABLE.
Is babble. Not funny is at all.

EURIPIDES *reappears, dressed as Perseus.*

EURIPIDES.
Ye gods, what strange, wild land is this?
1100   My wingéd sandals cleave the restless air –
To where? Know, stranger, Perseus is my name,
And here, this bundle in my hand, the Gorgon's
   head.

CONSTABLE.
The gorgeous head.

EURIPIDES.
Not gorgeous, Gorgon. *Please!*

CONSTABLE.
Gorgon cheese.

EURIPIDES.
One taste of this, they turn to stone.

CONSTABLE.
I know what what you mean. Bad cheese.

EURIPIDES.
Egad! What crag is this? What maid
Moored by this rock like sailing-ship to shore?

MNESILOCHOS.
Oh sir, kind gentleman, oh pity me.
Do set me free.

CONSTABLE.
Oi, shut your mouth.
Condemned to die. You shut your mouth.

MNESILOCHOS.
1110   I weep to see thee hanging there, fair maid.

CONSTABLE.
Fair maid? Look closer. Bad old man is here,
Is riffraff, sticky-fingers –

EURIPIDES.
Watch your tongue!
Her highness, Princess Andromeda, here you see.

CONSTABLE.
Look under here. And *here*. No princess is.

EURIPIDES.
Reach out to me; give me your hand, my love.
My friend, please help. All mortals sorrow share.
Perdition catch my soul, but I do love her.

CONSTABLE.
What you say? Is queer you like? I turn him
This way, that way, any way you say.   1120

EURIPIDES.
Untie the maid, dear constable. I'll take
Her in my arms, from bonds to bed. No, please.

CONSTABLE.
You want to fuck this tough old man, go round
The back. Find hole in backside...plank...then *push*.

EURIPIDES.
I'll just untie these chains.

CONSTABLE.
I fetch my whip.

EURIPIDES.
Nay, nay, I must.

CONSTABLE.
You see this snickersnack?
You see your head? One move you make, I slice.

EURIPIDES.
Ai-ee, ai-ee. What now? Shall I make a speech?
No, no, he's far too thick. I'll save my pearls   1130
For another, better time. For now, Plan C.

   Exit.

CONSTABLE.
That crazy bastard nearly make me SHOUT.

MNESILOCHOS.
Oh Perseus, please don't leave me dangling here.

CONSTABLE.
Not *more* princess? I fetch my whip. You stay.

Exit.

CHORUS.
Sing to Athene,
Sing to her now,
Goddess who loves the dance.

1140   Lady, you guard us,
Protect us,
You hold the keys.
Come down to us,
Hater of tyrants, come down to us.

Hear us calling now,
Your women.
Bring peace, come down.

Come, holy Twain,
Come to your shrine.
All men are barred,
1150   Barred from your festival,
The holy dances,
Torch-glow on smiling face.

Come down to us now,
Your worshippers wait.
Hear us, come to us,
Dance with us, sing with us.
We sing for you,
Dance for you. Come down to us.

Enter EURIPIDES, *dressed as a Madam. He speaks to the* CHORUS *as himself.*

EURIPIDES.
1160   Psst. Ladies. Peace. I offer peace.
I'll never libel or mock you again.
Promise. Cross my heart. My side of the bargain.

CHORUS.

And ours? What have you in mind for us?

EURIPIDES.

This poor planked man is my own close kin. A kind
Of uncle. Let me take him home. If you do,
I won't write another word about you. If you don't,
I'll wait till your husbands march home from war
And run and tell them all that's been going on.

CHORUS.

All, eh? We agree. You've persuaded us.   1170
But it's up to you to persuade that constable.

EURIPIDES.

And I know exactly how. Here, puss, puss, puss...

Enter DANCING GIRL.

Now, don't forget what I told you on the way.
The skirt a little higher. *Very* nice.
What else do we need? Yes: one of those Persian tunes.

Music. The DANCING GIRL *dances. Enter* CONSTABLE.

CONSTABLE.

Who make this buzzing? I sleep in there. Oh.

EURIPIDES.

It's all right. A rehearsal, that's all.
This young lady will be dancing later on.

CONSTABLE.

Dance now, rehearse. Is good. Now, please.

The GIRL *dances.*

Is jumping, yes. Ha-hey! Like flea on sheep.   1180

EURIPIDES.

That's enough, darling. You're getting warm.
Take off that dear little jacket. There.
Sit down. That's it, beside the constable.
Give me your foot. I'll loosen your sandal.

CONSTABLE.
    Oohoo. Aarooh. Aaroooaaroooaaroooh.
    Sit closer, closer. Oooooh. What's this?
    And this? So hard, so round, like turnip, oooooh.

EURIPIDES.
    Another dance. Don't be shy. You're shaking.
    You're surely not scared of the nice, kind
      constable?

The GIRL *dances again.*

CONSTABLE.
    See botties. Soft...smooth... High kicks, yes.

(*into his tunic*)

Not you. Lie down. You turn come soon. Oh, soon.

(*to the* GIRL)

So pretty she is. Such titties, such botties, such a –

EURIPIDES (*suddenly to the* GIRL).
    Right. Put this back on. It's time to go.

CONSTABLE.
1190   You let me kiss?

EURIPIDES.
    Of *course*.

The CONSTABLE *and the* GIRL *enfold each other.*

CONSTABLE.
    Oh, oh, oh, papapapapapapapapa-ee.
    Such tongue, is honey. You bed?

EURIPIDES.
    She certainly does not.

CONSTABLE.
    Is money you want?

EURIPIDES.
    What *do* you mean?

CONSTABLE.
    I pay, I pay.

EURIPIDES.
As much as...one drachma?

CONSTABLE.
Ooh, ooh, yes.

EURIPIDES.
Where is it, then?

CONSTABLE.
Ah. No drachma. You take this...

He hands over his quiver.

EURIPIDES.
How nice.

CONSTABLE.
You girl, go. I come.

Exit DANCING GIRL.

You stay, old woman, watch old man.
What name? First tell your name.

EURIPIDES.
Dunabunka.   1200

CONSTABLE.
Dunabunka. Not forget.

Exit.

EURIPIDES.
That's right, sprint.
Hermes, that was brilliant! He's gone –
And so should you be, when I get you free.
Stand up like a hero, stand up straight.

MNESILOCHOS.
I will, I will. Once I get out of *this*.

EURIPIDES.
Now come, like greyhound leashed from slips.
Thy wife, thy family wait.

MNESILOCHOS.
I'm coming, I'm coming.

Exeunt. Pause. Enter CONSTABLE, *dishevelled.*

CONSTABLE.
1210   She good little girl, know everything.
Old woman. Galoo. Now, where old woman gone?
Now where old man? Is trick. Old woman, old woman,
You play me games? Dunabunka.
Galoo. Old woman, old woman. Dunabunka.

CHORUS.
You want the old woman with the bagpipe?

CONSTABLE.
Yes, where she go?

CHORUS.
That way. Oh, and the old man too.

CONSTABLE.
In the yellow dress?

CHORUS.
1220   Couldn't be yellower.
Run. You may still catch them. *That* way.

CONSTABLE.
That tricky old woman. This way? Dunabunka.

CHORUS.
Up *there*. Over *there*. Not that way, *that* way.
You'll never catch them. Run. The *other* way.

CONSTABLE.
She run like wind. I never catch her now.
Dunabunka. Dunabunka.

Exit.

CHORUS.
Run, run, run, get knotted, run.
For today, we've done. We've had our fun.
It's hometime. Holy Twain, we pray,
1230   If you laughed at our play,
Grant first prize today.

Exeunt.

FROGS

Characters

XANTHIAS
DIONYSOS
HERAKLES
CORPSE
CHARON
AIAKOS
SERVANT GIRL
LANDLADY
PLATHANE
EURIPIDES
AESCHYLUS
PLOUTON

silent parts:

CORPSE-BEARERS
EURIPIDES' MUSE
MUSICIANS
SLAVES

FROGS

CHORUS OF HOLY ONES

A large open space. On one side, the door of HERAKLES'
house. On the other, the gateway of the Underworld.
Enter DIONYSOS, wearing a yellow costume covered with a
lion-skin, and carrying a club. Behind him, loaded
with luggage, enter XANTHIAS on a donkey.

XANTHIAS.
　　Hey, sir, shall I start with one of the old routines?
　　They never fail.

DIONYSOS.
　　Yes, if you must.
　　So long as it's not 'I've had this up to here'.
　　Not that again. I've had that up to here.

XANTHIAS.
　　Something more upmarket?

DIONYSOS.
　　'I'm knackered'? No.

XANTHIAS.
　　The Mother of all Funnies?

DIONYSOS.
　　Good idea –
　　Unless it's the one I think it is.

XANTHIAS.
　　Which one?

DIONYSOS.
　　When you shift your bags about, and shout
　　'I've got to dump my load'.

XANTHIAS.
　　Not quite. I had in mind,
　　'Won't someone relieve me – before I relieve myself?' 10

DIONYSOS.
　　Not now. I'll tell you when. When I want to puke.

XANTHIAS.
　　So what's the point of carrying all these bags,
　　If I can't get a laugh with them? They're all at it:
　　Ameipsias, Phrynichos, Lykis.
　　There's *always* a baggage scene.

DIONYSOS.
Except this time.
Leave all that clever stuff to them. I come away
From their plays years older as it is.

XANTHIAS.
Poor old shoulders. They've had it up to here –
20 And that's no joke.

DIONYSOS.
The whole thing's no joke. Here am I,
Dionysos, son of Juice, walking, on foot,
Left, right, left right, while you sit there in style –
Just to save you carrying half a dozen bags.

XANTHIAS.
You mean I'm *not* carrying them?

DIONYSOS.
How can you be? You're riding.

XANTHIAS.
I'm bearing the baggage.

DIONYSOS.
How, bearing it?

XANTHIAS.
Grin-and-bearing it.

DIONYSOS.
How can someone be bearing something,
When something's bearing *him?*

XANTHIAS.
Oh, I don't know.
30 All I know is, I've got to dump my load.

DIONYSOS.
So, dump it. If the donkey's doing you no good,
Let *him* carry it. *You* carry *him.*

XANTHIAS.
Ha! Very funny. I wish I'd served at sea.
I'd be a free man now[30], and you could –

DIONYSOS.
> Shh! We're here. We've reached...the door.
> The door I was making for. This door.
> I'll knock. Hello-oh. Anyone at home?

HERAKLES opens the door.

HERAKLES.
> Who's that hammering? Who d'you think you are?
> My god! What is it? Who *do* you think you are?

He goes inside, bursting with laughter.

DIONYSOS.
> You saw that?

XANTHIAS.
> What?

DIONYSOS.
> You took that in?

XANTHIAS.
> What in?   40

DIONYSOS.
> How scared he was –

XANTHIAS.
> That you were a loony. Yes.

HERAKLES opens the door again, still convulsed.

HERAKLES.
> I'm terribly sorry. I couldn't help it.
> I'm all right now. I'm biting my lip. Oh god, oh god.

DIONYSOS.
> That's quite all right. Don't be alarmed. Approach.
> I want to ask you something.

HERAKLES.
> Excuse me a moment.
> A lion-skin...a yellow dress...a *club*...?
> Are you...going somewhere?

DIONYSOS.
I served with Kleisthenes.

HERAKLES.
Ooh, sailor...

DIONYSOS.
50   We sank twelve or thirteen of them.

HERAKLES.
You and him..*between* you?

DIONYSOS.
Ask anyone.

XANTHIAS.
Then I woke up.

DIONYSOS.
The point is, I was sitting on deck,
Reading Euripides' *Andromeda*,
When I felt a sudden prick. Of desire.

HERAKLES.
How big?

DIONYSOS.
This big.

HERAKLES.
For a woman?

DIONYSOS.
No.

HERAKLES.
A boy, then?

DIONYSOS.
No.

HERAKLES.
A man?

DIONYSOS.
Don't be daft.

HERAKLES.
　　Not...Kleisthenes?

DIONYSOS.
　　This isn't a joke. It's serious.
　　It's eating me away. I just can't cope.

HERAKLES.
　　There, there. What are the symptoms?

DIONYSOS.
　　How can I explain?　　　　　　　　　　　　60
　　Make it simple...? Use words you'll understand...?
　　Have you ever craved, really craved, pea soup?

HERAKLES.
　　A million times. Pea soup!

DIONYSOS.
　　Is that quite clear? Shall I try again?

HERAKLES.
　　No, no. Pea soup's quite clear. If you see what I mean.

DIONYSOS.
　　Well, that's the kind of craving that's eating me.
　　For Euripides.

HERAKLES.
　　But he's a corpse.

DIONYSOS.
　　I *know* that.
　　I'm going to see him, and no one's going to stop me.

HERAKLES.
　　But he's...Down There. In the Underworld.

DIONYSOS.
　　I *know.*
　　I'll go as low as I have to. Lower.　　　　　　70

HERAKLES.
　　But *why?*

DIONYSOS.
I need a classy poet, fast.
Where are the snows of yesteryear? Not here.

HERAKLES.
You're joking. There's Iophon.

DIONYSOS.
Oh, really?
You're really recommending Iophon?
Some yesteryear. Some snow.

HERAKLES.
What about his Daddy?
Sophocles? If you must bring someone back,
Bring Sophocles. Who needs Euripides?

DIONYSOS.
Not fair to Iophon. Such a Daddy's boy.
Can he hack it on his own – or were those Daddy's
    plays?
In any case, he won't. Not Sophocles.
He's easy. He liked it here. He'll like it there.
Not like Euripides. He's such a scamp!
Give him half a chance, he's out of there.

HERAKLES.
Just a minute. What's wrong with Agathon?

DIONYSOS.
He's gone. Good friend,
Good poet, and now he's good and gone.

HERAKLES.
Gone where?

DIONYSOS.
The Banquets of the Blest.

HERAKLES.
What about Xenokles?

DIONYSOS.
To Hell with him.

HERAKLES.
Pythangelos?

XANTHIAS.
What about *me?*
Won't someone relieve me, before I relieve myself?

HERAKLES.
There are millions more of them out there:
The younger generation. Scribbling away,   90
Miles more words to the minute than Euripides.

DIONYSOS.
Barren leaves, dregs, chattering starlings.
They get one play put on, cock their legs once
Against Tragedy, you never hear of them again.
No, no, I want a really ballsy genius –

HERAKLES.
How d'you mean, ballsy?

DIONYSOS.
Technical expression.
Someone who gives inspiration a bit of welly.
'Air, Zeus' garden shed'; 'the foot of Time';   100
'My tongue it was that promised, not my brain.'

HERAKLES.
You go for that?

DIONYSOS.
I'm mad for it.

HERAKLES.
You're joking.
It's a load of old –

DIONYSOS.
Steady. Who's god of drama here?

HERAKLES.
It's just my opinion.

DIONYSOS.
Do *I* lecture *you* on food?

XANTHIAS.
They've forgotten I exist.

DIONYSOS.
Anyway, that's why I'm here. With all this stuff.
Dressed like you. I want you to tell me everything.
I mean, you've *been* there, the Underworld...
That time you went to steal Kerberos. *You* know.
110   I want you to tell me everything about the place:
Harbours, snack-bars, whore-houses, dosshouses,
Water-holes, roads, bed-and-breakfast joints
With the fewest bugs...

XANTHIAS.
They *have* forgotten I exist.

HERAKLES.
I don't believe this. You're *going* there? *You?*

DIONYSOS.
Don't start again. Just tell me a quick way down.
One that's not too hot, and not too cold.

HERAKLES.
120   There's such a lot to choose from. H'm. I know.
There's Kick-Chair-Slipknot Alley. Hanging
      yourself.

DIONYSOS.
Too much of a strain.

HERAKLES.
Stay-Out-in-the-Rain?

DIONYSOS.
Freeze to death, you mean?

HERAKLES.
Exactly.

DIONYSOS.
I'd get cold feet.

HERAKLES.
You want a short cut?

DIONYSOS.
Please. I'm not much of a walker.

HERAKLES.
Right. Straight up the road,
Turn left into Potter's Row...

DIONYSOS.
Then what?

HERAKLES.
Climb to the top of the tower.

DIONYSOS.
Then what?   130

HERAKLES.
When they start the torch-race,
When you hear them shout 'Ready, steady, go!',
You go as well.

DIONYSOS.
 Where?

HERAKLES.
Down.

DIONYSOS.
No thanks. I *hate* minced brain.
What about the other way?

HERAKLES.
What other way?

DIONYSOS.
The way *you* took.

HERAKLES.
Oh, that.
It's more of a cruise than a way. A bottomless lake –

DIONYSOS.
How do I get across?

HERAKLES.
There's an aged ferryman.

DIONYSOS.
Charon, you mean?

HERAKLES.
140   He'll take you over. The fare's two obols.

DIONYSOS.
Two obols? That's nearly half a drach.

HERAKLES.
No kidding. Once you get to the other side,
Past all the snakes and monsters –

DIONYSOS.
You can't scare me. Get on.

HERAKLES.
– you'll come to the Mud Marsh,
The Great Desolation of Dung. That's where they
    keep
Bastards who cheated their friends,
Or beat up their Mummies,
Or walloped their Daddies,
150   Or swore false oaths –

DIONYSOS.
– or quoted Morsimos,
Or danced with Kinesias –

HERAKLES.
Quite suddenly, there'll be a breath of flutes,
And it'll all turn bright and sunny, like up here.
You'll have reached the Myrtle Groves...
The Banquets of the Blest...men and women,
    feasting...

DIONYSOS.
Who are they?

HERAKLES.
The Holy Ones, who understand the mysteries –

XANTHIAS.
Like me and this donkey. I've got to put these down.

Can't wait any longer. Going, going...gone!   160

HERAKLES.
>They'll tell you everything you need to know.
>They'll put you right, on the road to Pluto's Place.
>Good luck.

DIONYSOS.
>I'll need it. Thanks.

>HERAKLES *goes in and shuts the door.*

Pick up the bags.

XANTHIAS.
>But I've only just –

DIONYSOS.
>Don't argue. Now.

XANTHIAS.
>Just a minute.

>*Enter a funeral procesion.*

Can't you get *him* to carry them?

DIONYSOS.
>What if he won't?

XANTHIAS.
>Then I will.

DIONYSOS.
>Aren't we lucky he came along? I'll have a word.   170
>I say. Excuse me. You, lying there.
>A little favour...? A bag or two...down there?

CORPSE.
>What bags?

DIONYSOS.
>Just these.

CORPSE.
>All those? Two drachmas.

DIONYSOS.
You're joking.

CORPSE (*to* BEARERS).
On we go.

DIONYSOS.
Can't we discuss this?

CORPSE.
Two drachs or nothing.

DIONYSOS.
Nine obols?

CORPSE.
I'd rather live!

Exit procession.

XANTHIAS.
Cheeky beggar. To Hell with him. I'll do it.

DIONYSOS.
I don't know what I'd do without you.
This way. Down to the jetty.

Enter CHARON *in his ferry-boat.*

CHARON.
180   Avast behind!

DIONYSOS.
Pardon?

XANTHIAS.
It's that lake he was on about. That ferry-boat.

DIONYSOS.
This must be Charon, then. Ooh-ar, me hearty.
See?

CHARON.
Any more for the Ground Floor, the Dogs,
The Last Resting Place, the Lower Depths?

DIONYSOS.
Yes. Me.

CHARON.
Get in, then, quick.

DIONYSOS.
. You go all the way to Hell?

CHARON.
You'll see. Get in.

DIONYSOS.
Xanthias, after you.

CHARON.
Oh, no you don't.   190
No slaves allowed – unless they served at sea.

XANTHIAS.
Ah. Flat feet. They wouldn't take me.

CHARON.
Tough. Start walking. The whole way round.

XANTHIAS.
Where shall I meet you?

CHARON.
At the Skull and Skeletons.
The pub by the Withered Rock.

DIONYSOS.
Have you got that?

XANTHIAS.
I've got it, I've got it.
I don't want it, but I've got it.

Exit.

CHARON.
Right. You. Sit to the oar.
Anyone else? Any more for the Die-lark?
Hey, what are you doing?

DIONYSOS.
Sitting on my oar. That's what you said.

CHARON.
200   You great fat... Here, sit here.

DIONYSOS.
All right.

CHARON.
Grab hold.

DIONYSOS.
All right.

CHARON.
Now, stop fooling about, and *pull*.

DIONYSOS.
Pull? Me? I've never rowed before.
Which end did you say you hold?

CHARON.
It's simple, once you start.
They'll help you.

DIONYSOS.
Who will?

CHARON.
Frog-swans. Singing. You'll see. Are you ready?

DIONYSOS.
I suppose so.

CHARON.
Right. LEAN-and-PULL, LEAN-and-PULL...

DIONYSOS *starts rowing to this rhythm. The air gradually fills with the sound of* FROGS. *Their song is in an entirely different rhythm, and puts* DIONYSOS *off his stroke.*

FROGS.
Brekekekex, koax, koax,
210   Brekekekex, koax, koax.

Children of the limpid lake,
Sing with us, till echoes break
Along the reedbeds by the shore,
Koax, koax.
Sing, as you never sang before,
For Dionysos, lord of Vine,
Who leads singing, leads laughter,
Leads revels in the shrine –

Leads fuzzy heads, the morning after.
Brekekekex, koax, koax.   220

DIONYSOS.
I'm getting a blistered behind,
Koax, koax,
And you don't seem to mind.

FROGS.
Brekekekex, koax, koax.

DIONYSOS.
You're going too FAR with your koax.
Is that all you ARE, koax?

FROGS.
In deep dark pools, where fat carp feed,
We plant and tend the sacred reed
For Apollo's lute. The Muses hymn us,
Expert divers, expert swimmers –
They love our song.
Horn-footed Pan agrees,   230
As he dances through the trees –
And he's not wrong.
Brekekekex, koax, koax.

DIONYSOS.
I getting sore.
My bottom's sweating,
Fretting,
Ready to roar –

FROGS.
Brekekekex, koax, koax.

DIONYSOS.
240   That's over the top.
    Please stop.

FROGS.
    In sunny, summer days,
    Our song was a mist, a haze
    Rising to heaven. Now, in the rain,
    We sing again,
    Diving and burbling,
    Singing and gurgling,
    For you, for you,
    A bubble of melody bursting through –

DIONYSOS.
    Brekekekex, koax, koax.
250   Ye gods, *I'm* doing it now.
    I got that from you.

FROGS.
    Well, give it back.

DIONYSOS.
    I'm on the rack.
    I'm rowing myself in two.
    I'd stop, but I don't know how.

FROGS.
    Brekekekex, koax, koax.

DIONYSOS.
    You're driving me mad.

FROGS.
    How sad.
    We're a musical crowd.
260   All night and all day,
    We open our gullets and say –

DIONYSOS.
    Brekekekex, koax, koax.
    How's that for loud?

FROGS.
　You won't beat us.

DIONYSOS.
　No fret, no fuss.
　I'll shout you down. I'll yell myself hoarse.
　I'll stop your koaxing, if need be by force.
　Brekekekex, KOAX, KOAX.
　No answer? Give in, KOAX?
　I knew I'd win, KOAX.

CHARON.
　Lay to! We're here. Ship the oar and step ashore.
　Fares, please.

DIONYSOS.
　Two obols. Here.　　　　　　　　　　　　　　270

　　He steps ashore. The boat disappears.

　Xanthias? Oo-oo. Xanthy.

XANTHIAS (*out of sight*).
　Ya-oo.

DIONYSOS.
　Come over here.

XANTHIAS (*appearing*).
　Welcome to Hell, sir.

DIONYSOS.
　What *is* there?

XANTHIAS.
　Mud...dark...

DIONYSOS.
　Did you see the Daddy-bashers and oath-breakers
　He told us about?

XANTHIAS.
　Can't *you?*

DIONYSOS.
　Oh my god. *Now* what?

XANTHIAS.
Now we get out of here. Fast.
This is where all the nasties are. *He* said.

DIONYSOS.
He said? And you believed him? He was piling it on,
Trying to scare me. Me – Mr Brave, Mr Iron
280   Resolve.
Typical Herakles: all mouth and monsters.
Twelve labours! I'll have thirteen any day.

XANTHIAS.
What's that?

DIONYSOS.
What? Where?

XANTHIAS.
Behind you.

DIONYSOS (*pushing him behind*).
Get over there.

XANTHIAS.
Now it's in front.

DIONYSOS (*pushing him in front*).
Get *there*, I said.

XANTHIAS.
A huge great beast.

DIONYSOS.
T-tell me.

XANTHIAS.
It's horrible. Keeps changing. Now it's a cow...
290   A mule...a pretty girl...

DIONYSOS.
Let's have a look.

XANTHIAS.
Too late. Changed again. She-wolf.

DIONYSOS.
  It's probably Empousa.

XANTHIAS.
  Fiery features.

DIONYSOS.
  Is one leg made of copper?

XANTHIAS.
  It is, and one of cowdung.

DIONYSOS.
  Where can I hide?

XANTHIAS.
  Come back!

DIONYSOS.
  Is there a priest in the house?
  A priest of Dionysos? Help!³¹

XANTHIAS.
  We're done for, Herakles.

DIONYSOS.
  Don't call me that down here.

XANTHIAS.
  Dionysos, then.

DIONYSOS.
  That's worse.   300

XANTHIAS.
  Bad girl! Shoo! This way, sir.

DIONYSOS.
  What d'you mean?

XANTHIAS.
  Out of this nettle, danger, we pluck this flower,
  Safety.

DIONYSOS.
  Eh?

XANTHIAS.
  Empousa's hopped it.

DIONYSOS.
  You're joking.

XANTHIAS.
  I promise.

DIONYSOS.
  Cross your heart.

XANTHIAS.
  And spit in your eye. Sir.

DIONYSOS.
  D'you know, I went quite pale.

XANTHIAS.
  You went pale? You should see that priest.

DIONYSOS.
310 What a brute! Where *did* she come from?
  Air, Zeus' garden-shed? The foot of time?

  A flute is heard, offstage[32].

  Hey!

XANTHIAS.
  What?

DIONYSOS.
  Can't you hear it?

XANTHIAS.
  What?

DIONYSOS.
  A breath of flutes.

XANTHIAS.
  And a whiff of torches. Nice.

DIONYSOS.
  Get your *head* down. Shh! We'll listen.

CHORUS (*offstage*).
   Iacchos, O Iacchos!
   Iacchos, O Iacchos!

XANTHIAS.
   It's a procession. The Holy Ones. The Blest.
   He told us. They sing and dance. It's them.   320

DIONYSOS.
   Get down. Shut up. Let's see.

   Enter CHORUS. *They are carrying the statue of
   Iacchos in a torchlit procession.*

CHORUS.
   Iacchos,
   Here in this holy place,
   Iacchos, O Iacchos,
   Dance with us,
   Sing with us.
   Toss your head,
   Flower-crowned,   330
   In the holy dance.
   Dance with us,
   Sing with us,
   Your worshippers,
   Your holy ones,
   Come, share our feast we pray,
   Come, crown this holy day.

XANTHIAS.
   What's that I can smell? Roast pork?

DIONYSOS.
   If you want some sausage, shush.

CHORUS.
   Iacchos,
   Shine in our darkness, lord.   340
   Iacchos, O Iacchos,
   Morning star,
   End night for us,

Shine for us.
All dance for you,
Old men shake off
Their years and dance,
Dance for you,
Your worshippers,
350   Your holy ones.
Here in this place of night
Dance for us, lord of light.

If you're not one of us,
If you don't know the words,
If you don't know the steps,
Keep away.
If you can't hold your drink,
If you can't take a joke,
360   If you can't make a joke,
Keep away.
If it's profit you want,
If it's 'I'm all right, Jack',
If it's 'I was elected, I'm making my pile,
I'm in charge, I've a mandate,
I'll rob and I'll cheat and I'll do as I like –
And if comedy playwrights make fun of me,
Cut off their subsidies' –
Please keep away.
Keep away.
Keep away.
There's no room for you here.
Only singers allowed,
370   Only dancers,
Who honour the gods
And dance our dance.

Dance!
In fields of flowers advance.
Sing!
380   Happy voices raise,
To the goddess of spring
Sing praise.

Persephone, praise! Demeter too,
Harvest-bringer, we honour you.

Dance!
Excite, inspire, entrance.
Sing!
With laughing eyes   390
Bring luck, bring laughter, bring
First prize.

To Iacchos again your voices raise.
To the lord of the dance, sing praise.

Lord Iacchos, along the sacred way
Sing with us, dance with us today.   400
Our spirits soaring, our hearts on fire
We'll follow you, we'll never tire.
O Iacchos, lord, come lead the dance.
We revelled last night from dusk till dawn;
Shoes down at heel, clothes frayed and worn.
Wartime economy and ration.
Who cares? We're dancing – who needs fashion?
O Iacchos, lord, come lead the dance.   410

There was twist, there was leap, there was twirl,
And then, right beside me, this girl –
She was bubbly and bouncy and pretty,
And one proud little, pert little titty –
O Iacchos, lord, come lead the dance.

DIONYSOS.
   I fancy some of that.

XANTHIAS.
   Me first.

CHORUS.
   Ladies and gentlemen, Archedemos.   420
   Mr Nobody. Takes a correspondence course,
   A law degree,
   Next minute he's Mr High-and-Mighty,
   Big cheese among the Living Dead Upstairs.

And another one: Kleisthenes.
Mr Lover-boy. Loses his fancy,
Come-Kiss-Me-Quick,
430 And he's sobbing and tearing his hair,
No chance now for fucking among the tombs.

Kallias comes to mind as well.
Mr Hips. Buys a lion-skin, sashays to sea –
Where else would he be? –
And bumps and grinds among the...

DIONYSOS.
Excuse me, I wonder if you know
The way to Plouton's Place. We've just arrived –

CHORUS.
No problem. You see that door?
440 You're nearly there.

DIONYSOS.
Xanthias, the bags.

XANTHIAS.
What's in here anyway, the kitchen sink?

CHORUS.
On, on,
To the flower-meadows, the holy dance,
The singing, feasting.
Women eager and waiting
To see me raise the sacred torch.

Iacchos, lord, come lead the dance.

450 In fields of flowers,
Rose-meadows,
Guide us, lead us,
Dancing, singing –

Iacchos, lord, come lead the dance.

For us alone the Sun
Still smiles below.
We see, we know,
Your holy ones –

Iacchos, lord, come lead the dance.

DIONYSOS.
So this is the place. I wonder how to knock...   460
How *does* one knock on doors down here?

XANTHIAS.
Any way you like. Get on with it.
Just remember one thing: you're Herakles.

DIONYSOS *knocks*.

DIONYSOS.
Open up! Ha-HO!

AIAKOS *throws open the door*.

AIAKOS.
Oo is it?

DIONYSOS.
Herakles the Strong.

AIAKOS.
Ho. *You* again.
Bastard. Conman. Bum.
Cheating, lowlife scum.
Ere before, weren't you?
Grabbed our Kerberos and snitched him.
Right under my nose. And now you're back.
We've been waiting for you:
The Big Black Ole of Ell.   470
The Gaping Gulf. Y-enas, mate.
The Grasping Gorgon oo'll grab your guts,
The Undred-eaded Unger-snake oo'll ug your eart,
The Pitiless Piranha oo'll pluck your pubes –
Oh, we've been waiting, mate. Don't go away.

He goes in.

XANTHIAS.
What's the matter?

DIONYSOS.
I've had an accident.

XANTHIAS.

480 Why not clear off while you've got the chance?
There may be more of them.

DIONYSOS.

You don't understand.
I've had an *accident*. Give me a sponge, quick.

XANTHIAS.

Where d'you want it?

DIONYSOS.

Put it on my heart. Oh, oh.

XANTHIAS.

Is *that* where you keep your heart?

DIONYSOS.

It slipped in the excitement.

XANTHIAS.

A right little Herakles *you* are.

DIONYSOS.

What d'you mean? I asked for a sponge, didn't I?
He wouldn't have asked for a sponge.

XANTHIAS.

He wouldn't?

DIONYSOS.

He'd have stood there, oozing.
Whereas *I* asked for a sponge and bounced right
490   back.

XANTHIAS.

I've never seen bravery like it.

DIONYSOS.

Weren't *you* afraid? All that shouting?

XANTHIAS.

Me? Hot air.

DIONYSOS.

All right, if you're so brave,

Change clothes with me.
You take the club and the lionskin.
Stiff upper lip!
I'll be you, and carry the bags.

XANTHIAS.
  All right. Why not?
  Xanthias, superhero. I like the sound of that.
  Well? What d'you think? Do I get the part?   500

DIONYSOS.
  Oh yes. You get the part all right.
  And I get the bags. Where are they? Right.

  The door opens. The SERVANT GIRL *comes out.*

SERVANT GIRL.
  Herakles, darling, there you are!
  Her Ladyship could hardly believe her ears, inside.
  Fresh rolls, bean stew, roast ox,
  And *masses* of cheesecake. *Do* come in...

XANTHIAS.
  No, really.

SERVANT GIRL.
  Please...
  Roast pigeon, those *darling* little tarts,   510
  A keg of wine. Come on.

XANTHIAS.
  Well, I –

SERVANT GIRL.
  I *daren't* let you slip away.
  Did I mention the dancing-girls?

XANTHIAS.
  What dancing-girls?

SERVANT GIRL.
  Young and pretty.
  The table's laid. There's shish-kebab.

XANTHIAS.

All right. Go in and tell the dancing-girls
520   I'll be with them right away, in person.

The SERVANT GIRL *goes in and shuts the door.*

Hey, you. Pick up the bags, and follow me.

DIONYSOS.

Just a minute, just a minute.
You didn't take me seriously just now?
I was joking. You, Herakles? I *mean...*
Stop messing about, and get those bags.

XANTHIAS.

All change again?

DIONYSOS.

Take off that skin.

XANTHIAS.

Ye gods!

DIONYSOS.

Precisely. Have you forgotten who I am?
530   And who *you* are? *You,* Herakles?
Take off that skin.

XANTHIAS.

Whatever you say.
And if you need help again, don't hesitate...

They change clothes.

CHORUS.

What a clever idea!
It's magnificent stuff!
When the sea's getting rough,
When the breaker looms near,
Just roll with the ship and avoid it.
Be a rascal, rogue, cheat,
Lying swine, politician;
540   Think up something neat,

Try a novel position,
Don't wait till disaster's destroyed it.

DIONYSOS.
There's a moral in this.
He just *got* to behave.
He's an ignorant slave,
He's not living in bliss,
He's not guzzling and snogging and kissing,
While his master stands by
With a tear in his eye,
With a groan and a cry,
With a sob and a sigh,
Looking on at the goodies he's missing.

DIONYSOS *is now dressed as Herakles again.*
Enter LANDLADY *and* PLATHANE.

LANDLADY.
My god, it's him. Plathane, it's him.
That bed-and-breakfast bastard   550
Who ate sixteen loaves at a single sitting.

PLATHANE.
That's the one.

XANTHIAS.
Oh-oh.

LANDLADY.
I've got the bill here.
Twenty portions of lamb, one drachma seventy-five.

XANTHIAS.
Big trouble.

LANDLADY.
Not to mention all that garlic.

DIONYSOS.
You're babbling, woman. There's some mistake.

LANDLADY.
Some mistake, all right. I suppose you thought

I wouldn't recognise you in that yellow dress.
I haven't even *mentioned* the pickle.

PLATHANE.
Or the cheese. Don't forget the cheese.
560   Rind and all. Don't forget the cheese.

LANDLADY.
And when I tried to give him the bill,
He looked at me all bristly and shouted 'Boo!'

XANTHIAS.
Oh, he's like that. Does that all the time.

LANDLADY.
Pulled out his sword like a maniac –

PLATHANE.
A maniac –

LANDLADY.
Chased me upstairs and locked me in the...
Well, *you* know. Then he legged it,
Taking half the carpet with him.

XANTHIAS.
That's him all over.

PLATHANE.
So what do we do?

LANDLADY.
Ladies and gents, have you seen Kleon down here?

PLATHANE.
570   Never mind Kleon. We need Hyperbolos.

LANDLADY.
Give me a stone. I'll stuff it down his gob.

PLATHANE.
Chuck him in the pit.

LANDLADY.
Fetch a fish-knife. Fast.
He filleted those kippers. I'll fillet *him*.

PLATHANE.

Nah, nah, Kleon's best. We need a bit of shout.

Exeunt.

DIONYSOS.

Ahem. Xanthias.

XANTHIAS.

Don't ask. Not Herakles again.   580

DIONYSOS.

Oh, go on. Xanthy.

XANTHIAS.

Have you forgotten who I am? And who *you* are?

DIONYSOS.

You're right to be angry. Hit me if you want to.
But you can keep it this time. I promise.
Cross my heart and hope to die.
And if that isn't true
You can spit in my eye
And my wife's eye too.

XANTHIAS.

Oh, if you put it like that...

They change clothes again.

CHORUS.

Now you're back in the part
That you had at the start,   590
And in that yellow dress,
You must try to impress,
You must screw up your eyebrows and roar.
You must act like a god,
You must rumble and curse,
You must do nothing odd,
Or you'll end up far worse,
Humping bags as you humped them before.

XANTHIAS.

Don't tell me, I know.

I must put on a show.
I entirely agree.

600 But the problem, you see,
Is: my master's a cheat and a coward,
And he'll con me again.
Hey! What was that noise?
Brace up! Take the strain.
You can deal with those boys,
You can do it! Just roar, long and...er...loward.

AIAKOS *comes out, with* SLAVES.

AIAKOS.
There's the dognapper. Grab him, quick.

DIONYSOS.
Someone's for it.

XANTHIAS.
Back! I warn you.·

AIAKOS.
Ho.
Smasher, Gnasher, Basher, out here, quick.

DIONYSOS.
610 Fantastic, isn't it? Steals what isn't his,
Then hits an officer.

AIAKOS.
Unbelievable.

DIONYSOS.
Worse: incredible.

XANTHIAS.
Look, I've never been here before.
I've never stolen a hair off your head.
If I have, may I go to Hell. Here's a fair offer:
Take my slave, and torture him. *Then,*
If you find I'm guilty, do what you like to me.

AIAKOS.
Torture him, eh? How would you suggest?

XANTHIAS.
Any way you like. Rack, thumbscrews, whip,
Bricks on the chest, vinegar up the nose – anything 620
Except oiling him with onion or lashing him with
  leeks.

AIAKOS.
You can't say fairer than that. But what if I...
Break him a little? You won't want damages?

XANTHIAS.
Damages? You do like your little joke.
No, no. Take him in, do what you like with him.

AIAKOS.
Take him *in?* No, here. Where you can see.
Hey, you, come out from behind those bags.
We want the truth. You're not going to lie, now are you?

DIONYSOS.
I'm not having this. One *is* an immortal god.
Lay one finger on me, you'll be sorry.

AIAKOS.
You're raving mad.   630

DIONYSOS.
I'm Dionysos, son of Zeus –
And he's the slave.

AIAKOS.
Did you hear what he said?

XANTHIAS.
Of course.
All the more reason for thrashing him.
If he's a god, he won't feel a thing.

DIONYSOS.
Just a minute. You say *you're* a god.
Why doesn't he hit you too? Blow for blow?

XANTHIAS.
Fair enough. And the first to scream or yell
Or show the slightest sign of pain, isn't a god.

AIAKOS.

640 You *are* a gent. I can always tell.
Right. Get undressed, the pair of you.

XANTHIAS (*as he strips*).
Had you any particular method in mind?

AIAKOS.
One blow each. First you, then him.

XANTHIAS.
Fine by me.

AIAKOS *hits him*.

AIAKOS.
There.

XANTHIAS.
Ready when you are.

AIAKOS.
I've just hit you.

XANTHIAS.
You're joking.

AIAKOS.
I see. His turn, then.

He hits DIONYSOS.

DIONYSOS.
Get on with it.

AIAKOS.
I've done it.

DIONYSOS.
I'd have felt the draught.

AIAKOS.
Back to the other one.

XANTHIAS.
Ready when you – hoo!

AIAKOS.
What d'you mean, yoohoo? Felt that, did you?

XANTHIAS.
Felt what? I was waving to the audience.   650

AIAKOS.
Tough little specimen. Back to the other one.

He hits DIONYSOS.

DIONYSOS.
Ho-ho-ho-ho-*HO*.

AIAKOS.
Pardon?

DIONYSOS.
Ho-ho-horsemen. Look.

AIAKOS.
You're crying.

DIONYSOS.
Can't *you* smell onions?

AIAKOS.
You can't *feel* anything?

DIONYSOS.
Not a thing.

AIAKOS.
Back over here.

He hits XANTHIAS.

XANTHIAS.
Oh my god.

AIAKOS.
What's the matter?

XANRTHIAS.
Thorn in my foot.

AIAKOS.
I don't get this. Back again.

He hits DIONYSOS.

DIONYSOS.
Zeus!

XANTHIAS.
He felt that all right.

DIONYSOS.
660   Of course I didn't. How does that song go?
'What's z-use of worrying?'

XANTHIAS.
We're getting nowhere. Hit him lower down.

AIAKOS.
Oi! Stick your belly out.

He hits him again.

DIONYSOS.
GOD! – of the misty mountains, God of the rolling
plains.

AIAKOS.
This is ridiculous. How am I supposed to tell
Which one of you's the god? Oh, come inside.
670   The boss'll know, and Her Queasiness the Queen.
I mean, *they're* gods as well. They'll know.

DIONYSOS.
What a good idea. A little *late,* but good.

They all go in.

CHORUS.
Muse of comedy, dance with us, join in the fun.
There's a sensible crowd in today – all but one.
No, no, don't moan.
We're talking Kleophon.
The babbler,
680   The gabbler,

Won't say a single word if forty-nine will do.
Ignore him, Muse! Don't let him dine with you.

Now it's time to break into the play
With some serious moments, and give
You some useful advice. And today
Our prescription is, 'Live and let live'.
There's a tangle, a muddle, a mess –
And democracy's suffering. What
Are we talking about? Pain and distress
For Phrynichos' followers – that lot.
So they voted against you? They're brave,   690
Honest citizens, good men and true.
'But they voted against us.' A slave
Does his duty, fights fiercely – for you,
For his city – he's praised and rewarded.
'So what? It seems all right to me.'
All right? When a slave is applauded
For one noble action, set free,
And *they're* punished for just one mistake?
Why not welcome them back to the fold?   700
What a fine contribution they'd make
If you let them come in from the cold.

I'll read the leaves, consult my silver ball,
Tell people's fortunes – and first of all
(Don't make a face)
It's Kleigenes' case.
The tailor.
The failure.   710
You'll come to Assembly, you'll vote for war and
    strife –
What else should we expect, with your domestic
    life?[33]

'What's he on about?', someone may ask.
'What's the problem? Why can't he explain?'
Well, I'll try. It's a difficult task,
Puts a serious strain on the brain,
But I'll try. We don't honour the brave.

We forget their achievements, their feats,
We devalue the service they gave,
Put them second to conmen and cheats.
It's exactly what happens with money.
720 Time *was*, coins were gold, bright and new,
Sleek and shiny, as yellow as honey –
And where are they now? Keeping *you?*
So, if someone's old, honest and fair
We reject him, and put all our trust
In jumped-up young orators, spouting hot air,
730 And surprised when their schemes all go bust.
Don't be fooled, fellow-citizens. Hail
The old stagers. Put *them* to the test –
At least then if we lose, if we fail,
We'll fail honestly, doing our best.

Dance. When it ends, enter AIAKOS *and* XANTHIAS.

AIAKOS.
He really is a gent, your boss.

XANTHIAS.
Huh! Boozing and schmoozing.
740 Of course he's a gent.

AIAKOS.
I mean, fancy him not mashing you to pulp
For pretending you were him and he was you.

XANTHIAS.
I'd like to have seen him try.

AIAKOS.
I love it, I love it.

XANTHIAS.
Pardon?

AIAKOS.
Talking big about the boss behind his back.
You really *are* a slave.

XANTHIAS.
What about
When he knocks you one, and you slope out muttering
And slam the door?

AIAKOS.
Can't beat it.

XANTHIAS.
And the keyhole game?

AIAKOS.
What keyhole game?

XANTHIAS.
Listening at keyholes
When he's gabbing to his friends –   750

AIAKOS.
My favourite.

XANTHIAS.
Then blabbing to the neighbours.

AIAKOS.
My other favourite.

XANTHIAS.
Give us your hand. Nah, give us a kiss.
We're soul-mates, mate. We've seen it all –

Noise from inside.

What was that? What the Hell was that?

AIAKOS.
Aeschylus. Euripides.

XANTHIAS.
Ah.

AIAKOS.
Rows, rows, rows.
Fighting and arguing. The Dead used to be so *quiet.*   760

XANTHIAS.
What's it about?

AIAKOS.

The thrones. The banqueting thrones,
Up beside His Nibs.

XANTHIAS.

I don't get it.

AIAKOS.

Look: the best artist, best singer, best playwright,
They each have a throne beside His Majesty
Whenever there's a party.

XANTHIAS.

Oh.

AIAKOS.

And if someone classier turns up,
They have to give up their throne to *him*.

XANTHIAS.

So what's making Aeschylus so cross?

AIAKOS.

He's had the Throne of Tragedy for years.
Because he's the best. No arguing.

XANTHIAS.

770   Till now, you mean?

AIAKOS.

Euripides, exactly.
As soon as he arrived, he started showing off.
They're a rough lot down here – muggers,
   murderers –
And when he started with his metaphors
And his hypotheses and his stichomythia
They lapped it up. Next thing, they vote
That he's the greatest, and he nabs the throne.
Aeschylus' throne.

XANTHIAS.

So kick him off.

AIAKOS.

We tried that.
The crowd turned nasty, demanded a proper trial,
To test who was best. Insisted on fair play.   780

XANTHIAS.

Those murderers and muggers?

AIAKOS.

It's Hell in there.

XANTHIAS.

But what about Aeschylus? Hasn't *he* got friends?

AIAKOS.

Like, people of taste? Like this lot here?

He gestures at the audience.

XANTHIAS.

So what can Plouton do?

AIAKOS.

His Nibs? He's organised a fight.
A word-fight, to sort it out.

XANTHIAS.

Just a minute.
Sophocles. Didn't *he* claim the throne as well?

AIAKOS.

As soon as he arrived, he shook his hand –
That's Aeschylus' hand – and gave him a great big
    kiss.
So Aeschylus budged up, made room on the throne.   790
But Sophocles said no. Well, not in his own voice:
He got that actor Kleidemides to read his part.
He'll act as first reserve, he says. (That's Sophocles.)
If Aeschylus wins, that's fine with him.
But if Euripides comes top, he'll challenge him
And start the whole thing off again.

XANTHIAS.

Proper little madhouse.

AIAKOS.

Wait till you see the scales.

XANTHIAS.

What scales?

AIAKOS.

For weighing the lines. False quantities.
800 And there's plumblines and set-squares and wedges
–0

XANTHIAS.

It's a building site.

AIAKOS.

For poetry: that's right – and yardsticks and
endstops.
Euripides insists it's all done proper,
Tragedy by tragedy, line by line, word by word.

XANTHIAS.

And Aeschylus is *taking* this?

AIAKOS.

A bull sits on my tongue, as the proverb says –
You know what he's like.

XANTHIAS.

Who's going to judge?

AIAKOS.

That was the problem.
Brains are in short supply down here.
We suggested Athenians, but Aeschylus said no.

XANTHIAS.

All those muggers and murderers? I'm not
surprised.

AIAKOS.

And the rest are no better: wouldn't recognise
A poet if they fell over one in the street.
So when your boss turned up –   810.

XANTHIAS.

The god of tragedy.

AIAKOS.

He ought to know what's what.

Fanfare from inside.

It's starting. We'd better go inside.
When the bosses get busy, stay out of their way.

He and XANTHIAS *go in. Fanfare. During the chorus
which follows,* ATTENDANTS *bring out thrones.*
PLOUTON *and* DIONYSOS *take their places.*

CHORUS.

Rumble of thunder. Word-warrior now
Rolls his eyes, knits his big, bushy brow,
Pawing, snorting for battle. His enemy, too.
Subtle arguments, polished and new,
Sharp as scalpels, to slice him in two.

Solemn sentiments, lofty and loud;
Massive adjectives, prancing and proud.
And the slippery, slithery sound
Of a word-wrestler wriggling around,   820
Twisting, turning and changing his ground.

With his word-mane contemptuously tossed
And his metaphors rough-hewn, embossed,
Hear the lord of high rhetoric roar,
Hear him rack up and stack up the score
As he grumbles and rumbles for more.

On the other side, shivers and spills,
Tongue-entanglements, mouth-mugging, thrills,
As he darts in and ducks down and dips
With a twirl and a twist of the hips
And a feather-light flick of the lips.

Enter EURIPIDES *and* AESCHYLUS.

EURIPIDES.

Oh, no. It's mine and I mean to have it.   830
Better poet – you, me? No contest.

DIONYSOS.
Well, Aeschylus? No comment? You did hear that?

EURIPIDES.
He heard. He's just like one of his own tragedies:
The silences are the best bits.

DIONYSOS.
That's not very nice.

EURIPIDES.
You don't know him like I do.
How can I describe him? Over-elaborate?
Torrents of verbiage? Mount-Etna-mouth?
Ask what *restraint* means, he'd have a fit.

AESCHYLUS.
840   *Restraint?* What do you know about restraint,
You...grocer's boy? What about the beggars you
    favour –
The stench, the filthy clothes, the bugs?
Don't talk to *me* about restraint.

DIONYSOS.
Hang on.
You'll have a fit if you don't hang on.

AESCHYLUS.
Hang on?
Not till I've shown this rag-and-bone man
Just what I really think of him.

DIONYSOS.
Someone bring a sou'wester.
There's going to be *such* a storm.

AESCHYLUS.
Do *I* write choruses like Cretan belly-dances?
850   Am *I* obsessed with incest?

DIONYSOS.
Hold your horses. Wind-lord, wait.
Stand here, Euripides, out of range.

It's a tornado, a forest fire, a wordwind.
Mind a flying phrase doesn't topple your *Telephos*.
It's getting rough. Down, Aeschylus.
We agreed on a contest, line by line.
Not blaring and flaring,
Not puffing and panting and ranting.

EURIPIDES.
Line by line? No problem *there*.   860
I'm quite prepared, and so are my tragedies –
Peleus, Meleager, and especially *Telephos:*
Lined up, ready for inspection.

DIONYSOS.
Aeschylus?

AESCHYLUS.
It's hardly an equal contest.

DIONYSOS.
What d'you mean?

AESCHYLUS.
I mean that when I died, my works lived on.
I haven't got them by me. His died with him –
You heard him: 'lined up, ready for inspection'.
Still, if we must, we must.   870

DIONYSOS.
Good. Bring incense, bring holy fire.
I'll have a little pray before we start.
For critical acumen, a *rigorous* approach.

(*to the* CHORUS)

And while I'm at it, *you* can sing a hymn.

CHORUS.
Muses, daughters of Zeus on high,
When it's tournament time,
When word-warriors gather and glower,
You check their equipment –
All metaphors mustered?

All adjectives polished?
All similes sharp?
880   They're ready. Sir Tingle-tongue,
Lord Mighty-mouth. It's art.
Are you ready? They're dying to start.

DIONYSOS.
That's better. Why don't you two pray as well?

AESCHYLUS.
O Mighty Mater, nurturer,
Thou seest thine acolyte. Vouchsafe.

DIONYSOS (*to* EURIPIDES).
Your turn. Here. Take the pot.

EURIPIDES.
I'd rather not.
One has powers of one's own, if you really must
    know.

DIONYSOS.
You're joking. Home-made gods?

EURIPIDES.
890   You could call them that.

DIONYSOS.
Well, pray to them, then. Powers of one's own!

EURIPIDES.
Space, fill one's brain.
Twist, take one's tongue.
It's wriggle-out-of-trouble time.

CHORUS.
How exciting! To watch while such wits
Stand displaying their glamour, their glitz!
Their razzle,
Their dazzle,
Inspires us and thrills us to bits.

900   This one's slippery, nifty and quick,
Fires off quotes that are slinky and slick

For the other
To smother
With word-blankets, woolly and thick.

DIONYSOS.
You start. And make it original.
No 'On the one hand...on the other hand'.

EURIPIDES.
I'll come to my own work in a minute. First
I'll show how this word-monger cheats his audiences.
(They were stupid enough before. But *then*,   910
All they knew was Phrynichos.)
The play begins. And who's that onstage?
Hooded and wrapped, can't see the face.
Is it Niobe? Achilles? Who knows? All they do
Is sit like dummies, not uttering a word.

DIONYSOS.
I noticed that.

EURIPIDES.
The Chorus starts spouting:
Torrents, waterfalls. Achilles: nothing.

DIONYSOS.
It worked for *me*. The trouble with modern plays
Is, *everyone* speaks *all* the time.

EURIPIDES.
It worked for you!

DIONYSOS.
What d'you mean?

EURIPIDES.
Cheap trick. Audience on edge of seats –
What's Niobe going to say? Play goes on,
And on, and on, and...nothing.   920

DIONYSOS.
It *is* a cheap trick.

(*to* AESCHYLUS)

What are you *doing?*

EURIPIDES.
He's wriggling. Can't take the strain.
Then, halfway through, just when everyone's
    relaxed,
She whips the cloak off her head and bellows
A great long speech with eyebrows and whiskers
    on,
Like the Demon Queen in a pantomime.
Who understands a word?

AESCHYLUS.
Now *look*...

DIONYSOS.
Be quiet.

EURIPIDES.
From beginning to end, it's gibberish.

DIONYSOS (*to* AESCHYLUS).
Stop grinding your teeth.

EURIPIDES.
Scamanders, sepulchres, bronze-clad vulture-
    eagles,
Words like the wall of a fortress,
Impossible to batter your way into.

DIONYSOS.
He has got a point.
I spent several sleepless nights myself,
Wondering what on Earth a tawny horse-cock is.

AESCHYLUS.
It's a figurehead on ships, you fool.

DIONYSOS.
Thank God for that. I thought it meant Eryxis.

EURIPIDES.
A horse-cock! We write tragedies about horse-cocks
    now?

AESCHYLUS.

All right, what are *your* tragedies about?

EURIPIDES.

Not horse-cocks or goat-leopards. I leave those to you.
I don't get *my* inspiration from a Persian carpet.
When you handed me Tragedy, she was in a bad, bad
    way:
Bloated with adverbs, plumped-up with particles,   940
So stuffed with syllables she could hardly move.
I put her on a diet right away. Pure logic,
A pinch of prosody, carefully-selected metaphors,
Non-fattening similes, a touch of this, a touch of that –

AESCHYLUS.

– and more than a touch of Kephisophon.

EURIPIDES.

I didn't start in the middle, or babble on.
The first person onstage told the audience
Exactly what to expect.

AESCHYLUS.

They knew before they came.

EURIPIDES.

In *my* plays, no one stands about doing nothing.
Everyone gets a say: wife, daughter-in-law,
Slaves, even old Granny in the corner.

AESCHYLUS.

Ridiculous.   950

EURIPIDES.

Democracy in action.

DIONYSOS.

Oh, don't let's start on politics.

EURIPIDES.

I taught *them* –

He gestures at the audience.

– how to argue.

AESCHYLUS.
You should have been mashed to mincemeat.

EURIPIDES.
I taught them to *use* language,
Arrange words *neatly:*
Careful examination, logical argument,
Look at everything twice, no stone unturned –

AESCHYLUS.
He's *proud* of it!

EURIPIDES.
I kept to ordinary matters in my plays,
Things everyone knows, we all understand.
960   *My* audience could follow every word.
I didn't baffle them with Kyknoses and Memnons,
All horsebrasses and hippomanic crests.
You want to know what we're like? Look at our
        admirers.
His are Phormisios, Megainetos the Maniac,
By-the-lord-Harry merchants, Tear-em-limb-from-
        limb;
Mine are lean and spry: Theramenes, Kleitophon –

DIONYSOS.
Theramenes? Lean and spry?
I think you mean Mean and sly.
Rolls into trouble,
Quick change of policy,
Quick turn of the coat,
970   And rolls right out again.

EURIPIDES.
Question everything, I taught them.
First principle in drama,
First rule in life:
Don't let anything go by.
'Why's that?
What's going on?

How? When?
Where did that come from?'
Beg pardon?
Whose idea was that?

DIONYSOS.
I know exactly what you mean.   980
They're all at it now.
Come home, call the slaves,
Start shouting and yelling.
'Who moved that jug?
Who scoffed that sardine?
How? When?'
Once all they did was sit
On a stool   990
Like *this*, and drool.

CHORUS.
Now it's your turn. He's stated his case.
Don't keep groaning. Don't make such a face.
No, don't roar,
Don't be sore,
Or you'll blow it and forfeit the race.

Play it cool. Play it safe. Play it smart.
Take your time. Take your place at the start.   1000
When we shout
'Let him out' –
Then get *in* there and take him apart!

DIONYSOS.
Word-lord, it's time. Mighty architect, answer.
White-water arguments. Open the floodgates.

AESCHYLUS.
Rather a comedown. Not what I'm used to.
Bandying arguments. Still, if I have to...
Can't have him crowing and claiming I'm
    speechless.
Answer me this, then: what makes a great playwright?

EURIPIDES.
Clever ideas, and a clear moral viewpoint.
Open the audience's eyes and alert them –

AESCHYLUS.
1010 What if you don't? If you drag them behind you,
Down to the gutter – ?

DIONYSOS.
Simple: you've had it.

AESCHYLUS.
Right then. Let's start with the audience I left
him.
Noble, uplifted, not market-place gossips,
Public-bar chatterers. Mine dreamed of
breastplates,
Proud waving helmet-plumes, gauntlets, greaves,
corselets –

DIONYSOS.
Steady! We're drowning in armour already.

EURIPIDES.
That made them better, eh? How did you do it?

DIONYSOS.
1020 Words of one syllable, Aeschylus. *Quietly*.

AESCHYLUS.
War-plays. I gave them my war-plays.

DIONYSOS.
Please name one.

AESCHYLUS.
Well, there was *Seven*.

DIONYSOS.
What seven?

AESCHYLUS.
Against Thebes. Against *Thebes*.
That got them going.

DIONYSOS.

Yes, especially in Thebes.
Started them training. Good tactics it wasn't.

AESCHYLUS.

The message was simple.
Even in Athens, you could have learned *something*.
What about *Persians*, then? Brimful of battle,
Stick-it-and-win-through. A masterpiece, *Persians*.

DIONYSOS.

AND what a ghost-scene! The Chorus all stand there,
Clapping their hands, going 'EE-a-oo-OH-ee!'

AESCHYLUS.

Teaching, instruction... the job of the poet.   1030
That's what we've always done. Orpheus, remember?
'Worship the gods and respect Mother Nature'.
Hesiod: farming, the seasons. Mousaios:
Oracles, cures. Then, of course, there was
    Homer.
Crammed with instruction: on strategy, tactics –

DIONYSOS.

Yes, and I wish Pantakles had been listening.
There he was, yesterday, on the parade-ground,
Trying to march while he fastened his helmet...

AESCHYLUS.

Plenty of *good* soldiers learned: look at Lamachos.
Anyway, *my* plays are stuffed full of Homer.   1040
Look at my characters: Teucer, Patroklos,
Wait-for-the-signal-then-leap-into-battle men:
Great-hearted heroes the audience could learn from.
None of your Phaidras, Medeas –
I never bothered with love-maddened females.

EURIPIDES.

You never bothered with females.

AESCHYLUS.
Of course not.
You were the expert on love-maddened females.

DIONYSOS.
Didn't you have some yourself? Quite a houseful¹⁴?
Models for every emotion you showed us?

EURIPIDES.
Stories. What harm did my Phaidra, Medea do – ?

AESCHYLUS.
1050   Plenty. They made every woman of spirit,
Woman of decency, rush and take poison.

EURIPIDES.
Phaidra, Medea – I didn't invent them.

AESCHYLUS.
No, but you put them onstage. Didn't hide them.
Children have teachers to teach them, and grown-
ups
Have playwrights. To set good examples.

EURIPIDES.
Examples?
Up, up, where it spurts from highest peaks
On Caucasus, ceiling of the world. Climb here,
Rock-pinnacles beside the stars, then down –
That's an example? Do *you* understand it?

AESCHYLUS.
Towering sentiments, towering speeches.
1060   Gods don't use language like ordinary mortals –
And they should dress better. *I* gave them costumes;
You gave them – why am I wasting my breath here?

EURIPIDES.
What?

AESCHYLUS.
Every person of stature or standing
You put in plays, comes out ragged and tatty –
Sobbing for sympathy, playing for pathos.

EURIPIDES.
So? What's the problem?

AESCHYLUS.
Is *that* an example?
Rich people dress up in rags. 'Cut my taxes,
Cold, I'm so cold, look I'm starving, I'm shaking' –

DIONYSOS.
Not underneath. Woolly underwear. Starving?
Posh little restaurant – 'Case won, let's party.'

AESCHYLUS.
Everyone's at it. You've taught them to quibble.
No one works out; they've abandoned their
    training;   1070
Teenagers tongue-wrestle; sailors on warships
Answer back, question their officers, argue.
Once it was 'Hard tack, sir, Aye-aye, sir, Now, sir' –

DIONYSOS.
Now it's all fiddling and faddling and farting:
'Whoops, we're adrift, dearie, pass us your hankie' –

AESCHYLUS.
Yes, and there's more
Here on shore.
'Do you want a good time?
Over here in the shrine.'   1080
All those unmarried mothers,
Sisters sleeping with brothers,
Crying 'Life isn't life any more'.
No one's safe in the streets:
It's all lawyers and cheats,
Politicians and loungers,
Tax-dodgers and scroungers,
All 'I'm all right, Jack',
Feeble, flabby and slack –

DIONYSOS.
The other day
I was watching that marathon, over the way,   1090

And there, right by the start
Was a slight little,
White little
Pug of a man,
A slug of a man.
He was puffing and blowing,
He couldn't get going.
All the others were lapping him.
People kept slapping him,
Charging him,
Barging him –
Till he made up his mind
And came up from behind
With a stonking great, zonking great fart.

CHORUS.
    How long can this last?
1100   It's frantic, it's fast.
    The Olympian strains
    Like a colt at the reins
    And the Brainbox goes bounding right past.

    Play dirty, play rough.
    Try some really hot stuff.
    Make him sweat, make him melt.
    Hit him! Pound, paste and pelt.
    Below the belt!

    This crowd here tonight
1110   Is remarkably bright.
    They'll follow you,
    Swallow you,
    Take every subtlety, feast on the fight.

    They're incredibly sharp.
    They won't shuffle or carp.
    So don't hold yourselves back.
    Get on track
    With a big-brain attack.

EURIPIDES.
It's time for Round Two. Opening Speeches.
And even there, our learned friend falls down.   1120
He's obscure and hard to follow.

DIONYSOS.
What Opening Speeches?

EURIPIDES.
Plenty.
Let's start with *Libation-Bearers*.

DIONYSOS.
Shh! Shh! *Libation-Bearers*. Aeschylus...?

AESCHYLUS.
Lord Hermes, who, with ever-watchful eye
Hast ever guarded this, my father's realm,
Protect me now, and give me thy support.
I have come back, returning home at last.

DIONYSOS.
What's wrong with that?

EURIPIDES.
A dozen things.

DIONYSOS.
But he's only said four lines.   1130

EURIPIDES.
With twenty mistakes in each of them.

DIONYSOS.
Quiet, Aeschylus! That's eighty mistakes already.

AESCHYLUS.
You want *me* to be quiet for *him?*

DIONYSOS.
It *is* his turn.

EURIPIDES.
Right from the start, he puts his foot in it.

AESCHYLUS.
Rubbish.

DIONYSOS.
I did try to warn you.

AESCHYLUS.
What foot in it? Prove it!

EURIPIDES.
Give me the lines again.

AESCHYLUS.
Lord Hermes, who, with ever-watchful eye
Hast ever guarded this, my father's realm...

EURIPIDES.
Orestes says this – do remind me –
At the tomb of his dead father?

AESCHYLUS.
1140   Of course he does.

EURIPIDES.
Yes. So let's get this right.
The father comes home from the Trojan War.
His wife (who's been planning the deed for years)
Bops his napper with a chopper – and *that's*
How Lord Hermes does his guarding?
That's his ever-watchful eye?

AESCHYLUS.
I said he guards
The *realm* with ever-watchful eye. *Realm*, not *helm*.

EURIPIDES.
Oh, right. But it's his father's realm –

DIONYSOS.
– which makes Orestes a grave-robber[35].

AESCHYLUS.
1150   Stay out of this.

DIONYSOS.
Sorry. Do go on.

AESCHYLUS.
Protect me now, and give me thy support.
I have come back, returning home at last.

EURIPIDES.
Brilliant, Aeschylus. The same thing twice.

DIONYSOS.
Thing twice?

EURIPIDES.
Thing twice.
I have come back, returning home at last.
'Come back', 'return' – the same thing twice.

DIONYSOS.
You're right! It's like saying to a neighbour,
'Lend me a pie-dish, or perhaps a dish for pie.'

AESCHYLUS.
You know nothing about it. He's splitting hairs.   1160
It's brilliantly expressed.

EURIPIDES.
Oh, how?
Please show me what I'm missing.

AESCHYLUS.
Orestes has been away,
So he 'comes back'. We all do that.
But he's also been in exile, so he 'returns'.

DIONYSOS.
That's brilliant! You can't knock holes in that.

EURIPIDES.
Of course I can. Orestes came on the quiet.
Afraid of arrest. That's not 'returning'.

DIONYSOS.
Dazzling! I wish I understood.

EURIPIDES.
We'll take the next two lines.

DIONYSOS (*to* AESCHYLUS).
1170   We'll take the next two lines.

AESCHYLUS.
On this sad grave I summon thee, grim ghost
Of my dead father. Hear me! Hearken now!

EURIPIDES.
There he goes again. 'Hear me!' 'Hearken!'
The same thing twice.

DIONYSOS.
He's talking to a corpse, you fool.
Twice, three times – he still won't get through.

AESCHYLUS.
What about you, anyway? How do you begin?

EURIPIDES.
I'll show you. And if I say anything twice,
If you find one syllable more, or less,
Spit in my eye.

DIONYSOS.
1180   Let's hear some, then.

EURIPIDES.
A happy man was Oedipus at first.

AESCHYLUS.
He wasn't. Condemned by the gods from birth,
To murder his father and marry his mother.
Before he was even born. A happy man, at first!

EURIPIDES.
As things turned out, most miserable.

AESCHYLUS.
There you go again. 'As things turned out'.
He was miserable from start to finish.
1190   Exposed at birth on a piece of pot,
In the cold, cold snow, in case he killed his Daddy;

Limping to Corinth on those poor swollen feet;
Marrying a woman old enough to be his Mummy,
Who actually *was* his Mummy; putting out his eyes –

DIONYSOS.
At least he never sailed with Erasinides.

EURIPIDES.
I say my opening lines are brilliant.

AESCHYLUS.
And I say they're rubbish. They're all the same.
You write them to a formula. I'll prove it, too.
I'll wreck the lot with a little saucebox[36].

EURIPIDES.
A saucebox?

AESCHYLUS.
A saucebox. Your openings are all the same.   1200
Any old words do nicely: a woolly vest,
A lump of coal, a saucebox. I'll show you.

EURIPIDES.
Oh, no you won't.

AESCHYLUS.
Oh, yes I will.

DIONYSOS.
Get *on!*

EURIPIDES.
Aigyptos, as the well-known story tells,
With fifty daughters in a big, broad boat,
Sailing to Argos –

AESCHYLUS.
Lost his little saucebox.

EURIPIDES.
He didn't. This isn't fair.

DIONYSOS.
I see what he means, though. Try again.   1210

EURIPIDES.
Great Dionysos, who in fawn-skins dressed,
Bears high the pine-torch in his holy hand,
Leading our revels –

AESCHYLUS.
Lost his little saucebox.

DIONYSOS.
Another saucebox. It's everywhere.

EURIPIDES.
Oh no. There's no sauce here, for starters.
Bewail the unhappy lot of mortals. See:
Yon prince, high-born and proud, lost all his wealth;
Yon starving beggar –

AESCHYLUS.
Lost his little saucebox.

DIONYSOS.
Euripides.

EURIPIDES.
Yes?

DIONYSOS.
1220   Best mop up now. It's getting everywhere.

EURIPIDES.
Rubbish. I'll try another.

DIONYSOS.
All right, but beware of the sauce.

EURIPIDES.
One day Agenor's son, great Kadmos, while
Leaving the city –

AESCHYLUS.
Lost his little saucebox.

DIONYSOS.
Give up.

EURIPIDES.
Give up?

DIONYSOS.
Or take out shares in a sauce factory.
You're drowning in it.

EURIPIDES.
I've thousands more, all sauce-proof.   1230
Once Pelops, son of Tantalos, while on
His way to Pisa –

AESCHYLUS.
Lost his little saucebox.

DIONYSOS.
Not Pelops too. For God's sake give it back.
Or buy him another one. They only cost one drach.

EURIPIDES.
I haven't finished. I said I'd thousands more.
Once great king Oineus –

AESCHYLUS.
Lost his little saucebox.

EURIPIDES.
You might at least let me finish the line.
Once great king Oineus, offering sacrifice   1240
To the gods in Heaven –

AESCHYLUS.
Lost his little saucebox.

DIONYSOS.
In the middle of a sacrifice? Awkward.
Who snaffled it?

EURIPIDES.
Zeus, lord of Heaven, as the story goes –

DIONYSOS.
I know what's coming. 'Lost his little saucebox'.
It's like a stye on the eye, that saucebox.
Oh, change the subject. Time for a chorus.

EURIPIDES.
A chorus? This is where I really score.
1250 He writes terrible choruses, and I can prove it.

He hurries out.

CHORUS.
What happens next?
What will he do?
I'm perplexed.
Aren't you?
We're talking genius here,
Not trash –
Has Euripides no fear?
How rash,
How brash,
To have a go at *him*,
To throw at *him*
Whatever comes to hand.
1260 It should be banned.

Enter EURIPIDES with MUSICIANS.

EURIPIDES.
Terrible choruses. I'll give you a sample.
I'll lump them all together.

DIONYSOS.
I'll count them with these pebbles.

Someone plays a flute introduction*.

EURIPIDES.
O clamorous clan-chief, the warfare is woeful –
Drub, drub the doom-drum, rush to the rescue.
We lake-lovers clamour for Hermes our helpmeet –
Drub, drub the doom-drum, rush to the rescue.

DIONYSOS (*shouting above the noise*).
Two thumps, Aeschylus.

EURIPIDES.
Bloodied, embattled, we wail for our warlord –   1270
Drub, drub the doom-drum, rush to the rescue.

DIONYSOS.
Three!

EURIPIDES.
Hark, it's a heaven-sound! Choir-voices chanting –
Drub, drub the doom-drum, rush to the rescue.
With a bang, with a boom, with a bang-bang, boom-boom bang –
Drub, drub the doom-drum, rush to the rescue.

Silence.

DIONYSOS.
Zeus, what a pounding. I'm black and blue all over.
I'd love a hot bath – not to mention earmuffs.   1280

EURIPIDES.
Hang on. There's more. With *this*, this time.
Lyre-work.

DIONYSOS.
So long as it's not that drum.

EURIPIDES.
A-winging through the welkin,
DaDUNG, DaDUNG, daDUNG,
Bird dog dogs bird birds dog,
DaDUNG, DaDUNG, daDUNG,
Spear-handed, handy-speared,
DaDUNG, DaDUNG, daDUNG,   1290
Sky-chargers, galloping, galloping,
DaDUNG, DaDUNG, daDUNG,
To succour Ajax,
DaDUNG, DaDUNG, daDUNG.

DIONYSOS.
Oh, Aeschylus. Where did you pick that up?
DaDUNG, DaDUNG? A donkey ride?

AESCHYLUS.
> Wherever I 'picked it up', I made good use of it.
> One wanders the garden of the Muses. One plucks
> at will.
1300
> Along a slightly different path from Phrynichos.
> And not like *him*. Where does he go for inspiration?
> The pub, the disco, the strip-club... I'll show you.
> Someone give me a lyre. No, what am I talking
> about?
> Who needs a lyre? Where's that girl with the
> castanets?
> Here, puss, here, puss. Puss-puss-puss.
> Ladies and gentlemen: the Muse of Euripides.

Enter EURIPIDES' MUSE.

DIONYSOS.
> Thank god she didn't bring her friends[38].

EURIPIDES' MUSE *dances as* AESCHYLUS *sings.*

AESCHYLUS.
> *Kingfishers, diving, arriving*
> *At the salt sea spray at the water's edge,*
1310
> *Chattering, spattering*
> *Their wings with watery wetness,*
> *Then flying high where spiders spin*
> *Spi-i-i-i-i-i-i-in*
> *Webs woven under roof-rafters,*
> *Up there on the ceiling,*
> *While the dolphin sings the song*
> *Sailors smile at,*
> *Leaping in the wavelets at the sharp ship's bows.*
> *O grapes! O vine-leaves clustering*
1320
> *Round the thick, strong stem,*
> *Unwearying woe-remover*
> *O! O! O! Come to me!*

(*to* DIONYSOS)

> You noticed that bit at the bottom?

DIONYSOS (*gazing at* EURIPIDES' MUSE).
  Oh yes.

AESCHYLUS.
  Didn't fit the metre.

DIONYSOS.
  Eh? Oh.

AESCHYLUS.
  Typical. All his choruses are the same.
  And this...this bump-and-grind-merchant
  Criticises me?
  It's not just the choruses.
  His solo songs are just the same.
  I mean, for example: 1330

  O gleamy gloom of Night,
  Dream-shapes, dream-messengers
  You send up, send up
  From Down Below, down, up,
  Ghost-messengers,
  Billowing, billowing,
  Glaring eyes,
  Blood, blood in glaring eyes
  And great long talons.
  Light me, light me a lamp,
  Fetch water in a pot,
  A droplet in a potlet,
  From limpid streamlets fetch
  And warm it well, that I may wash
  The nasty dream away.   1340
  God! O God
  Of the swelling, heaving sea,
  Look here. I say, look here,
  Slaves of the house, look here,
  Look what naughty Glyke's done:
  Grabbed hold of cock
  And scarpered.
  To the hills, the hills.
  Mania, you see to that.

Ah me, me miserable!
I sat there spinning,
Spi-i-i-i-i-inning,
Busy fingers flicking the flax,
Making little balls, balls,
To creep out of the house in the dawn-light
1350   *And sell in that stall in the market.*
And now he's gone, gone,
On fluttery, feathery winglets
My cock has flown.
Oh woe! Oh no!
Beat breast, breast beat,
Tears fall, fall tears.
Cretans, children of Ida,
Snatch quivers, bows,
Surround the house.
Artemis, dear, Diktynna's darling daughter,
Haste to the hunt,
Send doggies padding here,
1360   *Padding there, padding everywhere.*
Hekate, come,
Zeus' thunder-torches blazing in your hand,
Light me to Glyke's house
And let's have a really good look-see.

DIONYSOS.
No more singing. Please.

AESCHYLUS.
I quite agree.
There's only one real way to settle this.
We'll weigh the lines. It's time for the scales.

DIONYSOS.
The scales! The scales!
We'll weigh those tragedies like lumps of cheese.

The scales are set up.

CHORUS.
1370   It's amazing. It's hard to believe

What these supermen have up their sleeve.
Each one devises
A million surprises
For the other one soon to receive.

It's a good job we're here, and can view
It ourselves. For if any of you
Had outlined it,
Defined it,
We'd never have thought it was true.

DIONYSOS.
Right. Stand by your weighing pans.

AESCHYLUS.
There.

EURIPIDES.
There.

DIONYSOS.
Take hold and say a line each.
And don't let go till I say 'Cuckoo'. Right?   1380

AESCHYLUS.
Right.

EURIPIDES.
Right.

DIONYSOS.
Ready, steady, speak.

EURIPIDES.
O why did it have to sail, the good ship Argo?

AESCHYLUS.
O river Spercheios, where cattle drink...

DIONYSOS.
Cuckoo. Let go. Ah. His is lower.

EURIPIDES.
Why?

DIONYSOS.
  He put in a river, like a wool-merchant
  Wetting his fleeces to make them heavier.
  You put in a fast, light sailing-ship.

EURIPIDES.
  I get the idea now. Let's try again.

DIONYSOS.
  Take hold of the pans, then. Right?

AESCHYLUS.
  Right.

EURIPIDES.
  Right.

DIONYSOS.
1390 Ready, steady, speak.

EURIPIDES.
  Persuasion builds her temples in words alone...

AESCHYLUS.
  Alone of the gods, grim Death accepts no gifts...

DIONYSOS.
  Cuckoo. Let go. His is lower again.
  He threw in Death, the heaviest blow of all.

EURIPIDES.
  You mean Persuasion carries no weight at all?

DIONYSOS.
  Of course she doesn't. What is she? Words.
  Try to remember some really *massive* sentiment,
  Some really *solid* line, *immense* and *packed*.

EURIPIDES.
  There are so many...

DIONYSOS.
  I know.
1400 *Achilles threw two sixes and a four...*
  No dice? Find something else: it's your only
    chance.

EURIPIDES.
The hero hefted his bulbous, bronze-bound club...

AESCHYLUS.
Chariot on chariot, corpse on broken corpse...

DIONYSOS.
Cuckoo. He's done it again.

EURIPIDES.
How?

DIONYSOS.
Two chariots, two corpses.
You'd need a crane to lift them.

AESCHYLUS.
Look, forget lines. So far as I'm concerned,
He can sit in the scales himself, with his wife,
His kids, his manuscripts, Kephisophon –
With two well-chosen words, I'll outweigh the lot.   1410

DIONYSOS (*to* PLOUTON).
I don't know what to do. I like them both.
I want to be friends with both. How can I judge?
One's so clever...one's so *satisfying*.

PLOUTON.
You mean you can't fulfil your mission?

DIONYSOS.
Pardon?

PLOUTON.
You came to choose a poet and a poet you must
    choose.
One stays, one goes. Your mission must succeed.

DIONYSOS.
Thanks very much. Look, lovies, it's like this:
I came to fetch a playwright, take him back.

EURIPIDES.
What for?

DIONYSOS.

To sort the city out.

1420 To write some sensible plays and sort the city out.
Look, one more contest. Give some good advice –
Whoever gives the best, goes back with me.
All right? First problem: Alkibiades.
What's your opinion? They really need to know.

EURIPIDES.

What's *their* opinion?

DIONYSOS.

That's the problem: they can't decide.
One minute they want him out. The next they
    don't.
The next...you know the sort of thing. So, speak.

EURIPIDES.

How can we trust a citizen who's slow
To help his city, quick to help himself?

DIONYSOS.

1430 Oh, very good. Now, Aeschylus.

AESCHYLUS.

It's hardly sensible to keep a lion as pet.
But if you do, remember: lions bite.

DIONYSOS.

Well, that didn't help much. Brilliant, bright...
I still can't choose. We'd better try again.
Some specific advice, perhaps. To end the war.

EURIPIDES.

Kleokritos could use Kinesias as wings.
The pair of them could fly across the sea –

DIONYSOS.

I'm getting it. Fly across the sea... Go on.

EURIPIDES.

1440 They'd be carrying vinegar, in flasks.

Then, when they reached the enemy,
Aerial bombardment.

Baffled silence all round.

Or then, again...

DIONYSOS.
Go on.

EURIPIDES.
What you trust, distrust, and start to trust
What you distrusted heretofore.

DIONYSOS.
Brilliant!
Pardon?

EURIPIDES.
Group A, Group B. A in, B out, big trouble.
So change. B in, A out. Could work.   1450

DIONYSOS.
Amazing!
Did *you* think of that, or did Kephisophon?

EURIPIDES.
I did. Kephisophon thought of the vinegar-flasks.

DIONYSOS.
Right, Aeschylus.

AESCHYLUS.
A in, B out. Depends.
Who's in just now? The people's choice?
Good men and true?

DIONYSOS.
You're joking.

AESCHYLUS.
Bastards?

DIONYSOS.
Well –

AESCHYLUS.
> The people's choice. They *do* need help. I'm
> stumped.

DIONYSOS.
1460 Oh, don't be stumped, if you want to live again.

AESCHYLUS.
> I'll see for myself, up there, and then I'll say.

DIONYSOS.
> Oh, no. You have to give advice down here.

AESCHYLUS.
> *Make enemy land your own, your land their land.*
> *Make taxes ships. Who sails on silver coins"?*

DIONYSOS.
> Who sails on coins? D'you think he means lawyers?

PLUTO.
> It's time. Decide.

DIONYSOS.
> Ah. Right. Decide. I'll choose –
> The one my instinct tells me, deep inside.

EURIPIDES.
1470 Good. Ready when you are. You promised. Me.

DIONYSOS.
> *My tongue is was that promised, not my brain.*
> I'm taking Aeschylus.

EURIPIDES.
> You bastard! *Why?*

DIONYSOS.
> Because he's won. I say he's won. All right?

EURIPIDES.
> *You dare such a deed, and look me in the face?*

DIONYSOS.
> What d'you mean, such a deed? The audience
> agrees.

EURIPIDES.
O heart of stone! You'll leave me here to die?

DIONYSOS.
To die, to sleep, perchance... Just a minute.
You're dead already.

Exit EURIPIDES.

PLOUTON.
Step inside, at once.

DIONYSOS.
What for?

PLOUTON.
One for the road. Before you go.

DIONYSOS.
Oh, thanks.   1480
How very kind. No, no, please. After *you*.

He and AESCHYLUS *follow* PLOUTON *inside*.

CHORUS.
Well, that's that, then. The contest is done,
And the Sensible Candidate won –
Took first place
In a race
That was over before it was run.

And it's hardly a moment too soon.   1491-99
We were rapidly reaching high noon.
On the page,
On the stage,
Every lamebrain and lunkhead and loon

Who assaulted our eyes and our ears
Had reduced us to fury and tears
With their vile
Want of style
And their lunatic lack of ideas.

The entire population will gain   1487
From a poet so sound and so sane.

He'll tend us,
Defend us;
1490 We'll all bless that bulging great brain.

PLOUTON *and* AESCHYLUS *come out.*

PLOUTON.
1500 Bye-bye, Aeschylus.
Save our city,
Educate the fools.
There are plenty to choose from.
Please deliver these presents –
Or should I say hints:
Kleophon can have *this*⁴⁰,
Nikomachos *this*
And the Income Tax *these*.
Tell them to hurry:
We want them down here.
1510 If they're chicken, I'll come up there,
Hurry them, flurry them,
Snatch them and catch them
In person.

AESCHYLUS.
You got it.
And while I'm away
Please let Sophocles see to my throne,
Be my stand-in – well, sit-in –
As long as I'm gone.
As for that other one,
1520 Niminy-piminy,
Dazzle-'em, Frazzle-'em –
What *is* the man's name? –
Don't let *him* ever sit in it,
Even if he doesn't want to.

PLOUTON.
Lift your torches,
Lift your voices,
Make a procession,
Sing in his honour.

The CHORUS *forms up round* AESCHYLUS.

CHORUS.
    Spirits of darkness, grant us your blessing.
    Lead us and guide us, home with our poet.
    Let his majestic brain
    Help us end war and pain.   1530
    Those who like fighting, don't keep them guessing.
    'Swords into ploughshares'. 'Plant it and hoe it'.
    Mottoes for happiness,
    End of all strain and stress...

    Exeunt.

NOTES

NOTES

Wasps

1. This splendid word was coined by David Barrett, in his 1964 translation (Penguin Books). The Greek is *philheliastes* ('lover of jury-service'), which Barrett equally memorably translates as 'litigious maniac'.

2. Literally, 'as if he'd been sprinkling incense for the New Moon festival'. Incense was resinous dust, gathered in a pinch – but Aristophanes' secondary meaning is perfectly clear in Greek as well as in English.

3. The sequence which follows parodies a scene in Homer's *Odyssey*. Odysseus, trapped in the cave of the giant Polyphemos, escaped by clinging underneath Polyphemos' prize ram as it went out to pasture. He had already confused Polyphemos by telling him that his name was No One. I have restricted *Odyssey* references to the next line only, so that it can be cut if required, without damage to the joke.

4. Greek: 'No One of Ithaka, son of Clean Pair of Heels'.

5. Greek: 'It would be easier to keep an eye on Skione than on father.' Skione was a town, allied to Athens in the Peloponnesian War. It had recently defected to Sparta and the Athenians were trying to reclaim it.

6. Some productions equate the Chorus' wasp-stings with phalluses. This is not authentic: vase pictures suggest that insect-choruses, in the Greek theatre, had no phalluses.

7. Greek: 'She asked if I was trying to get up another tyranny of Hippias'. The pun is between Hippias (the last sole ruler of Athens, expelled 90 years before the play was written), and *hippeus*, 'horse-rider'.

8. In the original, the coins are in his mouth, and she French-kisses him to winkle it out.

9. In Greek, the girl's crime is going outside without permission – something women of all kinds, not just slave-girls, were not supposed to do.

10. In Greek, the dog's name is Labes, a blend of 'Grabber' and the name of Laches, a real-life general. In the same way, the Second Dog (here called Snitch) is intended to represent Kleon (one of whose nicknames was 'Dog'). The stolen cheese is 'Sicilian' – a reference to the recent scandal in which Laches was threatened with prosecution for taking bribes to betray his country during the Sicilian Expedition. It is possible that the (boy?) actors playing the dogs wore portrait masks caricaturing the politicians.

11. There follows the *parabasis* (address to the audience). Aristophanes mocks his rivals, and scolds his listeners for not appreciating his talent fully. The comment about ventriloquism refers to the fact that his first three plays were produced in the name of his sponsor Kallistratos. The memorable description of Kleon (lines 1030-7) appears again, slightly changed, in *Peace* 752-9. The 'vampires and spooks' (line 1038) are informers, probably the target of the play *Merchant Ships* (produced in 423BC, the same year as *Clouds*, and now lost). The bitter comments in lines 1043-50 refer to the failure of *Clouds* at its first performance (see page 96). The rest of the interlude returns to matters in hand, with the Chorus once more as Wasps.

12. 'Running entries' of this kind became a popular feature of later comedy. Scholars have worried that the interlude seems too short, that the drunk scene comes too soon after Philokleon's exit. Some rearrange the text; others say that Aristophanes probably inserted more verses of general or topical insult. (Certainly the metrical balance suggests that a few lines are missing.) But equally possibly, the shortness of the interlude is the whole point of the joke.

13. The dancers are sons of Karkinos ('Crab'), and Karkinos himself appears at the end. Possibly they were eccentric dancers like those in 20th-century music-hall. Some scholars say that they were played by the boys/ puppies we saw earlier.

Clouds

14. There was an extra joke here for the Greek audience. Phainarete, mother of the real Sokrates, was a midwife. Sokrates once jokingly called himself 'a midwife of thought'.

15. In the Greek theatre, it is possible that the permanent scenery for this play showed the inside of the Thinkery, and that for the opening of the play this was hidden by large wheeled screens, on which the outside doors were painted. (This would also explain why Strepsiades and Pheidippides apparently sleep in the street, outside their house.) When Strepsiades calls here for the doors to be opened, the screens would have been wheeled away by stage-hands, revealing the inside of the Thinkery and the groups of Students.

16. There follows the *parabasis* (address to the audience). The section spoken in Aristophanes' name by the Chorus-leader (lines 516-61) is prime evidence for the fact that our present text is a revision of the play. The rest is the usual mixture of topical jokes and elaborate music-numbers.

17. This 'business' is not authentic Aristophanes, but dates back to the earliest surviving commentaries on his plays, some 500 years after they were written.

18. For this passage, it is important to know (a) that Greek men and boys stripped naked for exercise, and (b) that visitors were welcome at training-sessions.

19. I have slightly simplified the argument about Payday: in Greek, it depends on a more complicated and much less comprehensible law. But I have left the style of Pheidippides' logic-chopping unchanged.

20. This and the succeeding items of 'business', to the end of the play, are traditional.

Birds

21. In the Greek, Euelpides says that he wants no seaside town, in case the Athenian galley arrives there with a constable on board to summons him. This happened to Alkibiades, the famous general, who sat out on the Sicilian Expedition just a few months before the play was produced. The reference below (lines 151-2) to Melanthios, the comic poet often mocked by Aristophanes, is totally obscure: perhaps Melanthios wrote a play involving disease and healing (perhaps along lines similar to Aristophanes' own later *Wealth*)? The joke about Opous (lines 152-3) seems, in Greek, to depend on the audience remembering a comedy, *The Opountian*, by Aristophanes' rival Eupolis – about which nothing is known, though it may have featured a one-eyed conman. ('The Opountian' appears later in *Birds*, line 1294, as a one-eyed crow.)

22. On the Melians, see Editor's introduction, page ix.

23. These and similar sounds may have been indications to the flautist to imitate bird-sounds, rather than words for the singer. All the bird-sounds may have been supplied instrumentally in this way. 'Tiou' is a single sound: the '-ou' is emphasised. In 'tioutinx', the stress is on the '-tinx'.

24. Original: '*Tereus:* And here's an owl. *Euelpides:* What are you saying? Who's brought owls to Athens?' 'Owls to Athens' was a proverb, identical to the English 'coals to Newcastle'.

25. Experts identify the actual birds listed as jay, turtle-dove, crested lark, reed warbler, wheatear, pigeon, merlin, sparrowhawk, ringdove, cuckoo, stockdove, firecrest, rail, kestrel, dabchick, waxwing, vulture and woodpecker.

26. This sequence is Aristophanes taking maximum advantage of the flautist's need to remove his mask before playing. Chairis was a favourite butt, possibly a long-standing member of the company.

27. Literally: In Tell-tale land by the water-clock
             exists a shameless,
             tongue-in-belly tribe,
             who sow, reap, harvest,
             gather ripe figs
             with their tongues.
             They're foreigners,
             Gorgiases, Philipposes,
             and because of those
             tongue-in-belly Philipposes,
             everywhere in Attica
             the tongue is sliced separately (at
             sacrifices)

Festival Time

28. Some authorities say that there was an extra point to this in the Greek: 'weaving wreaths' was a euphemism for prostitution.

29. In the original, and like most Athenian policemen in comedy, the Constable came from Scythia (modern Ukraine). The Athenians regarded this as all but the edge of the world, and its inhabitants as barbarians. The Constable's Greek is in an appropriately garbled dialect. I have sketched this in English, rather than choose any prescriptive dialect or defect, physical or mental: Dogberryish malapropisms, for example, sprang at one stage to mind.

Frogs

30. After the battle of Arginousai (see page xxx), all slaves who had fought and survived were granted their freedom.

31. In the original theatre there *was* a priest, in a seat of honour in the front row. Dionysos runs to beg him for

help, and offers to sit next to him at the party after the show.

32. This stage-direction is original.

33. In the original, Kleigenes is a laundryman who sells adulterated soap. He always votes for war rather than peace, in conformity with his habit of carrying a big stick in the street, to scare off muggers as he rolls home drunk.

34. Euripides divorced his first wife for adultery, and then married someone even flightier.

35. There *was* a highwayman Orestes in Aristophanes' time.

36. The Greek word *lekuthion*, 'little oil-jar', which I have translated 'sauce-box', is also slang for (a) the female genitals, and (b) 'wife'. Aeschylus is mocking not only Euripides' joggly rhythms, but also his domestic troubles.

37. Original stage direction. The words of the songs which follow, however, suggest additional instruments, perhaps wielded by Euripides himself. DaDUNG, daDUNG, daDUNG (Greek: tophlattothrat, tophlattothrat) represents the sound of someone strumming and finger-slapping a lyre, flamenco-style. As with other such noises in Aristophanes, it may indicate not words for the actor but instrumental 'breaks'.

38. Original: 'This Muse never played in the Lesbian mode'.

39. Aeschylus is making two serious political suggestions: (1) that the Athenians may do better in the war if they abandon their own territory, Attika, to the enemy and concentrate on attacking Spartan territory in the Peloponnese; (2) that taxes should be spent on building ships, not on paying jurors (not lawyers in the original) for wasting time on court-cases back home.

40. In Greek folklore, the three 'roads to death' were blade, noose and poison-pot. Hence Pluto's three 'presents' for leading politicians of the war-persuasion.

These translations follow the old Oxford Classical Text of Hall and Geldart, or new editions of individual plays currently being published by OUP, or both. All divergent readings and reallocations of characters are my own. I should like to recommend three books: K.J. Dover, *Aristophanic Comedy* (a general study, good on politics), C.H. Whitman, *Aristophanes and the Comic Hero* (interesting literary criticism), and Jeffery Henderson, *The Maculate Muse* (fascinating, not to say mind-boggling, on bawdy). My own book *The Theatre of Aristophanes* discusses Aristophanes as a practical playwright, going further into many of the issues raised in the Introductions and Notes to these translations.

WHO'S WHO

WHO'S WHO

Most names are transliterated from the Greek, but when an anglicised form is more familiar – as with Aeschylus – this has been retained.

Stressed syllable is in capitals. 'ai' sounds as the 'i' in 'ice'; 'ch' as in Scots 'loch'. * before a name means that that person has his or her own entry in this list.

ACHILLES (a-CHILL-ees). In myth, Greek hero who fought at Troy.

AESCHYLUS–AISCHYLOS (EESS-chil-oss or ESS-chil-oss). Real poet, quoted by Aristophanes' older characters, as typical of all that was fine about the good old days. Mocked by Aristophanes' younger characters as a wordy bore.

AESOP–AISOPOS (EE-sop). Legendary figure credited with collecting the folk-tales and anecdotes known as 'Aesop's Fables'. Aristophanes' older characters quote him as if he is some kind of fount of universal wisdom.

AGATHON (ag-AH-thohn). Real tragedian, contemporary and (possibly) friend of Aristophanes, who nevertheless mocks him for bad verse and for effeminacy.

AIAKOS (AI-a-koss). In myth, a king of such integrity that after death he was appointed one of the three Judges of the Dead.

AISCHINES (ess-CHEE-nees). Real politician, ridiculed as a big-talking do-nothing.

ALKIBIADES (al-si-BYE-a-dees, more correctly al-ki-bi-AH-dees). Real politician, a man of genius and personal charisma who constantly squabbled with the Athenian powers-that-were. The Athenians could neither live with him nor without him; in 404 he was assassinated.

ALKAIOS (AL-kai-oss). Real poet.

ALKMENE (alk-MEE-nee). In myth, the mortal queen with whom *Zeus slept to produce *Herakles.

ALOPE (a-LOH-pee). In myth, the princess of Eleusis near Athens. *Poseidon slept with her, and their son Hippothoön later became king of Athens.

AMEINIAS (am-ay-NEE-ass). Nothing known. Maybe the same person as *Amynias.

AMEIPSIAS (a-mayp-SEE-ass). Real comic playwright.

AMYNIAS (am-y-NEE-ass). Real general, mocked for effeminacy and swanking.

ANAKREON (an-a-KREE-ohn). Real poet.

ANDROKLES (an-dro-KLEES). Real politician, mocked for miserliness and immorality.

ANDROMEDA (an-DROM-e-da). In myth, a princess chained to a rock as food for a sea-monster, and rescued by *Perseus.

ANTIPHON (ant-i-FOHN). Real orator and politician.

ANTITHEOS (an-TI-thay-oss). Father of *Kritylla.

APOLLO–APOLLON (a-POL-loh). God of music, healing and prophecy (especially at his chief shrine at Delphi). Also known as Phoibos (or Phoebus), 'shining'.

ARCHEDEMOS (ar-CHED-ee-moss). Real lawyer, mocked for being not a native Athenian but a immigrant who wangled citizenship and then began impeaching true-born citizens.

ARIPHRADES (ar-i-FRAH-dees). Real flautist, mocked by Aristophanes for liking cunnilingus.

ARISTOMACHE (ar-iss-to-MAH-chee, 'best fighter'). Woman's name, probably imaginary – though in *Festival Time* she is said to be a veteran of the battle of Marathon.

ARTEMIS (AR-te-miss). Virgin goddess of hunting, childbirth and young creatures.

ASKONDAS (as-KOHN-dass). Boxer.

ATHENE (a-THEE-nee). Goddess of wisdom; patron of Athens.

AUTOMENES (ow-to-MAY-nees). Nothing known.

BAKIS (BAK-iss). Real soothsayer, but treated by Aristophanes as peddler of fraudulent gibberish.

BDELYKLEON (bdel-y-KLE-ohn, 'Kleon-puke'). Leading character in *Wasps*.

BIGGUN. Outlandish god 'from beyond the stars' in *Birds*. His Greek name, *Triballos*, is the name of a Thracian tribe regarded by the Athenians as untouched by civilisation.

CHAIREPHON (chai-REH-phon). Real friend and disciple of Sokrates. In comedy, he is a thin, swooping glutton, usually compared to a vampire bat.

CHAIRIS (CHAI-riss). Real flute-player, possibly a member of Aristophanes' company.

CHARMINOS (char-MEE-noss). Real admiral, notorious for losing six ships after an abortive sea-ambush.

CHARON (cha-ROHN). In myth, the aged ferryman who transported the souls of the dead across the River Styx into the Underworld.

DARDANIS (dar-dan-EES, 'the Trojan' or 'blaze'). Name of a torch-carrying slave-girl.

DAREIOS (dar-AI-uss or DAH-ree-oss). King of Persia, defeated at the Battle of Marathon (490BC).

DEMETER (dee-mee-TEER). Goddess of Harvest; mother of *Persephone (with whom she is 'The Twain').

DIAGORAS (dee-a-GOH-rass). (Real) Melian resident in Athens, summonsed for atheism, and specifically for mocking the Eleusinian Mysteries.

DIEITREPHES (dee-ay-TREF-ees). A (real) maker of wicker flasks, and a self-important, part-time soldier, he reached the heights of ambition when he was elected Hipparch, joint commander of the Athenian cavalry.

DIONYSOS (die-on-EYE-soss or dee-on-i-SOSS). God of ecstasy, intoxication, artistic inspiration and drama.

ECHO In myth, a beautiful nymph – till she fell in love with Narcissus, and pined away till she was nothing but a disembodied voice.

ELEKTRA (e-LEK-tra). in myth, *Agamemnon's daughter, who saved *Orestes from being killed with his father and then had to wait years till he was old enough to take vengeance for the murder.

EMPOUSA (EM-poo-sa). In myth, ghoul-servant of Hekate, goddess of midnight. Able to change shape at will, to take on the form of your worst nightmare.

EPHOUDION (ef-oo-DEE-ohn). Boxer.

EROS (EE-ross or e-ROHS). God of desire.

ERGASION (er-gas-EE-on, 'hard worker'). Invented name.

ERYXIS (ER-ix-iss). Real person; nothing known.

EUATHLOS (YOO-ath-loss, 'good fighter'). Real lawyer.

EUBOULE (yoo-BOO-lee). Legendary heroine of Athens.

EUELPIDES (yoo-el-PEE-dees, 'son of good hope'). Second lead in Birds.

EUPOLIS (YOO-po-liss). Real comic playwright.

EURIPIDES (yoo-RIP-i-dees or yoo-ri-PEE-dees). Real tragedian, mocked for atheism, trendy style, hostility to women, and because his mother kept a greengrocery stall.

EXEKESTIDES (ex-e-kes-TEE-dees). Real politician, mocked for being so repulsive that no one would offer him a home.

GLAUKETES (glow-KEHT-ees). (Real?) glutton.

GORGON. In myth, a monster whose glance turned mortals to stone. *Perseus killed it and cut off its head. The Gorgon's head was often painted on shields.

HARMODIOS (har-mo-DEE-oss). Athenian democratic hero, subject of popular songs of the good old days.

HELEN. In myth, daughter of Zeus and wife of *Menelaos. She was reputedly the most beautiful mortal in the world, and her abduction by Paris of Troy led to the Trojan War. In some versions of the myth, instead of being taken to Troy she was wafted to Egypt, where Menelaos sought her after the war. (This is where *Euripides' play *Helen* begins – one of the plays parodied in *Festival Time*).

HERA (HEE-ra). Consort of *Zeus, queen of the gods and supervisor of oaths, promises and the marriage-bond.

HERAKLES (he-RA-klees). In myth, the son of *Zeus and the mortal *Alkmene. Famous in Aristophanes as a gluttonous he-man.

HERMES (HER-mees). God who led dead souls to the Underworld; messenger god; doorkeeper; patron of thieves and tricksters. Aristophanes makes him an effeminate glutton.

HIPPYLLOS (HIP-i-loss). Nothing known.

HYMEN (hi-MEHN). God of marriage.

HYPERBOLOS (hi-PER-bo-loss). Real lampmaker and politician.

IACCHOS (YAK-choss or EE-ak-choss). In myth, one of the names of Bacchos/Dionysos, known only to initiates, and shouted by them in holy ecstasy.

IBYKOS (IB-i-koss). Real poet.

IOPHON (ee-o-PHON). Real playwright, *Sophocles' son.

IRIS (EE-ris). Rainbow-goddess, messenger between the gods and Earth.

ITYS (IT-iss). In myth, the son of *Tereus and Prokne.

KALLIAS (ka-LEE-ass). Real rich man.

KARKINOS (kar-KEE-nos, 'crab'). Real dancer.

KARDOPION (kar-do-PEE-on, 'little kneading trough'). Invented myth-hero.

KEPHISOPHON (ke-fee-so-FOHN). Real assistant of *Euripides. Aristophanes mocks his tragic pretensions, but also uses him because his name means 'river-babble'.

KERBEROS (KER-be-ross). In myth, the guard-dog of the Underworld. One of *Herakles' labours was to go to the Underworld and bring Kerberos back alive.

KINESIAS (kin-e-SEE-ass). (1) Real poet mocked for his *avant-garde* style. His lines are (in Greek) a mixture of his own (real) phrases and Aristophanes' parodies, and (in this English) a mixture of everyone from Keats to Hopkins, McLeish to Shakespeare. (2) Randy husband of *Myrrhine in *Lysistrata*. (Kinesias means 'Getting it up'.)

KLEIDEMIDES (klay-de-MEE-dees). Real actor, friend and possibly executor of *Sophocles.

KLEIGENES (klay-GE-nees). Apparently a laundryman, but nothing known.

KLEISTHENES (klays-THAY-nees). A favourite butt of Athenian comedians: camp, effeminate and pretentious: when he speaks, it is almost always in lines parodied from tragedy. No one knows if he existed in real life.

KLEITOPHON (klay-to-FOHN). Real philosopher, student of *Sokrates.

KLEOKRITOS (klee-O-krit-oss). Mocked for his ungainly shape and size. No one knows if he existed in real life.

KLEON (KLEE-on or klee-OHN). Real tanner who went into politics and was the most powerful man in Athens from 429BC until he was killed in battle. Nicknamed 'Dog' because of his yapping, snarling oratory. Virulently mocked by Aristophanes – and prone to retaliate with lawsuits.

KLEONYMOS (klee-OH-ni-moss). One of Aristophanes' favourite joke figures, mentioned over 30 times in the extant plays as a fat, greedy coward, who in the course of some battle threw away his shield and ran for safety. The battle may have been the real battle of Delion; Kleonymos may have been a real person; no one knows.

KRITYLLA (KRIT-ill-a, 'boss-eyed judge'). Character in *Festival Time*.

KTESIPHON (ktee-si-FOHN). Fat man; nothing else known.

KYKNOS (KIK-noss). In myth, the son of Ares, god of war.

LACHES (LA-chees). Real soldier, possibly (though not certainly) a rival of Kleon's at the time of *Wasps*.

LAISPODIAS (lais-po-DEE-ass). Real soldier, said to have concealed a withered leg by wearing his cloak in some exaggerated manner.

LAMACHOS (LA-ma-choss). Real general, who fought bravely in the war against Sparta but who is mocked by Aristophanes as a bone-headed warmonger. Perhaps his name is the reason: it means 'Too much fighting'.

LAMPON (LAM-pohn). Nothing known.

LEOGORAS (le-o-GOH-rass). Real politician, noted for wealth and love of luxury.

LETO (LEE-toh). Mother of *Apollo and *Artemis.

LYKIS (LIK-iss). Real comic playwright.

LYKON (LIK-ohn). Real politician.

LYKOURGOS (lik-OOR-goss). (1) Real grandfather of the famous Lykourgos (the orator and politician). (2) In *Festival Time*, a mythical king of Thrace, who opposed *Dionysos and suffered for it, and about whom *Aeschylus wrote a trilogy (now lost).

LYSIKRATES (liss-i-KRAH-tees). Possibly a real general, summonsed for taking bribes; no sure facts known.

LYSILLA (LISS-il-la). Woman's name.

LYSISTRATOS (lis-ISS-tra-toss, 'disbander of armies'). Real politician, mocked as a swaggerer.

MANES (MAH-nees). Slave's name.

MANIA (ma-NEE-a, 'wild one') Slave's name.

MANODOROS (man-o-DOH-ross, 'treasure'). Slave's name.

MEDEA (med-EE-a). In myth, a Colchian princess who married Jason, and who, when he left her for another woman, murdered their children to punish him.

MEGABATES (meg-a-BAH-tees). Real Persian satrap (provincial ruler). Probably mentioned in *Birds* because his name means 'Big-stepper'.

MEGAINETOS (meg-AI-ne-toss). Nothing known.

MEGAKLES (meg-a-KLEES, 'big-fame'). Imaginary person, but the name was common in the real, high-class Alkmaionid family.

MEIDIAS (may-DEE-ass). Real informer, a quail-breeder by trade.

MELANTHIOS (mel-anth-EE-os). Real poet and glutton.

MEMNON (mem-NOHN). Mythical war-hero.

MENELAOS (men-e-LAH-oss). In myth, king of Sparta and warrior husband of *Helen of Troy.

MENIPPOS (men-IP-poss). Real horse-breeder.

METON (ME-tohn, 'measurer'). Real astronomer, known for the 'metonic cycle': the period of 6940 days after which the Moon and Sun are in the same positions relative to one another as when they started.

MIKKA (mik-KA, 'tiny'). Character in *Festival Time*.

MNESILOCHOS (mnees-ILL-o-choss, 'remember the ambush'). Leading character in *Festival Time*: purportedly an elderly relative by marriage of *Euripides.

MORSIMOS (MOR-si-moss). Real dramatist.

MORYCHOS (MO-ru-choss). Real glutton and dandy.

MOUSAIOS (moo-SAI-oss). Real poet.

NAUSIMACHE (now-si-MAH-chee, 'Fighter at sea'). Name of an imaginary woman in *Festival Time*.

NIOBE (nee-OH-bee). In myth, queen who boasted that her children were finer than *Apollo and *Artemis – who promptly killed them.

ODYSSEUS (od-ISS-yooss or od-i-SYOOSS). In myth, the trickster-hero who devised the scheme of the Wooden Horse and later spent ten years wandering the world on his journey home.

OIAGROS (OI-a-gross). Nothing known.

OINEUS (oyn-YOOSS). In myth, a king who made sacrifice to all the gods – save one, with catastrophic results.

OPOUNTIOS (op-oon-TEE-oss). Real informer, one-eyed and shifty.

ORESTES (o-REST-ees). (1) In myth, the son of *Agamemnon and Klytemnestra, who killed his mother after she murdered his father. (2) A real Athenian mugger and highwayman.

ORPHEUS (OR-fyooss). In myth, the singer whose music could charm rocks, trees, even the spirits of the Under-world. Several real poems were attributed to him, and sung by devotees of his mystery cult.

PALAMEDES (pa-la-MEE-dees). In myth, hero and inventor, falsely accused (by *Odysseus) of treason during the Trojan War, and executed. Said to have invented the game of draughts, and several letters of the alphabet.

PANTAKLES (pan-ta-KLEES). (Real?) poet; nothing known.

PARIS (PA-riss). In myth, prince of Troy who judged between three goddesses, was awarded *Helen of Sparta as prize – and caused the Trojan War.

PASIAS (pa-SEE-ass, 'one-hundred-per-cent'). Imaginary fat man.

PEGASOS (PEG-a-soss). In myth, a winged horse which sprang from the blood of the *Gorgon killed by *Perseus.

PEISANDROS (pay-SAN-dross). Real fat coward.

PEISIAS (pay-SEE-ass). Nothing known.

PEITHETAIROS (payth-et-AI-ross, 'persuades companions'). Leading character in *Birds*.

PELEUS (PEEL-yooss or pel-YOOSS). In myth, was falsely accused of raping Hippolyte and was left to die in a region full of wild animals. The gods intervened, giving him a knife to defend himself with.

PENELOPE. In myth, the long-suffering and faithful wife of *Odysseus.

PERSEPHONE (per-SE-fon-ee, in Greek Persephassa). Goddess of the Underworld; daughter of *Demeter (with whom she forms The Twain).

PERSEUS (per-SYOOSS). In myth, the hero who killed the *Gorgon and rescued *Andromeda from the sea-monster. Hero of a lost play by *Euripides.

PHAIDRA (FE-dra). In myth, the wife of King Theseus, who fell in love with her stepson Hippolytos, and when he spurned her accused him to Theseus of raping her.

PHANOS (FAH-noss, 'tell-tale'). Nothing known.

PHARNAKES (far-NAH-kees). Nothing known.

PHAYLLOS (FA-ul-loss). Real athlete, of the previous generation.

PHEIDIPPIDES (fe-dip-PEE-dees, 'prudent horseman'). *Strepsiades' son in *Clouds*.

PHEIDON (FE-dohn, 'prudent, miserly'). *Strepsiades' father in *Clouds*.

PHILOKLEON (fil-o-KLEH-ohn, 'love-Kleon'). Leading character in *Wasps*.

PHILOKLES (fil-OK-lees). Real playwright, *Aeschylus' nephew.

PHILOKRATES (fil-o-KRAH-tees). (Real?) bird-seller.

PHILOKTEMON (fil-o-KTEH-mohn, 'loves-profit'). Imaginary plutocrat.

PHORMISIOS (for-MEE-si-oss). Real person, mocked for huge, shaggy beard.

PHRYNICHOS (FRI-ni-choss). (1) Tragic poet, from the shadowy generation before *Aeschylus. (2) Politician of Aristophanes' time. Aristophanes delights in confusing the two, as if the politician had written the fusty old plays.

PLATHANE (pla-THA-nee), 'cake-tin'). Woman's name.

PLOUTON (ploo-TOHN, 'rich'). In myth, brother of *Zeus and *Poseidon, and ruler of the Underworld. (His wealth came from the minerals buried in the earth).

POSEIDON (poss-i-DOHN or poss-AI-don). *Zeus' brother, god of the sea and one of the most senior Olympian gods.

PRODIKOS (PRO-dik-oss). Real philosopher.

PROMETHEUS (pro-MEE-thyooss, 'foresight'). In myth, a Titan, one of the powers who ruled the universe before the gods. He created the human race, and stole the gods' fire of intelligence to give to them.

PROTEUS (proht-YOOSS). In myth, sea-spirit and first king of Egypt.

PROXENIDES (pro-xen-EE-dees). (Real?) boaster.

PYTHAGORAS (Pie-THA-go-rass, more correctly pith-a-GOH-rass). Real philosopher and mathematician. To ancient Athenians, his name would have had the same aura as Einstein's does to us.

PYTHANGELOS (pith-AN-gel-oss). Real comic playwright.

SALAMBACCHO (sal-am-bak-CHOH). Real whore.

SEMELE (SE-me-le). In myth, mortal princess, raped by *Zeus; mother of *Dionysos.

SIMONIDES (si-mon-EE-dees). Real poet.

SOKRATES (sock-RAH-tees). Real philosopher, mocked by Aristophanes as a fraud who never bathed.

SOPHOCLES–SOPHOKLES (SOF-o-klees or sof-o-KLEES). Real poet, always spoken of with affection by Aristophanes.

SOSIAS (so-SEE-ass, 'thrifty'). Slave's name.

SOSTRATE (so-STRAH-tee, 'saviour of the army'). Woman's name.

SPINTHAROS (SPIN-tha-ross). Nothing known.

STRATONIKE (strat-o-NEE-kee, 'wins in battle'). Character in *Festival Time.*

STREPSIADES (strep-si-AH-dees, 'wriggler'). Leading character in *Clouds.*

SYRAKOSIOS (see-ra-kos-EE-oss). Real orator, with a twittery voice.

TELEAS (te-LAY-ass). Nothing known.

TELEPHOS (TEH-le-foss). Hero of (lost) tragedy by *Euripides.

TEREUS (teer-YOOSS). In myth, he raped his sister-in-law Philomela and tore out her tongue to prevent her telling. Philomela embroidered the story in a piece of cloth, and showed it to her sister Prokne. Prokne punished Tereus by killing their son Itys and serving him up in a stew. The gods changed Tereus into a hoopoe, and Prokne into a nightingale, forever singing 'Itys, Itys' in memory of the child she killed.

THEAGENES (thee-a-GAY-nees). Real boaster.

THEOGNIS (THEE-og-niss). Real tragic poet, mocked for his frigid style. Nickname was 'Snow'.

THEOPHRASTOS (thee-OH-frass-toss). Real politician (not the author).

THEOROS (THEH-oh-ross). Real person, one of Kleon's toadies.

THERAMENES (the-ra-MEE-nees). Real politician.

THRATTA (THRAT-ta, 'the Thracian'). Slave's name.

TIMOKLEIA (tim-o-KLEE-a, 'well-respected'). Woman's name.

TYNDAREUS (tin-DAR-yooss). In myth, the mortal husband of *Helen's mother Leda (with whom *Zeus slept in the form of a swan).

XANTHIAS (zan-THEE-ass, 'redhead'). Slave-name.

XENOKLES (zen-o-KLEES). Real actor and dancer.

XENOPHANTES (zen-o-FAN-tees). Real person, father of *Hieronymos.

XENYLLA (ZEN-ill-a). Woman's name.

XERXES (ZERK-sees). King of Persia, who invaded Greece in the 480sBC, and was defeated at Salamis (480BC) and Platea (479BC).

ZEUS (ZYOOSS; one syllable; not 'Zoos'). Ruler of gods and mortals.

A Note on the Translator and Series Editor

KENNETH McLEISH's translations, of plays by all the Greek and Roman dramatists, Ibsen, Freydeau, Molière, Strindberg and others, have been performed throughout the world on stage, film, TV and radio. His original plays include *I Will If You Will, Just Do It, The Arabian Nights, Omma* and *Orpheus*. His books include *The Theatre of Aristophanes, Guide to Shakespeare's Plays* (with Stephen Unwin), *The Good Reading Guide* and *Guide to Greek Theatre and Drama*. He was editor of the Drama Classics series for Nick Hern Books and a Fellow of the Royal Society of Literature.

J. MICHAEL WALTON worked in the professional theatre as an actor and director before joining the University of Hull, where he is Professor of Drama. He has published four books on Greek theatre, *Greek Theatre Practice, The Greek Sense of Theatre: Tragedy Reviewed, Living Greek Theatre: A Handbook of Classical Performance and Modern Production* and *Menander and the Making of Comedy* (with the late Peter Arnott). He edited *Craig on Theatre* for Methuen and is Series Editor of Methuen Classical Greek Dramatists. He has translated plays by Sophocles, Euripides, Menander and Terence and is Director of the Performance Translation Centre in the drama Department at the University of Hull.